A former Professor of Economics, E. Ray Canterbery is one of the most respected economist-writers worldwide. John Kenneth Galbreath, who knew both Michal Kalecki and John Maynard Keynes, called Canterbery, "the best."

Canterbery conducted research at the Truman Library in Independence, Missouri, which led to the biographical book, *Harry S. Truman: The Economics of a Populist President*. Canterbery is the author of many other acclaimed works. Among these are *Inequality and Supra-surplus Capitalism,* a sequel to John Kenneth Galbraith's *The Affluent Society,* and *The Rise and Decline of Global Austerity*. Before these came *The Global Great Recession,* which Canterbery and *Business Week* named. And, there were many others: the ones still in print can be viewed at Amazon.com. Some 57 of his many articles have been published in a collection titled *The Collected Works of E. Ray Canterbery* (Singapore, London: World Scientific Publishers, 2017). Some of his books are available in several languages.

"Canterbery served as President of the Eastern Economics Association in 1986-87 and of the International Trade and Finance Association in 1997-98. In January 1996, Prentice-Hall, Inc. selected him for one of their 100 Hall of Fame Economists Baseball Cards for significant contributions to the economics discipline," including "developing one of the first complete mathematical theories of foreign exchange."

The International Biography Centre in Cambridge, England includes Canterbery among 500 persons worldwide in its *Living Legends*, among 2000 scholars worldwide in its *Outstanding Scholars in the 21st Century*, among *One Thousand Great Intellectuals*, among *2000 Outstanding People* worldwide, and among *1000 Great Americans*. The American Biographical Institute includes

Canterbery in its *Great Minds of the 21ˢᵗ Century*, among many other awards. He is also is listed in selected issues of *Marquis Who's Who in the World* and *Who's Who in America*.

To those who have written of financial speculation, but especially my late friend, John Kenneth Galbraith and the late Charles Kindleberger.

E. Ray Canterbery

MANIAS, CASINOS, BUBBLES AND CRASHES

AUSTIN MACAULEY PUBLISHERS™

LONDON • CAMBRIDGE • NEW YORK • SHARJAH

A CIP catalogue record for this title is available at the British Library.

ISBN 9781528907286 (Paperback)
ISBN 9781528907293 (Hardback)
ISBN 9781528958523 (ePub e-book)

www.austinmacauley.com

First Published 2024
Austin Macauley Publishers Ltd®
1 Canada Square
Canary Wharf
London
E14 5AA

I thank every member of my family.

Introduction

"Irrational exuberance" is a phrase famously coined by Alan Greenspan, head of the Federal Reserve in December 1997. He used it in a luncheon speech at an annual meeting of the American Economic Association. The audience of economists sat in awe of him, in an almost worshiping mode, usually reserved for rock stars. Sensing an overpricing of some 20 percent in the Dow, Greenspan hoped to talk the market down without a crash. Though the market immediately recoiled in reaction to Greenspan's remarks, it quickly recovered. The Dow had climbed another 20 percent by spring 1998. Still concerned with overvalued assets Greenspan was reluctant to raise interest rates for fear of setting in motion the greatest stock market crash in American history. Greenspan apparently believed that an irrational bubble was driving the stock market. Some will see the irony, Greenspan, an outspoken opponent of and regulation of financial markets, repeatedly has praised such markets for their "efficiency". During the first crisis on his watch, he contemplated going back on the old Gold Standard.

Figure 1.1
Greenspan Contemplates Going Back on the Gold Standard

A variety of formal definitions of a bubble exist. However, the intuition remains the same. If the price of an asset is high today only because buyers believe that the selling price will be high tomorrow, a bubble exists. Put differently, today's price is not fully explained by fundamentals (variables having a direct effect on future income streams from, for example, equities). Often, it appears, a self-fulfilling prophecy is underway, because asset prices will cleave to the high side if buyers believe they will. In the short run, the high asset price is "justifiable," because it yields a return (dividends) equal to or greater than returns on alternative assets, including bonds.

Still, Greenspan's view is contrary to the theories of efficient capital markets based on rational expectations. In the stronger version of rational expectations all asset prices are not only always correct but reflect market fundamentals. In the rational bubble models, even the "bubbles" are "rational" because investors can believe that an asset's price is above its fundamental value but continue to hold the asset anyway. This reasoning applies to many "investors" and many assets. That is, each believes that someone else (a greater fool, perhaps) will buy the asset for a higher price in the future, preventing a pricking of the bubble. In a rational bubble, therefore, asset prices can deviate from their fundamental values for a long time, because the bursting of the bubble can be predicted and so there are no unexploited profit opportunities. A single player in the market, such as George Soros or Warren Buffet, can never beat the market. Not only will any differences from the "optimal forecast" of any asset's price (its fundamental value) sum to zero, so will differences from the optimal forecast of the bubble. Such deviations, therefore, are unpredictable; asset prices walk a random walk.

For now, we will not trifle with the efficient market theories. Suffice it to say that most historians and some economists side with Greenspan. Ultimately, they say, we much come to grips with the reality of financial excess, a form of mass hysteria. Patsy-Cline-like "crazy" behaviour—maniac, obsessed, haunted, mesmerized and orgasmic—leads to abnormal outcomes. When the players overdo financial opportunities, a mania follows, that must somehow end, usually an atrabilious end. In this view the great financial bull market of the 1990s in the US came to such a gruesome finale on Friday, the 13th of October 1989, with a mini-crash. This was followed in the early 1999s by a recession in reaction to the invasion of Kuwait by Iraq in July 1990, causing oil prices to soar. The Dow dropped 18 percent more in three months, from 2,911.63 from July 3rd to 2,381.99 in October.

Rather than differences in fundamental and bubble prices, it is sometimes useful to contrast tranquil markets with turbulent markets. A tranquil market has no internal contradictions and no external shocks; expectations based upon experience are confidently held and constantly justified. Current prices can be confidently expected without rational (or forward-looking) expectations. Still, internal contradictions can evolve in any market, especially in a financial market. Moreover, when a market turns from tranquil to turbulent, it is difficult to say whether the turbulence is "caused" by external shocks. If a market is so delicate that a shock causes it to collapse (become ill-liquid), we might even question the basis for the players' confidence based on experience or even forward-looking expectations. Besides since markets are interdependent, does one market adversely affecting a second, comprise an "external shock"? Since the interest rate on a long-term bond may be used as the discount rate on valuing equities, an unexpectedly dramatic fall in bond prices may be an "internal" shock to stock markets and prices. If an equity-market player believes that movements in bond prices do not matter, is the player being rational?

We cannot answer all such questions in an introduction, but we can shed some light on the issues involved. Certainly, irrational exuberance defies the rational individual behaviour and general equilibrium models based on rational behaviour, including Lucas' critique as well as rational bubbles in assets.[1] Then irrespective of theory, those who deny bubbles must go to the barricades against at least four great bubbles in modern history—tulipmania, the Mississippi Bubble, the South Seas Bubble, and the Great Crash of 1929. This is precisely what has happened; recently, rewriting the history of bubbles has become a cottage industry, barricades aside. If these revisionists were to write the history of the Titanic, the iceberg would have sunk! Meantime a dramatic end to the Great Bull Market of 1990s provides still another historical case.

We will proceed to restate the history of the classic bubbles. Notably, these revisions have been written by rational expectationists. Then, we will critique the revisionist histories of these bubbles. Along the way, we will consider the

---

[1] Lucus' Critique contends that it is naive to predict the effects of a change in economic policy entirely on historical data, especially highly aggregated historical data. More formally it states that the decision rule of Keynesian models cannot be considered as structural in the sense of being invariant to changes in government policy variables such as national debt. Economic equations estimated on one policy regime is unlikely to fit another policy regime.

standard model for such bubbles. Finally, though considering the lessons learned from history, we will suggest an alternative theoretical approach.

First, we return to the first great historic bubble, tulip mania.

Chapter 1
Tulip Mania

Kipper and Wipper

Perhaps the first financial crisis in history happened during the start of the Thirty Years War (1518-48). Beginning around 1521, city-states in the Holy Roman Empire began to heavily debase currency to raise revenue for the Thirty Years' War, as effective taxation did not exist. The name, Kipper and Wipper, refers to the use of tipping scales to identify not-yet-debased coins, which were then taken out of circulation, melted, mixed with baser metals such as lead, copper or tin, and re-issued. (Kipper and Wipper literally means "Tipper and See-saw".). When the states did not debase their own currency, but instead manufactured low-value imitations of coins from other territories and then spent them in yet other territories as far as possible from their own lands. They were hoping that the resultant damage would occur to the economies of those other regions rather than their own. It was a kind of "beggar thy neighbour" policy. This worked for a while, but after a time, the public caught on to the manipulation, resulting in pamphlets denouncing the practice, local riots and the refusal of soldiers and mercenaries to fight unless paid in real-non-debased money. Also, the states began to back their own debased coins in taxes and customs fees. Due to these problems, the practice largely stopped around 1523; however, the damage done was so large that it created financial instability in almost all the city-states of the area. The same thing re-occurred on a smaller scale near the end of the century and again during the middle of the 18th century; moreover, the debasement spread from Germany to Austria, Hungary, Bohemia and Poland.

What is interesting about this financial crisis is the *specie* (metal coin) was debased, not paper money. In contrast, the Tulipmania of 1536-37 related to speculation in the value to tulip bulbs. What ended the metal coin speculation? More and more mints were established until the debased metal coins were so worthless that children allegedly played with them in the street, which became the basis for the short story by Leo Tolstoy, "Ivan the Fool."

Speculative Mania with Tulips

Ordinarily, we think of tulips as something you tiptoe through. During the Dutch Golden Age, it was more like romping through the tulips. This was a period during which contract prices for bulbs of the recently introduced tulip reached extraordinarily high levels and then collapsed. At the peak of tulipmania, in March 1637, some single tulip bulbs were sold for more than 10 times the annual income of a skilled craftsman. A tulip, known as the *Viceroy Bulb* cost between 3,000 and 4,200 guilders (florins) depending on size. Skilled craftsman at the time earned about 300 guilders a year, which meant working a decade or more to buy one tulip. It is generally considered the first recorded speculative bubble. It was so spectacular that the term "tulipmania" is now often used metaphorically to describe any large economic bubble when asset prices deviate from intrinsic values.

The 1637 event was popularized in 1841 by the book, *Extraordinary Popular Delusions and the Madness of Crowds*, by the British journalist Charles Mackay. According to Mackay, at one point 12 acres of land were offered for a *Semper Augustus* bulb. Since about half of the Netherlands is below sea level, dry land is very valuable. Mackay claims that many such investors were ruined by the fall in prices, and Dutch commerce suffered a severe shock. Many modern scholars feel that the mania was exaggerated by journalist Mackay. True, research is difficult because of limited economic data from the 1630s--much of which come from biased and very speculative sources. Other flowers, such as the hyacinth, also had high initial prices at the time of their introduction, which immediately fell. The high asset prices may also have been driven by expectations of a parliamentary decree that contracts could be voided for a small cost--thus lowering the price to buyers.

The tulip became very special once it was introduced in Europe by Ogier de Busbecq, the ambassador of Ferdinand I, Holy Roman Emperor, to the Sultan of Turkey. Ogier sent the first tulip bulbs and seeds to Vienna in 1554 from the Ottoman Empire. Tulip bulbs were soon distributed from Vienna to Augsburg, Antwerp and Amsterdam. Its popularity and cultivation in the United Provinces (now the Netherlands) is generally thought to have started in earnest around 1593 after the esteemed Flemish botanist Carolus Clusius (1526-1609) had taken up a post at the University of Leiden and established the *hortus academicus*. In 1573 he was appointed prefect of the imperial medical gardens in lovely Vienna. Clusius planted his collection of tulip bulbs and found they could tolerate the harsher conditions of the Low Countries. Shortly, thereafter the tulip began to grow in popularity.

The tulip was different from every other flower known to Europe at the time, with a saturated intense petal colour that no other plant had. The appearance of the nonpareil tulip as a status symbol coincides with the rise of newly independent Holland's trade fortunes. No longer the Spanish, Netherlands, the economic resources could now be channelled into commerce and the country embarked on its Golden Age. Amsterdam merchants were at the centre of the lucrative East Indies trade, where one voyage could yield profits of 400 percent. The new merchant class displayed and validated its success, primarily by setting up grand estates surrounded by flower gardens, and the plant that had pride of place was the sensational tulip. Thus, tulips rapidly became a coveted luxury item, and a profusion of varieties followed. They were classified in groups: the single-hued tulips of red, yellow, or white were known as *Couleren*; the multi-coloured *Rosen* (white streaks on a red or pink background); *Violetten* (White streaks on a purple or lilac background); and the rarest of all, the *Bizarden* (*Bizarres*), (yellow or white streaks on a red, brown, or purple background). The multi-coloured effects of intricate lines and flame-like streaks on the petals were vivid and spectacular and made the bulbs that produced these even more exotic looking plants highly sought-after. It is now known that this effect is due to the bulbs being infected with a type of tulip-specific mosaic virus, known as the "Tulip breaking virus," so called because the virus "breaks" the one petal colour into two or more.

The biology of the tulip was itself a contributor to the supply-squeeze that fuelled the speculation, in that it is grown from a bulb that cannot be produced quickly. Typically, it takes 7 to 12 years to grow a flowering bulb from seed; bulbs can produce both seeds and two or three bud clones, or offsets, annually, but the "mother bulb" lasts only a few years. Properly cultivated, the "daughter offsets" will become flowering bulbs after one to three years. Before the "broken" tulips were developed, virus-free bulbs producing ordinary single-color variety were sold by the pound. Once affected by the virus, the "broken exotics" were an extremely limited commodity because the sought-after "breaking pattern" can only be reproduced through offsets, not seeds, as only the bulb is affected by the mosaic virus. Unfortunately, the virus that provided the sought-after effects also acted adversely on the bulb, weakening it and retarding propagation of offsets, so cultivating the most appealing varieties now took even longer. Taking this into account, quite probably from the time the speculation got started until its collapse, the number of rare bulbs that changed hands so feverishly never increased beyond the original number.

The pioneering Dutch were not limited to tulip innovations; they also developed many of the techniques of modern finance. They managed to create a market for tulip bulbs, where they were treated as durable goods. They wrote contracts before a notary to buy tulips at the end of the season (effectively futures contracts). A futures contract specifies quantities of a commodity or financial instrument at a specified price with delivery set at some future date. For example, a January futures contract for a pound of common tulip bulbs might be at a price of 35 guilders to be delivered in May. A short position is where the party is obligated to *sell* the underlying asset upon maturity of the contract. For example, a Viceroy might have a contract to sell in March at 2500 guilders, hence constituting a short sale. Being short is highly speculative. Short selling was banned by an edict of 1610, which was reiterated or strengthened in 1621 and 1630, and again in 1636. Short sellers were not prosecuted under these edicts, but their contracts were deemed unenforceable.

As the flowers grew in popularity, professional growers paid higher and higher prices for bulbs with the virus, and prices rose steadily. By 1634, in part because of demand from the romantic French, speculators began to enter the market. The contract price of rare bulbs continued to rise throughout 1535, but by November, the price of common "unbroken" bulbs also began to increase, so that soon any tulip bulb could fetch hundreds of guilders. That year the Dutch created a type of formal futures market where contracts to buy bulbs at the end of the season were bought and sold. Traders meeting in "colleges" at taverns and buyers were required to pay a 2.5 percent "wine money" fee, up to a maximum of three guilders per trade. Neither party paid an initial margin nor a mark-to-market margin and all contracts were with the individual counter-parties rather than with the Exchange. The Dutch described tulip contract trading as windhandel (literally "wind trade"), because no bulbs were changing hands. It was a virtual market. The entire business was accomplished on the margins of Dutch economic life, not in the Exchange itself.

By 1636 the tulip bulb became the fourth leading export product of the Netherlands, after gin, herrings, and cheese. Among these, only tulip bulbs could not be digested. The price of tulips skyrocketed because of speculation in tulip futures among people who never saw the bulbs. Many men made and lost fortunes overnight. Tulipmania reached its peak during the winter of 1636-37, when some bulbs were reportedly changing hands ten times in a day. The price of Dutch tulips increased by several hundred percent in the autumn of 1636, and the prices of the more exotic species of tulip bulbs were even larger. No deliveries were ever made to fulfil any of these contracts, because in February 1637, tulip bulb contract prices collapsed abruptly and the trade of tulips ground to a halt. The collapse began in Haarlem, when for the first-time buyers apparently refused to show up at a routine bulb auction. This may have been because Haarlem was then at the height of an outbreak of bubonic plague. While the existence of the plague may have helped create a culture of fatalistic risk-taking that allowed the speculation to skyrocket in the first place, this outbreak might also have helped to burst the bubble.

When tulipmania set in; prices began to rise wildly. The higher the prices went, the more attractive the bulbs became to buyers. Even common bulbs became part of the speculative bubble. Farmers, mechanics, seamen, footmen and nobles shifted out their usual industry and speculated in tulip bulbs. People apparently thought tastes would never turn against the bizarre and prices would rise toward infinity. The few who thought otherwise were left behind, feeling foolish, so the prices continued to climb, and their friends made great profits.

A herd instinct took over, and few could resist temptation. Near the end people were exchanging their personal property—jewels, furniture, land—for the bulbs that they expected would make them rich. In the final stage of the mania during January 1537, prices of ordinary tulip bulbs increased twenty-fold only to drop to about $1/20^{th}$ of their peak value in February.

Speculators began cautiously to take their profits as they now tiptoed out of tulips. Prices began to wilt, like petals in a dry summer. Though the Dutch government reassured citizens that "there was no reason for the bulbs to fall in price," dealers continued to go bankrupt. Eventually, most tulip bulbs became no more valuable than onions. The end was poetically, well, bizarre. Not only speculators but the conservative buyers and dealers went down with the bulb prices.

Figure 1.2
Wagon of Fools by Hendrick Gerritsz Pot

Followed by Haarlem weavers who have abandoned their looms they ride to their destruction in the sea of tipers, money changers, and the two-faced goddess Fortuna. The fate of those Haarlem weavers who abandoned their looms to join those speculating in tulips is neatly captured by Hendrick Gerritsz Pot. It is appropriately called "Wagon of Fools," in the illustration shown above. It too illustrates some of the reasons behind the speculation. The temptation to jump on the wagon exceeded the fear of being left behind. You can see the fear in the faces of those running behind, hoping to get on the wagon. Once on it, the ride was too much of an adventure to abandon. They are blown by the wind and fly a flag emblazoned with tulips: Flora, goddess of flowers, her arms laden with tulips, rides to their destruction in the sea along with tipplers, money changers and the two-faced goddess Fortuna. The painting gives the phrase "wind trade" a literal meaning.

Some Models to Explain Speculative Euphoria

We can explain some of the standard models that were inspired by tulipomania and other speculative orgies without resort to mathematics. The mathematical version is relegated to Appendix I.

Paul Samuelson associated tulipmania with "the purely financial dream world of indefinite group self-fulfilment.[2]" Samuelson's students, Karl Shell and Joseph Stiglitz stated that "the instability of the Hahn model is suggestive of the economic forces operating during 'speculative booms like the Tulip Bulb mania.[3]'" In his presidential address to the American Finance Association, Van Horne[4] invoked the possibility of tulipmania, in which a "single bulb sold for many years' salary," in what were then called perfect foresight models (today, called rational expectation models), Frank Hahn, Samuelson, Shell, Stiglitz, and others nonetheless argued that in the absence of futures markets extending into infinity, no market forces could prevent bubbles.[5] That is, bubbles could exist.

In many such models, every bubble eventually broke, requiring only that a speculator be sufficiently long lived to take profits. Robert Shiller, too, advanced the hypothesis that asset prices are driven by crowd behaviour or fads. Shiller wrote that the standard and accurate view, until the last few decades, has been that asset markets are driven by capricious investors acting based on fads and bubbles. He cites tulipmania as an example.[6] These are not careless writers; both Stiglitz and Shiller have won Nobel Prizes in economics.

In these models the terminal price of the asset becomes trivial, if the asset price increases more slowly than the discount factor. Then, only if the value of

---

[2] P. A. Samuelson, "Indeterminacy of development in a heterogeneous capital model with constant saving propensity. In E. Shell, ed., Essays on the theory of optimal economic growth, (Cambridge: MIT Press, 1967), p. 230.

[3] K. Shell, and J. E. Stiglitz, "Allocation of investment in a dynamic economy, Quarterly Journal of Economics, November 81, p. 593.

[4] J. Van Horne, "Of financial innovations and excesses, Journal of Finance, July 40 (3), 1984, p. 527.

[5] H.F. Hahn, "Equilibrium dynamics with heterogeneous capital goods, Quarterly Journal of Economics, November 80, 1966: 533-46, Samuelson, op. Cit., and Shell-Stiglitz, op. Cit.

[6] R. Shiller, "Stock prices and social dynamics, Brookings Papers 2: 1984: 457-98 and R. Shiller, "Fashions, fads, and bubbles in financial markets," paper prepared for Conference on Takeovers and Contests for Corporate control, February 1986.

the asset were just equal to the discounted value of the stream of returns it yielded, would no bubble exist. Otherwise, if no one has an infinite planning horizon, nothing could ensure that the asset price equalling the discounted stream of returns condition (the transversality condition) would prevail. Put differently, if the rate of price increase of an asset equals (or exceeds) the rate of interest then the share of the value of all assets accounted for by this asset would grow without bound, a condition inconsistent with long-run (fundamentals) equilibrium. A bubble would persist (not burst) only in the special case where the growth rate in the asset's price equals the interest rate. Though these models assume a fixed interest rate, a rising interest rate (as suggested previously) could cause a financial bubble to collapse. This has been the over-riding fear of the Federal Reserve authorities. Traditionally, the Fed, as it is affectionately called, prefers to try to "talk down" a bubble. Later, we will consider how well this has worked out for it.

Today's rational expectations' models, though bearing a family resemblance to the Samuelson-Hahn style models, make contrary claims. The evaluation of errors in an "optimal" forecast model (the sum of which is assumed zero), "proves" the efficient market hypothesis. As defined previously, a bubble in an asset price requires a comparison with its "fundamental" price. The fundamental price is derived from an estimation of returns received over time (such as dividends on stocks), sometimes an estimate of the terminal value of the assets, and the proper selection of a discount rate or rates for transforming future returns into current values. Once we have a formula for a price based on fundamentals, of course, we need a solution that includes a bubble. The initial bubble then can have innovation attached to it. We could conceive even of a model in which many innovations take place, perhaps into infinity, though infinity is a *very* long time.

Besides the assumption that forecast errors sum to zero, the main departures under rational expectations are an "information set" behind the equations and the assumption that the representative agent lives forever. In the Hahn-Samuelson model, a bubble would persist only if the representative agent lives forever. Samuelson and his followers, however, always knew that only an infinitely lived "representative" agent could prevent the bursting of a bubble but considered such a condition irrelevant in the real world. So much the worse for the real world because most of us would prefer to live forever.

Revisionist Interpretation

Peter M. Garber, a long time champion of rational expectations, disavowed irrational bubbles, gave us not so much a revisionist parable of tulipmania, as a revisionist interpretation. He claims that "most" of tulipmania was not obvious madness. This sounds like the phrase used by Zelda Fitzgerald—"Sometimes madness is wisdom"—at a display of her painting of flowers.[7] In Gerber's view, high but rapidly depreciating prices for rare bulbs is a typical pattern in the tulip bulb industry. "Only the last month of the speculation, during which common bulb prices increased rapidly and crashed, remains as a potential bubble".[8] We are reminded nonetheless that madness is not always wisdom.

"The market for bulbs was limited to professional growers until 1534, but participation encompassed a more general class of speculators by the end of 1534."[9] Formal futures markets in bulbs developed in 1535, the primary focus of trading before the collapse in February 1537. By the summer of 1535 traders began meeting in taverns in groups called "colleges" where trades were regulated by a few rules. Since bulbs are not available until June and must be replanted by September, any purchase between September and June must be a contract for future delivery. The impetus for higher prices initially came from a rising demand from wealthy Frenchmen competing to adorn their favourite women with the most bizarre of the flowers. The Frenchmen, ever the romantics, went from bazaar to bizarre.

As with today's futures markets, neither party intended delivery on the settlement date; only a payment equalizing the difference between the contract and settlement price was expected. Counter to Garber, other accounts of tulipmania *do* include speculation in common bulbs. Otherwise, there would not have been an increase of much more than a hundred percent in common tulip bulbs.

The timing of events was recorded by Posthumus:

---

[7] The phrase which named the Zelda exhibit was originally in French. For much more on Zelda (and Scott), see E. Ray Canterbery, Scott, A Novel of F. Scott Fitzgerald (London & New York: Austin Macauley, 2017).

[8] P.M. Garber, "Tulipmania," Journal of Political Economy, June 97, 1989, p. 535. While we quarrel with the revisionist interpretation that a bubble or bubbles did not exist, Garber's history is remarkably accurate and we don't mind repeating it.

[9] Ibid., p. 553.

At the end of 1534, the new nonprofessional buyers came into action. Towards the middle of 1535 prices rose rapidly, while people could buy on credit. About the middle of 1535 the cottages appeared; and soon thereafter the trade in non-available bulbs was started, while in November of the same year the trade was extended to the common varieties...[10]

Though he wrote of what was happening to common bulbs, N. W. Posthumus (1880-1960) was an uncommon man. He was a Dutch historian and political scientist. Following the rise of the Nazi party in Germany, Posthumus founded the International Institute of Social History. It was a place to retain socialist documents and histories safe from the ruthless Nazi regime and other governments. He was dismissed in 1942 by the government of occupied Netherlands and returned to his post only following the war. During the war, he managed to publish *Inquiry into the History of Prices in Holland*, which today remains widely cited.

Posthumus was accurate about the common bulbs. Besides, even if Garber is correct in claiming that the prices of bizarres, traded among the serious and wealthy tulip fanciers, reflected fundamentals, he does not and cannot dismiss the bubble in prices of the common bulbs. Beyond that, the pattern described by Posthumus is precisely what is usually seen in speculative bubbles. At first, professionals and wealthy people control trading, bidding only on bizarres or blue chips. Later, when something dramatic happens such as the dazzling prices paid for the bizarres, common people desire part of the action. They, of course, leap upon the Wagon of Fools. They buy the common bulbs, because they cannot afford the high-priced bulbs. Often, because they have minimal resources, they and the traders bringing their business to them must be innovative (using futures, margins, meeting conveniently in taverns) to participate in markets normally serving only the rich. It is another rich man-poor man story. Participation by the masses drove up the price of the common bulb, causing it to soar well above any fundamental price. If the NASDAQ increased twenty-fold in one month and fell to $1/20^{th}$ of its value the next, it would attract the attention of many people, especially those falling off the wagon.

We arrive at Appendix I with trepidation. It will not be every reader's cup of tea. If you are mathematically inclined, you will want to read it; otherwise, you

---

[10] N.W. Posthumous, "The tulip mania in Holland in the years 1536-37," Journal of Economic and business History, May 1, 1929, p. 444.

can go to the next chapter on John Law and the Mississippi Bubble. Appendix I goes with that chapter as well.

Appendix 1
Standard Model of Speculation[11]

In the standard model, people are risk-averse, and they discount future returns at a constant rate, R. Then, for example, the price of one equity share, P sub t, equals the expected discounted present value of the accrued dividends during the ownership period, D sub t+1, plus the price at which the share can be sold at the end of the ownership period, P sub t+1. Thus,

(1) P sub t = E sub t (D sub t+1 + P sub t+1) / (1 + R),

where E sub t (D sub t+1 + P sub t + 1) is the expected value of the future dividend and the future price based on information available at time t. An asset pricing formula can be derived from equation (1) by a recursive process. Update equation (1) by one time period to derive P sub t+2 and substitute the right-hand side of the expression for P sub t+2 into equation (1), giving:

(2) P sub t = E sub t [D sub r+1 + E sub t+1 (D sub t+2 + P sub t+2) / (1 + R)] / (1 + R).

Update equation (1) again, and substitute for P sub t+2 into equation (2). Use the law of iterated expectations, E sub t [E sub t+1) (D sub t+2)] = E sub t (D sub t+2), which assumes that the expected value today of what we will expect about the future when we have more information in the next period. This is simply what

[11] This appendix is based in part on E. Ray Canterbery, "Irrational Exuberance and Rational Speculative Bubbles, The International Trade Journal, Volume VIII, No. 1 (Spring 1999), pp. 7-8. Reprinted in E. Ray Canterbery, Beyond Conventional Economics (Singapore, London, New Jersey: World Scientific, 2016), Chapter 16.

we expect about the future today with much less information. After an infinite number of substitutions, the current price equals the expected present value of all future dividends or,

(3) $P_{f_t} = SUM\ [1/(1 + R)]^i\ E_t\ (D_{t+i})$.

In this equation, the subscript f defines price as the market fundamentals price, as defined above. Since the share is held infinitely long it has no terminal value. This is the fundamentals equation.

One way of introducing bubbles in the fundamentals equation is to consider equation (3) as only one mathematical solution to equation (1). Other solutions can include a bubble, denoted with B_t, or,

(4) $P_t = P_{f,t} + B_t$.

The bubble represents a deviation of the current market price of the asset from the value based solely upon fundamentals. To satisfy equation (1) the current value of the bubble must be the expected discounted value of the future bubble in the next period, or,

(5) $B_t = E_t\ (B_{r+1})\ (1 + R)$.

However, a bubble is a possible outcome of this model only if it is expected that the bubble will continue. Sometimes the bubble definition has been written as:

(6) $B_{t+1} = B_t\ (1 + R) + b_{t+1}$

Where

(7) $b_{t+1} = B_{t+1} - E_t\ (B_{t+1})$,

Whereas B_{t+1} is a bubble in the equity price, b_{t+1} is the innovation in the bubble at time $t + 1$ which has mean zero. Then, if bubbles exist, they must grow at the real rate of interest. Burmeister, Flood and Garber[12]discussed several indeterminacies in the homogeneous part of the solution to the difference equation (1). Since the bubble process is the homogeneous part of the solution, $(1 + R) > 1$ generates an explosive indeterminacy. If the bubble were negative in equation (5), it would be expected to be larger and negative over time until it exceeded the fundamentals price, a price that could not grow as fast as the bubble would shrink. The equity would have a negative price in finite time, something we never observe in the stock markets, though some stocks can disappear from the market. This result has led some economists to conclude that bubbles cannot exist. Alternative conclusions, however, could be either (1) the asset price is constrained by market institutions to a positive value or (2) the bubble equation is incorrect. After all, the Russian and some other stock markets can drop 90 percent in a few days without going all the way to 110 percent.

---

[12] See E. Burmeister, R.P. Flood, and P.M. Garber, "On the equivalence of solutions in rational expectations models," *Journal of Economic Dynamics and Control*, May 5, 1983: 224-34.

Chapter 2
John Law and the Mississippi Bubble

John Law: Economist, "British Dandy," and Central Banker

John Law (1671-1729) was the Alan Greenspan of the 17th century. Both were economists and served as head of banks. Greenspan was head of the Federal Reserve and Law helped to determine the fate of the Second Bank of the United States, which performed many of the functions of a central bank. Both were present any time financial bubbles expanded and collapsed. Law, like Greenspan, believed that money was a medium of exchange that did not constitute wealth. Law also believed that national wealth depended on trade, to which he devoted much of his life. Both took actions that could be called "illegal'". John Law was a reckless gambler whereas Greenspan was a careful planner who manipulated Presidents and bankers. Still, Law is credited with the beginnings of the First Bank of the United States, the first bank to perform many of the functions of a central bank. After many missteps, including the failure to use margin requirements, Greenspan is credited, perhaps falsely, with ending the stock market crash of 1987. He later admitted as much. A brief biography of John Law will reveal more.

John Law was appointed Controller General of Finances of France under the Duke of Orle'ans, regent for the youthful king, Louis XV. As a reward for faithful service, Philippe d'Orléans appointed Law as Controller General of Finances in 1720. This appointment, at the age of 49, gave him effective control over external and internal commerce in France. In 1716 John Law had established the Banque Générale (a.k.a. Bank General) in France. While it was nominally a private bank, three-quarters of its capital consisted of government bills and government-accepted notes. This effectively made it the first central bank of the nation. However, it did not perform one of the main functions of a central bank namely issuing a *national* currency. Law also was responsible for the Mississippi Company bubble and a chaotic economic collapse in France, which has been compared to the early17th century tulipmania in Holland. The Mississippi Bubble was concurrent with the South Sea bubble of England. Law's methods were emulated in the South Seas. What follows are details leading up to the establishment of the Bank General.

Law was a gambler and a brilliant mental calculator, known to win card games by mentally calculating the odds. He originated economic ideas such as "The Scarcity Theory of Value" and the "real bills doctrine," ideas that had unreasonably long lives. Scarcity remains the hallmark of modern economic theory; the real bills doctrine has been invoked by Lloyd Metzler and Donald Trump. Law's views also held that money creation will stimulate the economy (anticipating Milton Friedman and his followers), that paper money is preferable to metallic money, and that shares are a superior form of money since they pay dividends.[13] John Law was the equal of some of the intellectuals of his age, such as Locke and Newton. He equalled them in originality and profundity of intellect and his powers of thought and deed were almost equally balanced. Fittingly, this sagacious, daring man was tall, imposing, and dark-skinned. He combined the highest ambition and unshakable self-confidence with a peculiar sincerity and longing to clear from the minds of others those barriers to the exploitation of the world's wealth. Though, of different spheres of influence, Duke John Churchill Marlborough (1650-1722) was among Law's contemporaries that offered the same combination of ambition, boldness and charm. Yet Marlborough had a taint of falseness and self-love which was not in the financier.[14]

Law was born into a family of bankers and goldsmiths from Fife in Scotland. Goldsmiths were the first bankers. Born with a gold spoon in his mouth, he joined the family business at age fourteen and studied the banking business until his father died in 1688. Through his mother, Law was related to the family which the Revolution made the most powerful in Scotland, the House of Argyll. He was

---

[13] Milton Friedman held that the money supply and its growth rate determined virtually everything. Among "everything" was the inflation rate and employment. He influenced Presidents Nixon and Reagan. John Kenneth Galbraith called him the most influential economist of the twentieth century. There is irony afoot: others saw his ideas belonging to an earlier century.

[14] Marlborough was an English soldier and statesman whose career spanned the reigns of five monarchs.

a speculator at an early age, making his father proud. He subsequently neglected the firm in favour of more extravagant pursuits and travelled to London to live the "British Dandy" lifestyle. He quickly lost large sums of money in gambling, despite his affinity for the gaming tables.

On April 9, 1694, John Law fought a duel with Edward "Beau" Wilson in Bloomsbury Square in London. Wilson had challenged Law over the affections of Elizabeth Villiers. A single pass and thrust of his sword killed Wilson. Law was arrested, charged with murder and stood trial at the Old Bailey. He appeared before the infamously sadistic "hanging-judge" Salathiel Lovell and was found guilty of murder and sentenced to death. Awaiting execution in Newgate Prison, his sentence was commuted to a fine upon the grounds that the offense only amounted to manslaughter. Wilson's brother appealed and had Law imprisoned, but Law managed to escape to Amsterdam. Speculating in women was part of his image as a British Dandy.

Figure 2.1
John Law by Casimir Bathazar

This was a speed-bump on the way to fame as an economist. Law urged the establishment of a national bank to create and increase instruments of credit and the issue of banknotes backed by land, gold or silver. These were the most precious commodities at the time. The first test of Law's system came when he had returned to Scotland and contributed to the debates leading to the Treaty of Union 1707. A couple of years before that, he published a text, *Money and Trade Consider'd with a Proposal for Supplying the Nation with Money*. Lengthy titles were common in those days.[15] Law's efforts to create a national bank in Scotland were ultimately rejected, and he left to pursue his ambitions abroad. He spent a decade moving between France and the Netherlands, dealing in financial speculations. The grave problems with the French economy generated the opportunity to put his system into practice.

Law made his home in Place Louis-le-Grand, a royal square where he could host and entertain Parisian nobles. He gained the attention of such notables as the Duke of Orle'ans and found himself a regular in high-stakes gambling parties attended by only the most affluent of Paris. He was not content to confine his gambling to Paris or France. His tall stature and elegant dress allowed Law to charm his way across Europe's financial hubs, ranging from Amsterdam to Venice. These experiences included many visits with bankers and agrarian folk, influenced Law's theories on monetary policies and the importance of paper money as credit. His idea of a centralized bank which would deal with a new form of paper money was years ahead of its time, especially for French and American thinkers.

Law was a pioneer in banking, but he was not the first to attempt to establish a national bank. That honour goes to the StockHolms Banco a.k.a. Bank of Palmstruch, founded by Johan Palmstruch in 1656, before Law was born. Though the bank was private the king chose its management. However, the bank collapsed because it issued too many notes without the necessary collateral. Palmstruch, who was considered responsible for the bank's losses, kings almost never being liable, was condemned to death, but later received clemency. There will be more to this story. In 1668, the bank became the Riksens Standers Bank

---

[15] The most extensive account of Law's other writings is in Antoin E. Murphy, John Law: Economic Theorist and Policy-Maker (Oxford, England: Oxford University Press, 1997). Murphy is primarily responsible for completing the transformation of opinion about Law from a con man to an important economic theorist and successful (for a time) financial leader.

("Bank of the Estates of the Realm") and was operated under the auspices of the parliament to prevent interference by none other than the king. The name of the bank was changed to Sveriges Riksbank in 1866. Initially, the Riksbank was not allowed to issue bank notes.[16] In 1701 nonetheless permission was granted to issue credit-notes. To prevent forgeries, the Riksbank began to produce its own paper for bank-notes at a paper-mill, Tumba Bruk, founded in Tumba, on the outskirts of Stockholm. But the Riksbank did not function as a central bank until 1897, continuing to this day. This means that the European influence of John Law predated the establishment of a fully functioning central bank. Law, wearing his economist's hat, would have been impressed by the Riksbank instituting of the annual Nobel prize in Economic Sciences in 1968.

Law's Evolving System

Early on, Law had the idea of abolishing minor monopolies and private preparers of taxes. As we will see, there is some irony at work here. He planned to create a bank for national finance and a state company for commerce, ultimately to exclude all private revenue. This, of course, would create a giant monopoly of finance and trade run by the state, with profits to pay off the national debt. A council was called to consider Law's proposal, which included financiers such as Samuel Bernard. In the Fall of 1715, the council rejected the proposition. The wars of Louis XIV came to the rescue of Law's ideas. The wars left the country completely devastated, both economically and financially. A consequence was the shortage of precious metals which led to a shortage of coins in circulation, which in turn limited the production of new coins. After the death of Louis XIV seventeen months after Law's arrival, the Duke of Orle'ans presented law with the opportunity to showcase his ingenuity. On May Day, 1716, Law presented a modified version of his centralized bank plan to the Générale Banque in France, which eventually became the Bank of France. It in turn approved a private bank in which investors supplied one-fourth of an investment in currency backed by gold and the other parts in defunct government bonds. A key feature of the proposal was the issuance of the bank's own currency backed by gold. Thus, the currency could be redeemed by the weight of silver

---

[16] Bank notes or credit notes are forms of letters sent by a buyer a seller, usually to a bank, stating the amount credited to the buyer's account. It can also be used to assess the buyer's account balance in the event that a deposit has not been made.

from the original deposit of gold instead of relying on the fluctuation of livres, the French currency, which had been devaluing rapidly.

This banking platform enabled Law to pursue giant monopoly companies. He saw France bankrolling the endeavour with 100 million livres in the form of Mississippi Company stock. The fabled Mississippi Company, later renamed the Occident Company, eventually became a part of the Company of the Indies, financed in the same way as the private bank.

As Controller General of France, Law instituted many beneficial reforms, some of which had lasting effect, others were soon abolished. For one thing, he tried to break up large land-holdings to benefit the peasants; he abolished internal road and canal tolls; he encouraged the building of new roads; and the starting of new industries. In this process, he imported artisans from Italy and other counties by offering low-interest loans. Industry increased 60 percent in two years, while the number of French ships engaged in export went from sixteen to three hundred.

The Mississippi Company

Law bought The Mississippi Company in August 1717 to help the French colony in Louisiana. Its purpose was to monopolize trade with Louisiana and in Canadian beaver skins. ("Mississippi" comes from the river being in the Louisiana territory.) Law floated the Mississippi Company as a joint stock trading company called the Compagnie d'Occident (The Mississippi Company or literally, "Company of [the] West".[17] In turn, it was granted a trade monopoly of the West Indies and North America. The abolition of other "minor" monopolies guaranteed the trade monopoly. Law converted the government debt into *rentes* and offered the government an interest rate reduction. His idea was to generate a cash flow that could be leveraged into wonderfully expanding commercial activity. Indeed, the Mississippi Company managed to gain a monopoly in tobacco in September 1718 and the Senegalese Company (trading with Africa). In 1718 the bank became the Banque Royale ("Royal Bank"). As a

---

[17] Earlier examples of joint stock trading companies include the Dutch East Indies Company (1602) and the English East Indies Company (1600/1613). The trade of a joint stock trading company is always managed by a court of directors. This court is frequently subject to the control of a general court of proprietors. But the greater part of these proprietors seldom pretend to know much about the business.

royal bank its shares were guaranteed. The Company absorbed the Compagnie des Indes Orientales (Company of the East Indies), Compagnie de Chine (Company of China), and other rival trading companies and became the Compagnie Perpetuelle des Indes on May 23, 1719, with a monopoly of commerce on all the seas.

Meantime, the French government allowed Law to open a conventional, note-issuing bank, the Banque Generale. In January 1719, the Bank General was renamed the Banque Royale with a note issue guaranteed by the crown. While remaining in control of the bank he acquired the French East India and China companies. Then he created a conglomerate of all his companies (the Compagnie des Indes) which monopolized all French trade beyond Europe. Law issued shares against the conglomerate at 1,000 livres per share to acquire the right to mint new coinage valued at weights of gold or silver which varied greatly during Law's regime. Share prices rose to 1,000 livres on the market to match the face value of shares within a few months. Between August and December 1719 Law took over the administration of the French tax system. Share prices soared to 3,000 livres.

Early in 1719, the French government allowed Law to issue 50,000 new shares in the Mississippi Company at 500 livres with just 75 livres down and the rest due in nineteen additional monthly payments of 25 livres each. The share price rose to 1,000 livres before the second instalment was even due. Ordinary citizens flocked to Paris to participate. From this success, Law offered to pay off the national debt of 1.5 billion livres by issuing an additional 300,000 shares at 500 livres paid in ten monthly instalments. By mid-year the Mississippi Company had issued more than 600,000 shares and the par value of the company stood at 300 million livres. During the summer the share price skyrocketed from 1,000 to 5,000 livres and continued to rise through year-end. The price ultimately reached the dizzying heights of 15,000 livres per share. The term *millionaire* was first used. Little wonder when John Law received that award of Controller General.[18]

---

[18] For more on the South Sea and Mississippi Companies, see the section in Wikipedia on the "South Sea."

The Mississippi Bubble

Before we paddle too far up the Mississippi, we need to restate the definition for a bubble. An asset bubble is trade in an asset at a price or price range that strongly deviates from the corresponding asset's intrinsic value. It could be described as a situation in which asset prices appear to be based on implausible or inconsistent views about the future. The tricky part in all this is the finding of an asset's intrinsic value. Because it is difficult to observe intrinsic values, bubbles are often conclusively identified only in retrospect, once a sudden drop in prices has happened. This is convenient for those who believe that bubbles cannot occur; that is, the market price is always and everywhere the intrinsic value of the asset. No less a personage than Alan Greenspan argued that financial and other asset bubbles could never exist. He apparently changed his mind after a few bubbles broke on his watch.[19]

Getting back to the John Law story, Law proceeded to refund the national debt (with a face value of 1,400 million livres but a market value of much less) with new shares sold at 5000 livres per share, payable in monthly instalments. Conveniently, payment could be made in the notes issued by Law's Banque Royale. By August 1720 he had acquired the government debt guaranteeing him a steady flow of income from the treasury. Then, share prices immediately rose to 10,000 livres. By now he was France's Controller General and Superintendant Generale of Finance, while heading the Banque Royale. Law now was CEO of a private conglomerate that controlled France's overseas trade and the development of its colonies, collected France's taxes, minted its coins and held three-quarters of France's national debt. By controlling all markets, Law could issue junk equity to buy junk bonds. Not surprisingly, King Louis XV was a principal shareholder.

---

[19] As I have noted in my publications, a variety of formal definitions of a bubble exist. Intuition remains the same. If the price of an asset is high today only because buyers believe that the selling price will be high tomorrow, a bubble exists. Put differently, today's price is not fully explained by fundamentals (variables having a direct effect on future income streams from, for example, equities). Often, it appears, a self-fulfilling prophecy is underway, because asset prices will cleave to the high side if buyers believe they will. Initially the high asset price is "justifiable," because it yields a return (dividends) equal to or greater than returns on alternative assets including, say, bonds.

The stock prices are in 1000s of livres. The principal events related to price levels are identified. We can observe the effects of each event, climaxing with Law's Price Deflation Proposal which apparently pricked the bubble.

The Bubble is Pricked

Law's Banque Royale issued new bank notes to fund each new issue of shares. Sensing the debasing of the bank's notes, people began to sell shares, converting their capital gains into gold. By the end of January 1720, share prices fell below 10,000 livres. The king, seeing the downside to this venture and an insider trader if there ever was one, sold his shares back to the conglomerate at 9,000 livres per share. He made a princely gain. The Banque Royale ceased supporting the share prices with new bank notes. Despite Law's devaluation of bank notes relative to gold (Law's Price Deflation Proposal), share prices had fallen to 2,000 livres by September 1720 and to 1,000 livres by December. By September 1721 the share prices had fallen to 400 livres or roughly to its value in May 1719. This is roughly equivalent of the Dow going from 1,000 to 10,000 in 1 1/2 years, then crashing to 400, a decline of 96 percent, one year later.

A Revisionist's View: Mississippi Was Not a Bubble

Not everyone has faith in bubbles. To be fair, we should consider the other side of the argument. Peter M. Garber claims that Mississippi was not a bubble.[20] This, despite his excellent historical account in the article "After all," he writes, "behind the price rise lies Law's program to revitalize the French economy through financial innovation and fiscal reform." As to the downward slide in share prices, "it is even easier to understand, given the radical shifts in monetary policy and the intimate connection of Compagnie shares to Banque Royale note emissions."[21] A rational macro-model underpinned John Law's program, for "elements of [Keynesian economics, supply-side economics, monetarism] were primary components of Law's scheme."[22] Rational expectations were at work because the French buyers of the shares had this convincing model apparently embossed on their silk cockades. "It is the centrepiece of most money and

---

[20] P. M. Garber, "Tulipmania," *Journal of Political Economy* Vol 97 (June 1989), pp. 535-60.

[21] *Ibid.*, p. 46.

[22] *Op. cit.*, p. 47.

macroeconomics textbooks produced in the last two generations and the lingua franca of economic policymakers concerned with the problem of underemployed economies."[23]

My first reaction to this revisionist view is "wow!" It is quite a stretch to think that John Law in 1720 understood economic texts published in the 20th century. Worse, Keynesian economics, supply-side economics and monetarism clash. Each is a different macro-model. In Keynesian economics, aggregate demand drives the system. In supply-side economics, tax cuts comprise the only acceptable policy. In monetarism, only the money supply matters. Besides, the spillover to the French economy was immediate and most notable in food prices. By May 21, 1720, Law was forced to deflate the value of banknotes and cut the stock price on Mississippi Company stock. As the public rushed to convert banknotes to coin, Law was forced to close Banque Generale for ten days, then limit the transaction size once the bank reopened. The queues grew longer, the Mississippi Company stock price continued to fall, and food prices soared by as much as 60 percent. Food is a necessity while company stock is a luxury.

The fractional reserve ratio was one fifth, and a Royal edict to criminalize the sale of gold was decreed. A later Royal edict decreed that gold coin was illegal, which was soon reversed, leading 50 people to be stampeded to death. The rush to convert paper money to coins led to sporadic bank hours and riots. Squatters now occupied the square of Palace Louis-le-Grand and openly attacked the financiers that inhabited the area. Under these circumstances and the guise of night, John Law fled Paris some seven months later.

From Paris, Law went to Brussels--impoverished. He spent the next few years gambling in Rome, Copenhagen and Venice. Despite the glamour of such places, he never regained his former prosperity. Law knew he could never return to Paris after the death of Orle'ans in 1723. Law was granted permission to live in London, having received that pardon in 1719. He lived there for four years and then moved to Venice where he contracted pneumonia and died a pauper in 1729. This was a bad Hollywood ending, one hardly fit for someone presumably living under the spell of rational expectations.

Next, we consider the South Sea Bubble, to which John Law's systems were applied.

---

[23] *Ibid.*

Chapter 3
The South Sea Bubble

Like so many movie stars, the South Sea Company had more than one name. For example, the British Singer Adele's real name is Adele Louise Blue Adkins. Likewise, the official name of the South Sea Company is "The Governor and Company of the merchants of Great Britain, trading to the South Seas and other parts of America, and for the encouragement of fishing." We can be excused for simply referring to Adele or especially to the South Sea Company. It too was British, being a joint-stock company founded in 1711, created as a public-private partnership to consolidate and reduce the cost of the national debt. At the time, Britain was involved in the War of the Spanish Succession and Spain controlled South America. Except for Brazil, Spanish is still the spoken language of South America.

There was no realistic prospect that trade would take place and the company never realized any significant profit from its monopoly, this despite the conventional wisdom that monopolies monopolize profits. Spain was also trading in the same region. In 1720, in return for a loan of 7 million pounds to finance the war against France, the House of Lords passed the South Sea Bill, which allowed the South Sea Company a monopoly in trade with South America. The company underwrote the English National debt, which stood at 30 million pounds, on a promise of 5 percent interest from the Government. Despite the absence of profits from trade, company stock rose greatly in value as the South Sea Company expanded its operations dealing in government debt, peaking in 1720 before collapsing to a little above its original issue price. This rise and subsequent fall of company stock prices is known as the South Sea Bubble.

There is considerable irony in all this. Before its collapse, the South Sea Company promoted the Bubble Act of 1720. The Act forbade the creation of joint-stock companies without a royal charter. It forbade companies like the

South Sea Company. A little background will help us to summarize what happened. A considerable number of people were ruined by the share collapse, and the national economy was consequently greatly diminished. As is so often the case the founders of the scheme engaged in insider trading, using advance knowledge of when the national debt was to be consolidated to make large profits from purchasing debt ahead of others. Worse, huge bribes were given to politicians to support the Acts of parliament required by the scheme. Company money was used to deal in its own shares, and selected persons purchasing shares were given loans backed by those same shares to spend on purchasing more shares. In this pyramid scheme, the expectation of vast wealth from trade with South America was used to encourage the unwitting public to buy shares, despite the limited likelihood that would ever happen. We would be wrong to say that no trade ever happened. But the only significant trade was in slaves, which the company failed to handle profitably.[24]

It wasn't just South Sea Company stock that went through the roof; other stocks soared along with the manic speculative activity. Persons went wild as stocks increased in the South Sea and other 'dodgy' schemes, and huge fortunes were made, only to be lost. When the bubble burst, the South Sea Company Directors were arrested, and their estates forfeited. Some 462 members of the House of Commons and 112 Peers in the South Sea Company were involved in the crash. Frantic bankers thronged the lobbies of Parliament and the Riot Act was read to restore order. Royalty was not exempt; King George I became involved as his two mistresses, the Countess of Darlington and the Duchess of Kendal were deep into the South Sea Company and were blamed by commoners for responsibility. Upon Parliamentary inquiry, John Aisliabie, Chancellor of the Exchequer, and several members of Parliament were expelled in 1721. These and the Company Directors were the fall guys. The rest went, as it were, Scot-free.

Parliaments and congresses have a way of dealing with their mistakes. In this instance, a parliamentary inquiry was held after the crash to discover its causes. As usual, several politicians were disgraced, and persons found to have profited unlawfully from the company had assets confiscated proportionate to their gains. This does not mean that a just redistribution of wealth took place. Rather, as is so often the case in these matters, most of the speculators were rich men who

---

[24] For more details, see Richard S. Dale, et. Al. "Financial Markets can go mad: evidence of irrational behaviour during the South Sea Bubble," *Economic History Review*, 58 (2), 2005: 233-271.

remained comfortably rich after losing in the share's decline. Others had little to lose and remained uncomfortably poor. Porters and ladies' maids who had bought their own carriages became destitute almost overnight. Clergy, Bishops and the Gentry lost their life savings; much of the country suffered a catastrophic loss of money and property. The gullible few whose innate greed had lain behind this mass hysteria demanded vengeance.

What happened next will surprise only the naïve. The South Sea Company was restructured and continued to operate for more than a century after the Bubble burst. Those who admire central bankers will appreciate what happened next. The headquarters of the company were in Threadneedle Street at the centre of the financial district in London. During the turmoil, the Bank of England also was a private company dealing in national debt. The crash of its rival consolidated its position as banker to the British government. The Bank of England became the central bank, still conveniently located on Threadneedle Street. One Robert Walpole, who had the foresight to be against the South Sea Company from the get-go, took charge and sorted through the financial mess. As just reward, he was made Chancellor of the Exchequer. There he divided the National debt that had been the South Sea Company into three, among the Bank of England, the Treasury and a Sinking Fund. The Sinking Fund was made up of a part of the nation's income that been put aside for such contingencies. Stability eventually returned.

Historical Background

As ever, some history preceded the calamity. In August 1710, Robert Harley was appointed Chancellor of the Exchequer. By now the government had become reliant on the Bank of England. At the time, the Bank of England was a privately-owned company, chartered some 16 years earlier, and which had obtained a monopoly as the lender to (yes) Westminster, in return for arranging and managing loans to the government. However, the government had become disenchanted with the service it was receiving from a monopoly and Harley began to seek new ways to improve the national finances.

A fresh Parliament met in November 1710 with the resolve to end the national financial crisis. At the time, it was fighting two wars: a war with France, which was not to end until the 1713 Treaty of Utrecht, and the Great Northern War, which was not ended until 1721. Harley nonetheless came well prepared, with detailed accounting of the national debt. This was not an easy undertaking since the debt had been accumulated by different departments which arranged their own loans as the need arose. Finally, in January 1711 the House of Commons agreed to appoint a committee to investigate the entire debt mess. The committee included Harley; the two Auditors of the Imprests, whose task was to investigate government spending; Harley's brother Edward; and Paul Foley, his brother-in-law. [25] This was not the first nor the last time that nepotism reigned. The Secretary of the Treasury, William Lowndes, was also included; he had had responsibility for re-minting the entire debased British coinage in 1696. Finally, John Aisliabie who represented the October Club, a group of 200 MPs who had tied their votes together in a neat bundle, was added to the committee.[26]

Harley's initial concern was to find £300,000 to meet the quarter's payroll for the British army operating in Europe under the redoubtable Duke John Churchill Marlborough (1650-1722).[27] This amount was again provided privately, by a consortium of Edward Gibbon, George Caswall and Hoare's Bank. Well, you must wonder what the Bank of England was up to. The Bank had been operating an unsuccessful state lottery on behalf of the government. Another lottery was started in 1711 with no better success. What was Harley to do? He sold tickets to John Blunt, a director of the Hollow Sword Blade Company, which despite its name was an unofficial private bank. In what was the first successful English state lottery, ticket sales begun on March 3, 1711 had completely sold out by the 7th. Success breeds success, and there shortly followed another, larger lottery. "The Two Million Adventure" or "The Classis" had tickets costing £100 with a top prize of £20,000 while every ticket winning a prize of at least £10. The prizes were paid in the form of a fixed annuity over a period of years, so that the government held the prize money as a loan until it was paid out to the winners. The marketing, of course, was handled by members of the Sword Blade syndicate with Gibbon selling £200,000 of tickets and earning £4,500 in commissions. The only sure winner was the syndicate. Blunt did even better, selling £993,000 worth of tickets. Again, family members were the only ones to

---

[25] Imprests comprise an advance of money from a fund used by a business for small items of expenses to be restored to a fixed amount periodically.

[26] Some of the details herein are gleaned from the classic Jon Carswell, *The South Sea Bubble* (London: Cresset Press, 1950), pp. 40, 48-50.

[27] Marlborough was an English soldier and statesman whose career spanned the reigns of five monarchs.

be absolutely trusted, and Charles Blunt was made Paymaster of the lottery with expenses of £5,000.

The Company, At Less-than-Immaculate Conception

The tally on the national debt, upon investigation, was £9,000,000, and there was no allocated income to pay it off. Edward Harley and John Blunt had devised a scheme to consolidate this debt in much the same way that the Bank of England had consolidated previous debts, though the Bank still held a monopoly. Holders of the debt would be required to surrender it to a new company, the South Sea Company, which in return would issue shares of the same amount. In turn the government would pay the Company 6 percent interest plus expenses (£568,279 10s) annually. The interest would be distributed as a dividend to shareholders. This sounded handsome enough but there was more: The Company was given a monopoly of trade with South America, seemingly a potentially lucrative enterprise. The enthusiasm for this new arrangement was dampened by the fact that South America was controlled by Spain which happened to be at war with England.

Figure 3.1
The Night Singer of Shares

NOTE: The "night singer of shares" sold stock on the street during the South Sea Bubble--Amsterdam 1720

We should say more about John Blunt. He was among the entrants to the promising profession of scrivener or scribe in the year of the Glorious Revolution (1688). The scrivener copied letters and legal papers for mostly the nobility. They were predecessors to the legal profession. At the comparatively late age of twenty-five Blunt was an apprentice to Daniel Richards, Scrivener or scribe. Like his father, who was a prosperous shoemaker in Rochester, Blunt was a Baptist. He was burly and overbearing, glib, ingenious, and determined. He was well fitted to make his way in the business jungle, and from the get-go was successful. Only four months after setting up as a scrivener he married a lady of the respectable Warwickshire family named Elizabeth Court, and in 1691 he became a liveryman.[28] In the techniques of his profession he was unequalled; and his coarse character contained just that trace of titanism[29] which was to carry him for a moment or two to the summit of politics and finance.

Blunt was making his way to fortune in an England that was advancing to power and civilization at a rate never equalled before. It was an age of giants, great achievements and unparalleled confidence. Isaac Newton and John Locke were transforming science and philosophy, Johnathan Swift had published *Gulliver's Travels*, and Daniel Defoe had penned *Robinson Crusoe*. Joseph Addison and Richard Steele founded *The Spectator*, a daily of 3000 circulation widely read in the coffee houses of London in 1711. In Cornwall steam power was set to work. The British Isles was brought under a single political system— Ireland by force, Scotland by diplomacy. The English armies that the Blunts helped shoe campaigned over the Continent and won a series of land victories against the greatest European power in battle on a scale not to be seen again for nearly a century. Augustan England was a Britain of the commercial as well as the political revolution, charged with a new and intoxicating energy.

Europeans applied the term "South Seas" only to South America and surrounding waters, not to any other ocean. The arrangement not only held out the potential for future profits but also encouraged a desire to end the war,

---

[28] Rather than an owner or worker in a livery stable, here "Liveryman" meant he was a member of a livery company.

[29] Titanism is a spirit of defiance of authority, conventional society, and the established order.

necessary if any profits were forthcoming. The original suggestion for the South Sea scheme has sometimes been credited romantically to Daniel Defoe (c.1660-1731), it is more likely the idea of William Paterson (1658-1719), one of the founders of the Bank of England as well as the ill-fated Darien Scheme, the failure of which contributed to Scotland's agreement to unite with England in 1707. Defoe is remembered as the novelist and spy who wrote *Robinson Crusoe.*

The Darien Scheme was an unsuccessful attempt by the Kingdom of Scotland to become a world trading nation by establishing a colony called "Caledonia" on the Gulf of Darien in the late 1690s. The general idea was to provide an overland route between the Pacific and Atlantic oceans. Among other things, collusion between the English East Indies Company and the English government and a siege by Spanish forces doomed the scheme. As the Scottish Company was backed by 25-50 percent of all the money circulating in Scotland, the failure of the Company almost completely ruined the entire Lowlands. Still, the adventure led to a novel and a stage play, which were only slightly less crazy than the South Sea scheme.

Edward Harley was handsomely rewarded for the South Seas Scheme; he was made the Earl of Oxford on May 23, 1711 and was promoted to Lord High Treasurer. Now with a more secure position, he began secret peace negotiations with France. Since the lotteries were discredited, some of the debt intended to be consolidated under the scheme was available in the open market before the scheme was announced, at a discounted rate of £55 per £100 nominal value. This conveniently allowed anyone with advance knowledge to buy debt cheap and sell at an immediate profit and made it possible for Harley to bring further financial supporters into the scheme, such as Theodore Janssen (1658-1748). He had arrived on the scene some eight years before the Revolution at the age of twenty-two with a small fortune he was to build into one of the largest London had seen. Janssen was made a director of the South Sea Company and was arrested (along with the other directors) when the Scheme collapsed. However, he was treated gingerly and retained much of his fortune of some £50,000.

Despite the founders' knowledge that there was no realistic expectation they there would ever be a trade to exploit, the potential for great wealth nonetheless was widely publicized at every opportunity, to encourage interest in the scheme. The objective of the founders was to create a Company which they could use to become wealthy, and which offered future scope for further government deals.

The Flotation

The Charter for the South Seas Company, drawn up by John Blunt, was based on that of the Bank of England. Blunt was paid £3,846 for his services. Directors would be elected every three years while shareholders would meet twice a year. The Company employed a Cashier, Secretary and Accountant. The Governor was intended to be an honorary position, and the position was later customarily held by the ruling monarch. The charter allowed the full court of directors to nominate a smaller committee to act on any matter on its behalf. In a show of ethical decorum directors of the Bank of England and of the East India Company were disbarred from being a director of the South Sea Company. Any ship of more than 500 tons owned by the Company was to have a Church of England clergyman on board. Having God on the Company's side was comforting to the directors.

The exchange of government debt for stock was to happen in five separate lots. The first two, totalling £2.75 million from about 200 large investors, had already been arranged before the company's charter was even issued on September 10, 1711. The government exchanged £0.75 million of its own debt held by different departments. Individual office holders in the government were responsible for money in their charge and were at liberty to invest it to their own advantage before it was required. Harley exchanged £8,000 of debt and was appointed Governor of the new company. Blunt, Caswall and Sawbridge together provided £65,000, Janssen £25,000 of his own plus £250,000 from a foreign consortium, Decker £49,000, and Sir Ambrose Crawley £36,791.

Jacob Strawbridge (c.1665-1748) began life with a considerable fortune. Strawbridge became an original director of the South Sea Company, which conveniently banked with his firm. He later became a partner in the firm of Turner, Sawbridge and Caswall, bankers, operating under the name and charter of the Sword Blade Company. He returned to Parliament as a Whig in 1715 and voted against the peerage bill which he had been put down as to be spoken to by Craggs's senior and his own partner, Sir George Caswall. When the South Sea fraudulent behaviour came out at the beginning of 1721 Sawbridge, with the other directors in the Commons, was expelled from the House, committed to the custody of the sergeant at arms and examined by the South Sea Committee of the Commons. He was questioned about entries in the books of his firm purporting to show that £50,000 of the £574,000 South Sea stock which was supposed to have been issued as bribes to Members of Parliament under George Caswall had been sold at a profit of £250,000 for Charles Stanhope, the secretary to the Treasury. The evidence exonerates Stanhope from any knowledge or share of this transaction. Strawbridge declared that he, Jacob Sawbridge, had bought the stock for himself and his partners and had entered it under a fictitious name so that their staff would not know that it belonged to them.[30]

A bill was introduced confiscating the estates of the directors and other guilty parties for the relief of their victims. Sawbridge petitioned the House for lenient treatment because of ignorance and inadvertency, without any unlawful views or designs, a weak defence against the severe charges. He could keep £5,000 of a fortune of £77,000; this proportion shows that the Commons classed him among the more rascally of the directors. As with all the directors, he was also prohibited from sitting in Parliament or holding public office.

The South Sea Company created a coat of arms with the motto *A Gadibus usque ad Auroram* (from Cadiz to the dawn) and rented a large house in the City as its headquarters. Seven sub-committees were created to handle its everyday business, the most important being the "Committee for the affairs of the company". The Sword Blade company was retained as its banker and on the strength of its new government connections issued notes in its own right, notwithstanding the Bank of England monopoly. The task of the Company Secretary was to oversee trading activities; the Accountant Grigsby, was responsible for registering and issuing stock; and the Cashier Robert Knight acted as John Blunt's personal assistant at a salary of £200 pounds per year. The Sword Blade bank—that is what it was—was a cut above the other companies.

Expanding Trade—Slave Trade, That Is

The stated goal of the South Sea Company was expanded trade for the British Isles. What resulted was the expansion of the slave trade. The War of the Spanish Succession ended March 1713, when the Treaty of Utrecht granted Britain an *Asiento,* a contract giving permission, lasting 30 years to supply the Spanish colonies with 4,800 slaves yearly. It was a special kind of Gentleman's Agreement. Britain was permitted to open offices in Buenos Aires, Caracas, Cartagena, Havana, Panama, Portobello and Vera Cruz to arrange the slave trade. One ship of no more than 500 tons could be sent to one of these places each year (the *Navio de Permiso*) with general trade goods. Thus, trade in goods was

---

[30] For many of the details, see Carswell, *Ibid.,* pp. 56-58

limited. A quarter of the profits were to be reserved for the King of Spain. There was provision for two extra sailings at the start of the contract. The *Asiento* was granted in the name of Queen Anne and then contracted to the South Sea Company.

By July the Company had arranged contracts with the Royal African Company to supply the necessary African slaves to Jamaica. £10 was paid for a slave aged over 16, £8 for one under 15 but over 10. Two-thirds were to be male, and 90 percent adults. The Company trans-shipped 1,230 slaves from Jamaica to America in the first year, plus any that might have been added (against standing instructions) by the ship's captains on their own behalf. On arrival of the first cargoes, the local authorities refused to accept the *Asiento*, which still had not been officially confirmed there by the Spanish authorities. The slaves were eventually sold at a loss in the West Indies. It was poetic justice, at last. In 1714 the government announced that a quarter of profits would be reserved for the Queen and a further 7.5 percent for a financial adviser, Manasseh Gilligan. Some Company board members refused to accept the contract on these terms, and the government was obliged to reverse its decision.

Despite these setbacks, the Company maintained its business, having raised £200,000 to finance the operations. In 1714 2,680 slaves were carried, and for 1716-17, 13,000 more, but the trade continued to be unprofitable. An import duty of 33 pieces of eight was charged on each slave (though for this purpose some slaves might be counted only as a fraction of a slave, depending on quality). One of the extra trade ships was sent to Cartagena in 1714 carrying woollen goods, despite a warning that there was no market for them there, and they indeed remained unsold for two years.[31]

Musical Chairs as the Board's Management Changes

There is a potential downside when a company is heavily dependent on the goodwill of the government. When the government changed, so too did the Company board. In 1714 one of the directors who had been sponsored by Harley, Arthur Moore, had attempted to send 50 tons of private goods on board the Company ship. He was quickly dismissed as a director, but the result was the beginning of Harley's own fall from favour with the Company. Indeed, on July

---

[31] Much of the detail regarding names and numbers in this section is based on John Carswell, *The South Sea Bubble*, *Op. cit.*, especially pp. 47-59.

27, 1714, Harley was replaced as Lord High Treasurer because of a disagreement that had broken out within the Tory faction in Parliament. Queen Anne had the temerity to die on August 1, 1714. At the election of directors in 1715 the Prince of Wales (the future King George II) was elected as Governor of the Company. The new King George I and the Prince of Wales both had significant holdings in the Company, as did some prominent Whig politicians, including James Craggs the Elder, the Earl of Halifax and Sir Joseph Jekyll. James Craggs, as Postmaster General, was responsible for intercepting mail on behalf of the government to obtain political and financial information. All Tory politicians were removed from the board and replaced with businessmen. The Whigs Horatio Townshend, brother in law of Robert Walpole, and the Duke of Argyll were elected directors. What happened was like the Democrats being replaced by Republicans in the U.S. Congress.

As so often happens, the new government led to a revival of the Company's share value, which had fallen below its issue price. The previous government had failed to make the interest payments to the Company for the last two years, owing more than a million pounds. The new administration insisted the debt be written off but allowed the Company to issue new shares to stockholders equalling the value of the missed payments. At around £10 million, this now represented half the share capital issued in the entire country. In 1714 the Company had 2,000 to 3,000 shareholders, more than either of its rivals.

As ever, politics sways like the strongest branch on the strongest tree. Once again, by the time of the next director's elections in 1718, a schism *within* the Whigs broke that proverbial branch. Walpole's faction supporting the Prince of Wales strongly disagreed with James Stanhope's supporting the King. Not only were Argyll and Townshend dismissed as directors of the Company, but so too were the surviving Tories--Sir Richard Hoare and George Pit. Predictably, King George I became Governor. The schism fell short of a "midnight massacre," for four members of Parliament retained directorships, as did six persons holding government financial offices. Finance often prevails and true to form, the old reliable Sword Blade Company remained bankers to the South Sea Company, and even had flourished despite the Company's dubious legal position. The very wealthy Blunt and Sawbridge remained South Sea directors, and they had been joined by Gibbon and Child. Meanwhile, Caswall had retired as director to concentrate his energies on the Sword Blade Business; this was like a chess piece moving from king to queen, or vice versa. Nature often acts as an eraser, and in

November 1718 subtracted Governor Sir James Bateman and Deputy Governor Samuel Shepheard from the population. Save for the honorary position of Governor (the King), this left the Company suddenly without its two most senior and experienced directors. No one is indispensable; they were just as quickly replaced by Sir John Fellowes as Sub-Governor and Charles Joye as Deputy.[32]

War and the Refinancing of Government Debt

Besides warring parties, the most disruptive event is war itself. In 1718 war broke out with Spain once again. The Company's assets in South America were seized, which cost the Company about £300,000. Prospects for trade, which had always been remote, become grim. The Company had purchased ships and had been planning new ventures; this went up in the smoke of cannon fire. Now events in France began to influence the future of the Company. John Law, exiled after killing a man in a duel, had travelled around Europe before settling in France. In his new country, he founded a bank, which in December 1718 became the Banque Royale, national bank of France, at a time when Law was granted sweeping powers to control the economy of France, which operated largely by royal decree. His remarkable success was known in financial circles throughout Europe, and now came to inspire Blunt and associates to make greater efforts to grow their own concerns.

In February 1719, Craggs explained to the House of Commons a new scheme for improving the national debt. He suggested converting the annuities issued after the 1710 lottery into South Sea stock. By Act of Parliament, the Company was granted the right to issue £1,150 of new stock for every £100 per annum of annuity which was surrendered. The government would pay 5 percent per annum on the stock created, which would halve their annual bill. The conversion was voluntary, amounting to £2.5 million of new stock if all converted. The Company was to make an additional new loan to the government pro-rata up to £750,000, again at 5 percent. It seems that 5 percent was a magical interest rate, perhaps the real or natural rate.

The offer was presented to the public by the South Sea Company in July 1719. Meanwhile, in March there was an abortive attempt to restore the Old Pretender, James Edward Stuart, to the throne of Britain, with a small landing of troops in Scotland. They were defeated at the Battle of Glen Shiel on June 10.

---

[32] Again, Carswell, *Ibid.*, pp. 67-75 is the source of some details and the names.

The Sword Blade Company spread a rumour that the Pretender had been captured creating a general euphoria that pushed the South Sea share price from £100, where it had been lingering in the spring, to £114. Annuitants were still paid out at the same money value of shares, the Company keeping the profit from the rise in value before issuance. About two-thirds of the in-force annuities were exchanged.

The 1719 scheme was a resounding success from the government's perspective, and they sought to repeat it. Negotiations took place between Assliabie and Craggs for the government and Blunt, Cahier Knight and his assistant and Caswell. Janssen, the Sub-Governor and Deputy Governor were also consulted but negotiations remained secret from most of the Company. News from France was of fortunes being made investing in Law's bank, whose shares had risen sharply. Money was moving around Europe, and other flotations threatened to soak up available capital; for example, two insurance schemes in December 1719 each sought to raise £3 million.

Plans for a new scheme were made to take over most of the unconsolidated national debt of Britain (£30,981,712) in exchange for Company shares. Annuities were valued as a lump sum necessary to produce the annual income over the original term at an assumed interest rate of 5 percent which favoured those with shorter terms still to run. The government agreed to pay the same amount to the Company for all the fixed term repayable debt as it had been paying before, but after seven years the magical 5 percent interest rate would fall to 4 percent on both the new annuity debt and that taken over previously. After the first year, the Company was to give the government £3 million in four quarterly instalments. New stock would be created at a face value equal to the debt, but the share price was still rising and sales of the remaining stock, i.e., the excess of the total market value for the stock over the amount of the debt, would be used to raise the government fee plus a profit (of course) for the Company. The greater the price rise in advance of conversion, the greater profits would be made by the Company. Before the scheme, payments were costing the government £1.5 million per year. Thus, the total government debt in 1719 was over £50. The distribution of the debt was:

- £18.3 million held by three large corporations.
- £3.4 million by the Bank of England
- £3.2 million by the British East India Company

- £11.7 million by the South Sea Company
- Privately held redeemable debt amounted to £16.5 million
- £15 million consisted of *irredeemable* annuities, long-fixed-term annuities of 72-87 years, and short annuities of 22 years remaining to expire.

The purpose of this conversion was like the first one: debt holders and annuitants might receive less return in total, but an illiquid investment was transformed into shares which not only could be easily traded but were appreciating in price. Shares backed by national debt were considered a safe investment and a convenient way to hold and move money. Besides, it was far easier to move and safer than metal coins. The only alternative safe asset, land, was much harder to sell and it was legally much more complex to transfer ownership.

Figure 3.2
South Sea Hous, Dividend Hall

What were the benefits to the government? The government received a cash payment and lower overall interest on the debt. Importantly, it also gained control over when the debt had to be repaid, which was not before seven years but then at its discretion. This avoided the risk that debt might become repayable at some future point just when the government needed to borrow more and could be forced into paying higher interest rates. The payment to the government was to be used to buy in any debt not subscribed to in the scheme, which although it helped the government it also helped the Company by removing possibly competing securities from the market, including larger holdings by the Bank of England.

We are reminded that the main competitor to the South Sea Company was the Bank of England. The plan was presented to the board of the South Sea Company on January 21, and the Chancellor of the Exchequer John Aisliabie presented it to Parliament the next day. The House was stunned into silence and jaws dropped but recovered sufficiently to propose that the Bank of England be invited to make a better offer. In response, the Company increased its cash payment to £3.5 million, while the Bank proposed to undertake the conversion with a payment of £5.5 million and a fixed conversion price of £170 per £100 face value Bank stock. On February 1, the Company negotiators led by Blunt raised their offer to £4 million plus a proportion of £3.5 million depending on how much of the debt was converted. They also agreed that the interest rate would be reduced after four years instead of the original seven and agreed to sell on behalf of the government £1 million of Exchequer bills (formerly handled by the Bank). The House had an offer it could not refuse and accepted the South Sea bid. The stock of the Bank of England fell sharply.

The price of South Sea Company stock was now trading at £123, so the new issue amounted to an injection of £5 million of new money into a booming economy just as interest rates were falling. British Gross Domestic Product (GDP) was estimated as £64.4 million. This means that the debt to GDP ratio was about 50.6.

The South Sea Bubble

The Company began to talk up its stock with "the most extravagant rumours" of the value of its potential trade in the new World. Except for the unprofitable slave trade, there never was a potential for trade gains. Anyway, rumours were followed by a wave of speculative frenzy. The share price had risen from the time the scheme was proposed—from £128 in January 1720, to £175 in February, £330 in March and, following the scheme's acceptance £550 at the end of May.

What may have supported the Company's high multiple (its P/E ratio) was a fund of credit (known to the market) of £70 million available for commercial expansion which had been made available by substantial support from Parliament and the King. Shares were sold to politicians at the current market price; however, rather than paying for these shares, the recipients simply held on to what shares they had been offered, with the option of selling them back to the Company when and as they chose, receiving as "profit" the increase in market price. This method won over the heads of government, the King's mistress, et al. also had the advantage of binding their interests to the interests of the Company. To secure their own profits, they had to help drive up the price of the stock. Meanwhile, by publishing the names of their elite stockholders the Company managed to sustain its aura of legitimacy, which attracted and kept other buyers.

In a single year, the South Sea stock went up from about £100 to almost £1000 per share. This would be like the Dow Jones Index rising from 20,000 to 200,000 in one year. There was a countrywide frenzy—herd behaviour—as all types of people, from peasants to lords, developed a feverish interest in investing in primarily South Seas stock, but in stocks generally. It was in August 1720 that the price reached £1,000.

The Bubble Bursts

At £1000 a sell-off brought the shares back to £100 per share before the year was out, triggering bankruptcies among those who had bought on credit, and increasing selling, even short selling—selling borrowed shares in the hope of buying them back at a profit if the price fell. In the dizzying month of August 1720, the first of the instalment payments of the first and second money subscriptions on new issues of South Sea stock were due. Earlier in the year John Blunt had come up with an idea to prop up the share price: The Company would lend people money to buy its shares. As a result, many shareholders could not pay for their shares except by selling them. No less a personage than Isaac Newton made a fortune when the bubble was expanding, but in the end lost everything. Newton was quoted as saying, "I can calculate the movement of the stars, but not the madness of men." This bubble was not confined to Britain. A scramble for liquidity happened internationally as "bubbles" were also bursting in mid-aid in Amsterdam and Paris. The collapse coincided with the fall of the Mississippi Company of John Law in France. Thus, the price of South Sea shares began to decline even more.

The Bubble Act

Many joint-stock companies had been created that made extravagant (sometimes fraudulent) claims about foreign or other ventures or bizarre schemes. The South Sea Company was not the only company seeking to raise money in 1720. Others represented potentially sound, although novel, schemes, such as the founding insurance companies. These were nicknamed "Bubbles." Some of the companies had no legal basis, while others, such as the Hollow Sword Blade Company acting as the South Sea's Banker, used existing chartered companies for purposes entirely different from their creation. The York Buildings Company was set up to provide water to London but was purchased by Case Billingsley who used it to purchase confiscated Jacobite estates in Scotland, which then formed the assets of an insurance company.

Figure 3.3
Tree Caricature from South Sea Bubble Cards

NOTE: These bubble cards were very popular and were widely traded.

In the House of Commons on February 22, 1720 John Hungerford raised the question of bubble companies, and persuaded the House to set up a committee,

53

which he chaired, to investigate. He identified many companies which between them sought to raise £40 million in capital. The committee investigated the companies, establishing a principle that companies should not be operating outside the objects specified in their charters. This raised a potentially embarrassing question for the Hollow Sword Blade Company. However, difficulty was avoided by flooding the committee with MPs who were supporters of the South Sea Company and voted down the proposal to investigate the Hollow Sword by 75 to 25. Stanhope, who was a member of the committee, received £50,000 in "resalable" South Sea stock from Sawbridge, a director of the Hollow Sword. Ironically, Hungerford had previously been expelled from the Commons for accepting a bribe.

The Bubble Act was henceforth devoted to creating charters for the Royal Exchange Assurance Corporation and the London Assurance Corporation. The companies were required to pay £300,000 for the privilege. The Act required that a joint stock company could only be incorporated by Act of Parliament or Royal charter. The prohibition on unauthorized joint stock ventures was not repealed until 1825. Oddly, the passage of the Act gave a boost to the South Sea Company, with its shares leaping to £890 in early June. This peak, however, encouraged people to start to sell. To counterbalance the selling the Company's directors ordered their agents to buy, which succeeded in propping the price up at around £750. We have indicated what happened after a price of £1,000 was reached.[33]

By the end of September, the stock had fallen to £150. The failures now extended to banks and goldsmiths (the holders of gold) as they could not collect loans made on the stock. Thousands of individuals were ruined, including many members of the aristocracy. With the outrage of investors afoot, Parliament was recalled in December and the indispensable investigation began. In a report in 1721, it revealed widespread fraud among the company directors and corruption in the Cabinet. Among those implicated were John Aisliabie, the Chancellor of the Exchequer, James Craggs the Elder, the Postmaster General, James Craggs the Younger, the Southern Secretary, and even the reputable Lord Stanhope and Lord Sunderland, the heads of the Ministry. Craggs the Elder and Craggs the Younger both died in disgrace; the remainder were impeached for their corruption. The Commons found Aisliabie guilty of the "most notorious, dangerous and infamous corruption," and he was imprisoned.

---

[33] For some of the details, see Carswell, *Op. cit.*, pp. 116-117.

And so, the bursting of the South Sea Bubble coincided with many downfalls and subsequent deaths.

Next, we consider a somewhat happier outcome for Alexander Hamilton and the Panic of 1792. Still, there were troubles along the way.

Chapter 4
Alexander Hamilton and the Panic of 1792

Panic is a sudden uncontrollable fear or anxiety, often causing wildly unthinking behaviour. Hold that thought. A financial panic is a situation in which financial assets suddenly lose a large part of their normal value, often related to banks, while many recessions have coincided with such panics. Such panics are usually accompanied by wildly unthinking behaviour by persons acting in herds. The Panic of 1792 was a financial credit crisis that happened during the months of March and April 1792, precipitated by the expansion of credit by the newly formed Bank of the United States as well as rampant speculation on the part of William Duer, Alexander Macomb, and other prominent bankers. Duer, Macomb, and their colleagues attempted to drive up prices of U.S. debt securities and bank stocks, but when they defaulted on loans, prices fell, causing a bank run. Simultaneous tightening of credit by the Bank of the United States served to heighten the initial panic. Secretary of the Treasury Alexander Hamilton deftly managed the crisis by providing the banks across the Northeast with hundreds of thousands of dollars to make open-market purchases of securities, which allowed the market to stabilize by May 1792.

Figure 4.1
A Picture of Panic

NOTE: This prosaic painting of what "Panic" might feel like resonates with many public and private individuals. It might have registered the feelings of Alexander Hamilton or "the herd" when they confronted the Panic of 1792. The painting could have been used in the stage and screen productions of "Alexander Hamilton," if not in the audience.

Alexander Hamilton (1755-1804) was a major player before and after the Panic. He was an American statesman and one of the Founding Fathers of the United States. He was an influential interpreter of and promoter of the U.S. Constitution, as well as the founder of the nation's financial system, the Federalist Party, the U.S. Coast Guard, and the *New York Post* newspaper. As the first Secretary of the Treasury, Hamilton was the main author of the economic policies of the George Washington administration. He took the lead in the funding of the states' debts by the Federal government, as well the establishment of a national bank, a system of tariffs, and friendly trade relations with Britain. His vision included a strong central government lead by a vigorous executive branch, a strong commercial economy, with a national bank and support for manufacturing, plus a strong military. All this was challenged by Thomas Jefferson and James Madison who formed a rival party. They favoured strong states based in rural America and protected by state militias as opposed to a strong national army and navy They denounced Hamilton as too friendly toward Britain and toward monarchy in general, and too oriented toward cities, business and banking. There is some irony in the Jefferson-Hamilton discord. When Jefferson and Aaron Burr tied for the presidency in the electoral college of 1801, Hamilton helped to defeat Burr, whom he found unprincipled, and to elect Jefferson despite philosophical differences.

Figure 4.2
Alexander Hamilton

In 1784, Hamilton founded the Bank of New York which became one of the longest operating banks in American history; it stayed in business for over 220 years before it merged with another bank in 2007. He was one of the men who restored King's College, which had been suspended since 1775 and severely damaged during the War, as Columbia College in New York City, later named Columbia University. Long dissatisfied with the weak Articles of Confederation, he played a major leadership role at the Annapolis Convention in 1786. He drafted its resolution for a constitutional convention, and in doing so brought his long-time desire to have a more powerful, more financially independent federal government one stop closer to reality. He was chosen as a delegate for the Constitutional Convention. Not content with the final Constitution, he signed it anyway as a vast improvement over the Articles of Confederation and urged his fellow delegates to do so also. Hamilton went on to recruit John Jay and James Madison to write a series of essays defending the proposed Constitution, now known as The Federalist Papers. Hamilton wrote 51 of the 85 essays, published and supervised the entire project. Today, the Federalist Papers are still used an original source of interpretation of the U.S. Constitution.

George Washington appointed Hamilton as the first U.S. Secretary of the Treasury on September 11, 1789. He left office on the last day of January 1797. Much of the structure of the government was worked out in those five years, beginning with the structure and function of the cabinet itself. Before the adjournment of the House in September 1789, they requested Hamilton to make a report on suggestions to improve the public credit by January 1790. The national debt, Hamilton concluded, was the price paid for liberty. Hamilton divided the debt into national and state, and further divided it into foreign and domestic debt. Hamilton suggested consolidation of the state debts with the national debt and label it as Federal debt.

Figure 4.3
1795 Eagle Obverse, Early Minted Coin

Hamilton's report on a National Bank was a projection from the first Report on the Public Credit. He based his ideas for a Bank on the theories of Adam Smith, extensive studies of the Bank of England, the blunders of the Bank of North America and his experience in establishing the Bank of New York. He suggested that Congress charter the National Bank with a capitalization of $10 million, one-fifth of which would be handled by the Government. Since the Government did not have the money, it would borrow the money from the bank itself, and repay the loan in ten even annual instalments. The rest was to be available to individual investors. The bank was to be governed by a twenty-five-member board of directors that was to represent a large majority of the private shareholders which Hamilton considered essential to his being under a private direction. Hamilton's bank model had many similarities to that of the Bank of England, except Hamilton wanted to exclude the Government from being involved in public debt, but provide a large, firm, and elastic money supply for the functioning of normal businesses and usual economic development, among other differences. For tax revenue to ignite the bank, he wanted increase taxes on imported spirits, rum, liquor and whiskey. In other words, he favoured a sin tax to fund the virginal bank. After a great debate that involved Jefferson, Washington reluctantly signed the bill to establish the Bank of the United States.[34]

Alexander Hamilton had an untimely death. When Vice President Burr ran for governor of New York State in 1804, Hamilton crusaded against him as unworthy. Burr took offense and challenged him to a dual. Burr mortally wounded Hamilton, who died the next day.

Hamilton has been the subject of several biographies, the best-known being Ron Chernow, *Alexander Hamilton* (New York: Penguin Books, 2004). Recent interest has led to a well-received Broadway play, *Hamilton: an American Musical*, which had a long run.

The Bank of the United States

It all began with Alexander Hamilton and the Bank of the United States. In December 1790, Hamilton had called for the creation of the Bank of the United

---

[34] The details are gleaned from Ron Chernow, *Alexander Hamilton* (New York: Penguin Books, 2004). See also Richard Brookhiser, *Alexander Hamilton, American* (New York: Simon & Schuster, 2000).

States, and in February 1791 President George Washington signed the charter allowing it to open. During the initial public offering for the Bank, investors paid $25 for a stock, called a scrip, and were required to make three additional payments in six-month intervals totalling $375. These payments were to be 25 percent in specie and 75 percent in U.S. debt securities. Demand for stock in the newly formed Bank was significant, and prices for scrips increased dramatically for the first several weeks, reaching $280 in New York and reportedly over $300 in Philadelphia by mid-August. The market shifts were not sustainable, and within days prices began to fall rapidly. Hamilton stepped in by working with William Seton, the cashier of the Bank of New York, to authorize the purchase of $150,000 of public debt in New York to be covered by government revenues. By September 12, prices had recovered, and Hamilton's timely intervention had not only stabilized the market but also laid the groundwork for his cooperation with the Bank of New York, which would later be crucial in ending the Panic of 1792.

Causes of the Panic

In late December 1791, the price of securities began to increase once again, and the eventual crash in March 1792 caused many investors to panic and withdraw their money from the Bank of the United States. One of the primary causes of the sudden run on the bank was the failure of a scheme created by William Duer, Alexander Macomb and other bankers in the winter of 1791. Duer and Macomb's plan was to use large loans to gain control of the U.S. debt securities market because other investors needed these securities to make payments on stocks in the Bank of the United States. Besides that, Duer and Macomb were creating their own credit by endorsing one another's notes and did so in hopes of creating a new bank in New York to overtake the existing Bank of New York. It was a bold plan. On March 9, 1792 Duer stopped making payments to his creditors and simultaneously faced a lawsuit for actions he had taken as Secretary of the Treasury Board in the 1780s. As Duer and Macomb defaulted on their contracts and found themselves in prison, the price of securities fell more than 20 percent, all in the matter of weeks.

The Panic of 1792 was further instigated by the sudden restriction of previously overextended credit by the Bank of the United States. When the Bank of the United States first began accepting deposits and making discounts in December 1791, it expanded credit extensively. By January 31, 1792 monetary liabilities exceeded $2.17 million and discounts reached $2.58 million a very large sum at the time. Speculators took advantage of this new credit source, using it to make withdrawals from the Bank of New York, which placed undue stress on the bank's reserves. From December 29 to March 9, cash reserves of the Bank of the United States decreased by 34 percent, prompting that bank to not renew nearly 25 percent of its outstanding 30-day loans. To pay off these loans, many borrowers were forced to sell securities that they had purchased, which caused prices to fall sharply.

William Duer and the Crash

William Duer was born in England in 1743, the son of a very successful West Indian planter. Educated at Eton, Duer settled in America in 1773, became sympathetic with the colonist's grievances against Britain and, at the same time, he quickly began to hold positions of importance in New York society. Duer regaled his friends and associates at dinner at his home on Broadway, not far from Wall Street. At his wedding to Catherine Alexander, the bride was given away by George Washington.

Duer became a member of the Continental Congress, a New York judge and a signer of the Articles of Confederation. He was also secretary to the Board of the Treasury (appointed by Alexander Hamilton), a position that made him privy to the inner working of American finance in the late 1780s. While Hamilton was honest and never profited from his government position, Duer saw nothing wrong with using insider information to make a fast buck. The Duer-Hamilton relationship was to have its trying moments. Duer had been instrumental in helping Hamilton establish the Bank of New York. In return, Hamilton would later attempt to bail Duer out of some major problems.

Duer had made his fortune in land and speculating on the Revolutionary debt. In 1791, he resigned his Treasury position and entered into a partnership with Alexander Macomb, one of New York's richest and most prominent citizens. They agreed to combine Macomb's money and Duer's speculative talents and insider connections with the Treasury Department. Duer began speculating on Bank of New York stock when there were rumours that it was to be bought by the Bank of the United States. If true, the stock was sure to rise. But while long in the market with Macomb, he was short (betting that the stock would go down) Bank of New York in his own account. If the merger failed, Duer and Macomb would lose, but Duer, on his own would make a fortune. Since his agreement with Macomb called for using Macomb's money, not his own, all Duer had to lose by double-crossing his partner was honour, a sacrifice he seemed perfectly willing to make.

The behaviour of bond prices in New York during this time, the prices are as a percent of par value. The volatility, including breaks in the series, is evident. The price went from below par (78), soaring to about 13 percent above par, before settling at about 4 percent above par. Thereafter, trading in the bond ceased but resumed at 13 percent above par. The price peaked at 25 percent above par, only to fall, with a break in between, to below par value.

Again, volatility is evident with sharp breaks in the price. The wide gap shows where trading in the stock ceased after reaching a high of $745, only to resume at a much lower level of $545. It rallied somewhat but soon fell to $540. It was a wild ride for bonds and stocks, reflecting the great uncertainty of the times.

We resume with Hamilton and Duer. Hamilton, unaware of Duer's duplicity, but appalled at his speculative activities wrote on March 2, 1792, "This time, there must be a line of separation between honest Men & knaves, between respectable Stockholders and dealers in the funds, and mere unprincipled Gamblers." Duer became the centre of attention and many were only too anxious to lend him money in hopes of getting in on the bandwagon. He began to buy other bank stocks for future delivery, betting that rising prices would enable him to pay for them when the time came. However, at the same time, there were others who had an interest in seeing that prices fell, namely the Livingston clan, one of the richest families in the New York area. To ensure this, they began to withdraw gold and silver from their bank deposits, contracting the local money supply and forcing banks to call in loans, thus instituting a credit squeeze. Interest rates soared by as much as one percent a day.

The Livingston activity was ruinous for Duer and his followers who had borrowed to speculate. Desperate, he tried to borrow more to cover his obligations, but there was none to be had. With his resounding fall, panic ensued. Immediately, Duer was thrown in debtor's prison and Macomb ended up there as well. Alexander Hamilton, however, rode to the rescue and ensured that the country did not suffer. He ordered the Treasury to purchase several hundred thousand dollars' worth of federal securities to support the market and he urged banks not to call in loans. Soon, calm returned. It would be 195 years, until the great crash of 1987, before the federal government once again moved decisively to prevent a panic.

Because Duer often traded on insider information, he earned the distinction of being the first to do so. Within a month of his collapse and the crash that followed, the auctioneers and dealers resolved to move themselves in from the street and the coffeehouses and to find a more permanent location. It became apparent that the marketplace needed a central location so that dealings could be better controlled and better records kept. In May 1792, dealers and auctioneers entered the Buttonwood Agreement. Meeting under a buttonwood tree, today the location of 68 Wall Street, the traders agreed to establish a formal exchange for the buying and selling of shares and loans (bonds).

What was the fate of William Duer? The ever-loyal Hamilton tried to intervene on his behalf but was only able to obtain a short reprieve. Duer soon ended up back in prison and he died there in 1799.[35]

Hamilton's Crisis Management

In mid-March 1792, Alexander Hamilton began the political and economic manoeuvring necessary to contain the credit crisis affecting markets across the country. The charter creating the Bank of the United States had also set up a Sinking Fund Commission composed of Vice President John Adams, Secretary of State Thomas Jefferson, Attorney General Edmund Randolph, Chief Justice John Jay and Secretary of the Treasury Alexander Hamilton, charged with resolving the financial crises. On March 21, 1792, with Jay absent from voting, the commission split on the decision to allow open-market purchases. Having received notice from William Seton that the Bank of New York was in trouble, Hamilton wished to have the government make purchases as it had in 1791 but was unable to do so while Jefferson and Randolph stood opposed. While still waiting for Jay's formal and deciding vote, Randolph began to side with Hamilton on March 25, and with only Jefferson dissenting, the commission authorized $100,000 in open-market purchases of securities.

In a series of letters to Seton at the Bank of New York, Hamilton introduced several other measures to restore normalcy to the securities market. He encouraged the bank to continue offering loans collateralized by U.S. debt securities, but at a slightly increased rate of interest—seven percent instead of

---

[35] The foregoing was based on two *sources*: Charles Geisst, *Wall Street: A History* (Oxford: Oxford University Press, 2004) and John Steele Gordon, "The Great Crash of 1792," *American Heritage* magazine, May/June, 2000.

six. To persuade the Bank of New York to lend during the panic, Hamilton also promised that the U.S. Treasury would buy from the bank up to $500,000 of securities should the Bank of New York be stuck with excessive collateral. Similarly, Hamilton supported the Bank of Maryland's lending by offering to have the U.S. Treasury cover loans made to merchants paying duties. By April 15, after Hamilton authorized an additional $150,0000 of open-market purchases by the Bank of New York, Seton reported that market demand was returning to normal.[36]

In just under a month, Hamilton was thus able to stabilize the securities market and prevent the panic from inducing a recession. By exerting his power as Secretary of Treasury and persuading several banks to continue offering credit throughout the crisis, Hamilton was able to limit the amount spent by the Sinking Fund Commission to $243,000—roughly $100,000 less than what was spent during the smaller panic in 1791.

Economists and economic historians have given Hamilton high marks for handling the crisis. Hamilton's management appears to have anticipated "Bagehot's Dictum" by approximately 80 years.

This prescription, that, in crisis central banks should "lend freely, against good collateral, at a penalty rate" is still considered the gold standard for managing a financial panic as the "lender of last resort". It began with Hamilton but ended up on Bagehot's platter much later.

---

[36] Details of Hamilton's actions are found in David J. Cowan, Richard Sylla, & Robert E. Wright, "Alexander Hamilton, Central Banker: Crisis Management During the U.S. financial Panic of 1792," *Business History Review*, Vol. 83 Spring 2009.

Chapter 5
The Panic of 1819 and the Second Bank of the United States

The panic of 1819 was the first major peacetime financial crisis in the United States. It was followed by a general collapse of the American economy persisting through 1821. The Panic announced the transition of the nation from its colonial commercial status with Europe toward an independent economy, increasingly characterized by the financial and industrial imperatives of central bank monetary policy, making it susceptible to boom and bust cycles.

Though driven by global market adjustments in the aftermath of the Napoleonic Wars, the severity of the downturn was compounded by excessive speculation in public lands, fuelled by the unrestrained issue of paper money from banks and business concerns. The Second Bank of the United States (BUS), itself deeply enmeshed in these inflationary practices, sought to compensate for its laxness in regulating the state bank credit market by initiating a sharp curtailment in loans by its western branches, beginning in 1818. Failing to provide metallic currency when presented with their own bank notes by the BUS, the state-chartered banks began foreclosing on the heavily mortgaged farms and business properties they had financed. The ensuing financial panic, in conjunction with a sudden recovery in European agricultural production in 1817 led to widespread bankruptcies and mass unemployment.

The financial disaster and depression provoked popular resentment against banking and business enterprise, and a general belief that federal government economic policy was fundamentally flawed. Americans, many for the first time, became politically engaged to defend their local economic interests. The New Republicans and their American System—tariff protection, internal improvements and the BUS—were exposed to sharp criticism, eliciting a vigorous defence.

This widespread discontent would be mobilized by Democratic-Republicans in alliance with Old Republicans, and a return to the Jeffersonian principles of limited government, strict construction of the Constitution, and Southern pre-eminence. The Panic of 1819 marked the end of the Era of Good Feelings and the rise of Jacksonian nationalism.

Post-War European and American Economies

The United States and the United Kingdom signed the treaty of Ghent on December 24, 1814, ending the War of 1812. The British government effectively relinquished its mercantilist policies towards the United States, preparing the way for the development of free trade and the opening of America's vast western frontier.[37]

As for Europe, it was undergoing a period of disorganization as it readjusted to peacetime production and commerce in the aftermath of the Napoleonic Wars. The general effect was a decline in prices throughout the Western world, due to a scarcity of metallic sources of currency (i.e. gold and silver). Britain had advanced its industrial capacity to fully meet its wartime demands, but post-war continental Europe was temporarily too devastated to absorb Britain's surplus manufacturer goods. Moreover, European agriculture production, exhausted by years of warfare, was unable to feed its own population. The United States economy was not immune to the chaos that afflicted Europe, and therein lay the roots of the Panic of 1819.

American manufacturers faced U.S. markets swamped with British products, produced by low-paid workers and priced well below competitive prices and forcing many factories out of business. Continental Europe, its agrarian output crippled by the recent war offered new markets for American staple crops, particularly cotton, wheat, corn and tobacco. As prices soared for agricultural goods, a speculative agrarian land boom ensued in the South and West United States, encouraged by liberal terms for government public land sales. The entire post-war American economy was based on a land boom. The inflationary bubble grew from 1815 to 1818, obscuring the general deflationary trends in world

---

[37] Much of what follows is based on three major sources: Harry Ammon, *James Monroe: The Quest for National Identity* (New York: McGraw-Hill, 1971); George Dangerfield, *The Awakening of American Nationalism: 1815-1828* (New York: Harper & Row, 1965); and Murray Rothbard, *The Panic of 1819: Reactions and Policies* (New York: Columbia University press, 1962.

prices.

Laissez Faire Banking and the Imperatives of Republican Enterprise

With the failure to re-charter the First Bank of the United States in 1811, regulatory influence over state banks ceased. Credit-friendly Republicans—entrepreneurs, bankers, farmers—adapted the imperatives of laissez-faire finance to the precepts of Jeffersonian libertarianism—equating land speculation with "rugged individualism" and the frontier spirit. Private bank interests and their allies sought to evade or resist any threat to the profitability of their local enterprises, including the regulatory influence of government bank limiting easy credit. There followed an enormous expansion in state-chartered banking, with chartered institutions increasing from 88 in 1811 to 208 in 1815, mostly in mid-Atlantic states.

During the war with the United Kingdom (1812-1815), the American government turned to these new banks for loans, encouraging proliferation of paper money. This practice tended to shift specie into the more conservatively lending New England banking apparatus, depleting the newer banks of their hard money reserves. In response, the U.S. government acquiesced in a suspension of specie payments from state banks to prolong the wartime lending. The arrangement persisted in the war's aftermath, allowing old and new banks to profitably lend without regard to their metallic currency reserves. A speculative bubble formed because of these inflationary practices threatening the health of the economy. By 1814, calls for a new central bank and a resumption of regulatory controls were heard from powerful capitalist and economic nationalists in the Republican Party leadership.

Resurrection of the Bank of the United States

With the collapse of the Federalist Party at the end of the War of 1812, the Democratic-Republican Party found itself in control of the national government. Some of the traditional Jeffersonian agrarian precepts—especially strict construction of the Constitution—had softened due to difficulties during the war arising from lack of infrastructure, unregulated banking and the shortage of manufactured material, as well as the prospect of developing the vast natural resources with westward expansion. A mild nationalist outlook took hold among the "New Republicans," neo-Federalists led by Speaker of the House Henry Clay and Congressman John C. Calhoun. A three-part program dubbed the American System, incorporating some of the Hamiltonian projects championed by the Federalists, proposed to create a stable economy through a centralized banking system, stimulated by an ever-widening web of transportation and communication, through which domestic manufactures could eventually reach all parts of the Union. Advocates of the American System called for a protective tariff to encourage manufacturing, a federally funded program for internal improvements and a revival of the First Bank of the United States to regulate finance.

Astor, Girard and Parish

In the crucible of the War of 1812, the Treasury of the United States had been compelled to offer $16 million in government war bonds to stave off bankruptcy due to military costs and wartime loss of revenue. Financier Stephen Girard, an immigrant from France who was the fourth wealthiest person ever, business magnate John Jacob Astor, who was the fifth wealthiest persons of all time, and merchant David Parish bought up these government securities and rescued the nation's credit. Though their influence, and in alliance with Republican Congressmen John C. Calhoun and Henry Clay, they sought to augment their investment by proposing that the securities be exchangeable for stock in a new Bank of the United States.

Secretary of State James Monroe supported the Bank's revival, wishing to bind those highly regarded and pro-Republican business figures to government financial operations. Republicans in the South and West joined with moneyed interests in the Mid-Atlantic States to support Hamiltonian banking mechanisms for democratizing a national system of currency and credit.

Figure 5.1

Pro-BUS congressman John C. Calhoun, a strong supporter of the War of 1812, argued forcefully that the federal government had a constitutional obligation to regulate bank credit as a part of the national money supply. In January 1816, he introduced a bill of incorporation in the House of Representatives for a government bank. The measure was passed by Congress and signed by President James Madison in April 1816. Opposition to the Bank came from two fronts: the orthodox "Old Republicans" who regarded an enlargement of the central government as an assault on personal liberty and a violation of Jeffersonian agrarianism, and state chartered private banking interests, who favoured paper money, but considered federal regulation of local banking operations to be anti-Republican. These ideologies and interests would be arrayed against the central bank during the Andrew Jackson administration (1829-1837) and would destroy the institution by 1833. The Second Bank of the United States began operations in January 1817 under a twenty-year charter.

Figure 5.2

Neo-federalist Expectations for A Central Bank

The revival of the Second Bank of the United States had two primary objectives: (1) to reverse the post-war inflationary practices of state-chartered banks by inducing resumption of convertibility, and (2) to expand the opportunities for the common man to acquire bank credit, promoting enterprise and orderly and profitable westward expansion. The regulatory mechanism of the BUS resided in its fiscal duties as depository for the U.S. Department of the Treasury. As such, the Bank accepted circulating state bank paper money from individuals, Businesses and importers when they paid taxes or custom duty fees. The central bank immediately credited these payments to the U.S. Treasury with its own metallic reserves. The BUS, in turn, anticipated that the state banks which had issued the paper money would upon demand redeem their currency with gold and silver—"convertibility"—reimbursing the government bank.

To remain solvent, the state banks would, ideally, constrain their lending of paper money—however profitable—so as not to cause the BUS to become a significant creditor and deplete their specie reserves. Failing this, the Second Bank of the United States would, in theory, cease to honour the bank notes of those financial institutions that refused to promptly settle their government accounts with hard money—a recipe for bankruptcy.

The central bank's direct influence on inflationary lending was limited to those chartered banks whose paper currency was extensively used to remit funds to the government (i.e. tax and duty payments). The BUS and its branches had little or no direct control over commercial paper created by unchartered lending outfits. All that was necessary to start a bank was plates, presses and paper; a church, a tavern or a blacksmith shop would be a suitable site. These unregulated credit operations would to some extent interpenetrate the regulated banking system especially in the regions of wildcat banking.

Prologue to Panic: 1816–1818

President James Madison and Secretary of the Treasury Alexander Dallas fully approved the elevation of William Jones—one of the federally appointed bank directors—to BUS President in October 1816. Jones, formerly a member of Madison's cabinet, owed his promotion more to his political acumen than his skills as a banker. Financier and co-director Stephan Girard were troubled at Jones' promotion, concerned that he could never provide disinterested leadership of the Bank, and businessman John Jacob Astor doubted Jones' ability to wield the Bank's regulatory powers effectively. Jones extended the institution's resources literally in accordance with the post-war "national exuberance", generating large dividends for its stockholders. His administration of the Bank resonated with Secretary Crawford's lenient policy regarding public land receipts the form of chartered-bank script when specie was scarce nationally.

The Second Bank of the United States (BUS) began operations in January 1817 as fiscal agent of the United States Treasury. After February 20, 1817, the BUS was scheduled to begin to receive all government revenue in legal tender as required by its charter. Hard money shortages prevailed because U.S. exports exceeded imports and Peruvian and Mexican gold and silver sources failed to replenish specie reserves. Due to this scarcity, the terms of the Bank's incorporation provided for private subscribers to invest with a combination of metallic currency and government stock. Further, they were granted an indulgence by Bank directors that effectively waived the specie requirement. Ultimately, investors could purchase Bank shares on the security of the stock itself. Under its charter guidelines the BUS was expected to acquire specie totalling $28 million by the time it opened for business, but with only $2 million secured when it commenced operations; the Bank was compelled to purchase specie at usurious rates from the London financial markets in 1817 and 1818, over-burdening BUS credit.

As the February 20 deadline approached to resume convertibility, the private (i.e. state-chartered) banks withheld cooperation from BUS officials, loath to submit to the regulatory influence of the central bank—and diminish the large profits derived from the issue of unredeemable paper. On February 1, 1817, an association of bankers from Pennsylvania, New York, Maryland and Virginia met with the new Secretary of the Treasury William H. Crawford and BUS president William Jones, arranging a compromise which undermined the ability of the central bank to assert is role as creditor to the private banks.

The directors of the Second Bank, with Secretary Crawford's imprimatur, promised to refrain from collecting public deposits held in state banks until July 1, 1817. Moreover, they agreed to greatly expand the Bank's credit—at a discount of $6 million—before proceeding to collect public debt from the state institutions. In effect, the central bank transformed the private banks into creditors, inviting them to draw specie from BUS reserves months before the Bank of the United States assumed its regulatory functions. Under these ominous terms the Bank was at last launched—its operational success already at risk.

The eighteen branch offices of the BUS in 1817 operated with little oversight from the Philadelphia headquarters, nor from the U.S. Treasury. This policy stemmed in part from a social philosophy that prevailed among Republicans during the era of Good Feelings that wished to Republicanize credit practices and encourage westward migration. As to the migration, the United States government encouraged settlement of these lands by offering public land at $2 per acre (160-acre minimum), though auctioneering tended to retard sales and raised prices slightly. The terms required a down payment of one-fourth of the total cost and the balance in four annual payments. Failure to pay in full in five years meant forfeiture. Public land debt ballooned from $3 million in 1815 to $17 million in 1818. The U.S. Treasury accepted land payments in the form of bank notes issued by western and southern state banks. These institutions often lacked enough specie reserves to back up their vastly over-extended credit. If the land boom continued, the Treasury Department was compelled to accept depreciated bank notes for its public land sales, undermining government efforts to pay down the war debt, but serving to stave off private bank failures.

The onset of the financial panic was triggered by the Second Bank of the United States when it initiated a sharp credit contraction beginning the summer of 1818. The timing could not have been worse. The eruption of Mount Tambura in 1815 had created the "Year Without a Summer" causing European agriculture to fail that year. The link between the frontier land boom and overseas markets for staple goods was dramatically revealed when Europe finally recovered from its post-war harvest shortages and began producing bumper crops in 1817. American planters and farmers who had expanded production to exploit the European demand, discovered agricultural prices declining by half, even as production increased. Southwestern plantations were devastated when Britain began to increase its imports of East India cotton to avoid purchasing the high-priced U.S. cotton. India enjoyed not only a longer growing season and lower cost of freight to Britain, but also more cotton-devoted land than the Louisiana Purchase. Tench Coxe, a Pennsylvanian political economist and delegate to the Continental Congress, warned of the substantial evil exhibited in the rivalry created by foreign competition. Coxe has been dubbed by many as the father of the American cotton industry. Cotton values began to waver in 1818 and threaten to burst the speculative bubble. A general contraction in lending was induced in response to these developments in Europe.

In August 1818 with credit dangerously overextended, BUS branch offices began to reject all state-chartered bank notes under the direction of William Jones. Exceptions were made for notes issued as revenue payments to the U.S. Treasury. In October 1828, the U.S. Treasury demanded a transfer of $2 million in specie from the BUS to redeem bonds on the Louisiana Purchase. State banks in the West and South, unable to provide the required specie, began to call in their loans on the heavily mortgaged lands they had recklessly financed. Cash poor farmers and speculators found their land values dropping 50 percent to 75 percent. Banks began foreclosing on the properties and transferring them to their creditor, the Second Bank of the United States. When news arrived in January 1819 that the value of cotton had broken—dropping 25 percent in a single day—the ensuring panic drove the economy into recession. William Jones quietly resigned from his position as BUS president and was replaced by South Carolinian Langdon Cheves.

Tight Money by The BUS Heightens the Panic

The limited curtailment policy initiated by William Jones was rigorously applied by his successor, the former Congressman from South Carolina, Langdon Cheves. Among his backers were U.S. President James Monroe, The BUS directors Stephen Girard and Nicholas Biddle and those stockholders who wanted The Second Bank (BUS) leadership that was fiscally conservative and

74

immune to political influence. But it was not what the doctor ordered. The tight money policy Cheves implemented—a principled effort to cope with the financial disaster—had the effect of deepening the depression, undermining the recovery that was already underway. Through public land debt relief legislation, Cheves managed to reduce the Second Bank's land debt by $6 million within a year of assuming his position as the BUS president. Specie drain was also reversed to a great extent, increasing from $2.5 million in 1819 to $3.4 million by 1820. It further rose to $8 million by 1821. As an added consequence, bank notes in circulation were reduced by about $23 million within a span of four years from 1815-1820.

Employing these stern procedures, Cheves placed the Bank on sound footing in early 1819. In retrospect, it would be difficult to design a more inept policy than that followed by the Second Bank of the United States in dealing with the Panic. In the end the Bank was saved but the people were ruined.

While monetary policy was mismanaged during the crisis, The Second Bank of the United States did not cause the Panic. Rather, the Panic of 1819 was compounded by many factors beyond the direct control of the central bank. There was the overexpansion of credit during the post-war years, the collapse of the export market after the bumper crop of 1817 in Europe, low prices of imports from Europe which force American manufacturers to close, financial instability resulting from both the excessive expansion of state banking after 1811 and the unsound policies of The Second Bank of the United States, and widespread unemployment.

After the Fall

President Monroe, interpreting the economic crisis in the narrow monetary terms then current, limited governmental action to economizing and ensuring fiscal stability. All of which simply made matters worse. He acquiesced in suspending specie payments to bank depositors, setting a precedent for the Panics of 1837 and 1857. Although Monroe agreed that improved transportation facilities were needed, he refused to approve appropriations for internal improvements without constitutional amendments. Yet the economy needed a yank from the expenditure for infrastructure.

James Monroe continued to deal with effects rather than with causes. Back in 1821, Congress passed the Relief for Public Land Debtors Act. The bill allowed debtors who owed money on land purchased from the government to keep the part of land they had already paid for and relinquish the remaining amount. It further extended the schedule of payments by several years, with a discount for quick payment. Except for New England states, most of the country strongly supported the measure. Many state legislatures, particularly in rural western states, passed extra relief measures for debtors.

Another response to the Panic was monetary expansion, primarily at the state level. In Tennessee, Kentucky and Illinois, state banks suspended specie payments and issued large amounts of inconvertible notes. However, most other states avoided inflationist policies and enforced the payment of specie. Every state nonetheless witnessed vigorous debates on the merits of each policy. Treasury Secretary Crawford advocated restricting bank credit as a measure to prevent future crisis. Banking regulation was primarily a state responsibility, and several states passed regulations in the years following the Panic that required banks to maintain certain fixed ratios of capital to ensure their ability to convert to specie.

A further effect of the Panic of 1819 was increased support for protective tariffs for American industry. Vocal protectionists, such as Philadelphia printer Matthew Carrey, blamed free trade for the depression and argued that tariffs would protect American prosperity. Generally, support for tariffs was strongest in the Mid-Atlantic States and was opposed by export-heavy southern states.

Attention Shifts toward Poor Relief

The Panic brought attention, for the first time, to issues regarding debt relief policy as well as poor relief. City and state governances began to more effectively approach the public policy reform issue surrounding the poor. For once, a classification system was created (able-bodied vs. disabled, temporary vs. long-term, etc.). Public attention to solving poverty issues consequently led to public education systems. Public support for protective tariffs was once again great.

When the "Tariff of Abominations" was implemented in 1829, regional discontent led to the outbreak of the Nullification Crisis. The Crisis was seen as a critical precedent for democratic action. Whatever the case, the Panic of 1819 marked the arrival of the modern business cycle into the United States.

Chapter 6
The Panic of 1873 and the Long Goodbye

The American Civil War was followed by a boom in railroad construction. Some 33,000 miles of new track were laid across the country between 1858 and 1873. Much of the craze in railroad investment was driven by government land grants and subsidies to the railroads. At that time, the railroad industry was the nation's largest employer outside of agriculture. And it involved not only large amounts of money but also great risk. A large infusion of cash from speculators caused abnormal growth in the industry as well as overbuilding of docks, factories and ancillary facilities. At the same time, too much capital was involved in projects offering no immediate or early returns.

Meanwhile, the German Empire decided to cease minting silver thaler coins in 1871, causing a drop in demand and downward pressure on the value of silver; this had an adverse effect in the USA, where much of the supply was mined. As a response, the United States Congress passed the Coinage Act of 1873, which changed the country's silver policy. Before the Act, the US had backed its currency with both gold and silver, and it minted both types of coins. The new Act moved the United States to a *de facto* gold standard, which meant it would no longer buy silver at a statuary price or convert silver for the public into silver coins (though it would still mint silver dollars for export in the form of trade dollars).

On the lighter side, traditional folk songs were some of the most popular fare of the 1870s. The American Civil War had ended and the conflict was therapeutic. Much of the passion from that era remained in some post-war songs. Some of the hits included "Good-bye, Liza Jane," "My Grandfather's Clock" and "Carry Me Back to Old Virginny". Rutherford B. Hayes used the song "The Boys in Blue will see it Through" as his presidential campaign song. There were also protest songs such a "Daughter of Freedom! The Ballot be Yours", a suffrage song.

As to fashions, 1870s fashion in European and European-influenced clothing is characterized by a gradual return to a narrow silhouette after the full-skirted fashions of the 1850s and 1860s. By 1870, fullness in the skirt had moved to the rear, where elaborately draped overskirts were held in place by tapes and supported by a bustle. This fashion required an underskirt, which was heavily trimmed with pleats, flounces, rouching and frills. This fashion was short-lived (though the bustle would return in the mid-1880s) and was succeeded by tight-fitting silhouette with fullness as low as the knees--the cuirass bodice, a form-fitting, long-waisted, boned bodice that reached below the hips. And then there was the princess sheath dress with very tight-fitting sleeves. Square necklines also were common.

Daly dresses had high neckline that were either closed, squared-off or V-shaped. Sleeves of morning dresses were narrow throughout the period, with a tendency to flare slightly at the waist early on. Women often draped overskirts to produce an apron like effect from the front. Evening gowns had low necklines and very short-off-the-shoulder sleeves were worn with short (later mid-length) gloves. Other characteristic fashions included a velvet ribbon tied high around the neck and trailing behind for the evening (the origin of the modern choker necklace). Newly fashionable tea gowns, an informal fashion for entertaining at home combine Pre-Raphaelite influences with the loose sack-back styles of the 18th century. Seaside dress in England had its own distinct characteristics but still followed the regular fashions of the day. Seaside dress was more daring, frivolous, eccentric and brighter. Even though the bustle was extremely cumbersome, it was still a part of seaside fashion.

Corsets were a main stay, to coin a pun. The emphasis was placed on the bust, waist and hips. A corset was used to help mould the body to the desired shape. This was achieved by making the corsets longer than before, and by constructing them from separate shaped pieces of fabric. To increase rigidity, they were reinforced with many strips of whalebone, cording or pieces of leather. Steam-moulding, patented in 1868, helped to create a curvaceous contour. Properly corseted, one would be most uncomfortable.

There is less to be said of men's fashions. Innovations in the 1870s included patterned or figured fabrics for shirts and the general replacement of neckties tied in bowknots with the four-in-hand and later the ascot tie. Frock coats remained fashionable, but new shirr versions arose, distinguished from the sack coat by a waist seam. Waistcoats (US vests) were generally cut straight across the front and had collars and lapels but collarless waistcoats were also worn. Three-piece suits consisting of a high-buttoned sack oat with matching waistcoat and trousers, called ditto suits or (UK) lounge suits, grew in popularity. The sack coat might be cutaway so that only the top button could be fastened. The cutaway morning coat was still worn for informal day occasions in Europe and major cities elsewhere. Frock coats were required for more formal daytime dress. Formal evening dress remained dark tailcoat and trousers. The Frock coat was fastened lower on the chest and had wider lapels. In the year of the Panic Levi Strauss and Jacob Davis began to sell the original copper-riveted blue jeans in San Francisco. These became popular with the local gathering of gold seekers, who wanted strong clothing with durable pockets. The gentlemen were more comfortable than the ladies.

To resume with the emphasis on women, hair was pulled back at the sides and worn in a high knot or cluster of ringlets, often with a fringe (bangs) over the forehead. False hair was commonly used. Bonnets were smaller--to allow for the elaborately piled hairstyles and resembled hats except for their ribbons tied under the chin. A smallish hat, some with a veil, were perched on top of the head, and brimmed straw hats were worn for outdoor wear in summer.

So much for our brief foray into fashions; now you can imagine a properly corseted woman and man in a cutaway morning coat with panic on their faces. The panic of 1873 was a financial crisis that triggered a depression in Europe and North America that lasted from 1873 until 1879 and was longer in some countries such as France and Britain. In Britain, for example, it started two decades of stagnation known as the "long Depression" that weakened the country's economic leadership. The Panic was known as the "great depression" until the events of the 1930s set a new standard; yet to be broken.

Causal Elements

There were several underlying causes of the Panic; American Post-Civil War inflation, rampant speculative investment (overwhelmingly in railroads), and the demonetization of silver in Germany. The large trade deficit in the USA, ripples from economic dislocation in Europe resulting from the Franco-Prussian War (1870-71), property losses in the Chicago (1871) and the Boston (1872) fires, as well as other factors put a massive strain on bank reserves, which plummeted in New York City during September and October 1873 from US$50 million to $17 million. But the first symptoms of the crisis were financial failures in the Austro-Hungarian capital, the delightful Vienna, which spread to most of Europe and North America by 1873.

The American Civil War was followed by a boom in railroad construction. Some 33,000 miles of new track were laid across the country between 1858 and 1873. Much of the craze in railway investment was driven by government land grants and subsidies to the railroads. At that time, the railroad industry was the USA's largest employer outside of agriculture, and it involved great amounts of money and risk. A large infusion of cash for speculators caused abnormal growth in the industry as well as overbuilding of docks, factories and ancillary facilities. At the same time, too much capital was involved in projects offering no immediate or early returns.

The decision of the German Empire to cease mining silver thaler coins in 1871 caused a drop-in demand and downward pressure on the value of silver; this had a damaging effect in the USA, where much of the supply of silver was then mined. As a response, the United States Congress passed the Coinage Act of 1873, which changed the country's silver policy. Before the Act, the United States had backed its currency with both gold and silver, and it minted both types of coins. The Act moved the United States to a *de facto* gold standard, which meant it would no longer buy silver at a statutory price or convert silver from the public into silver coins (though it would still mint silver dollars for export in the form of trade dollars). The Act had an immediate effect of depressing silver prices. This hurt Western mining interests, who labelled the Act "The Crime of 73". Its effect was offset somewhat by the introduction of a silver trade dollar for use in Asia, and the discovery of new silver deposits at Virginia City, Nevada, resulting in new investment in mining activity. But the coinage law also reduced the domestic money supply, which raised interest rates, thereby hurting farmers and anyone else who normally carried heavy debt levels. The resulting outcry raised serious questions about how long the new policy would last. This perception of instability in U.S. monetary policy caused investors to shy away from long-term obligations, particularly long-term bonds. This problem was compounded by the railroad boom, which was in its later stages at the time.

NOTE: The source is Wikipedia, the Free Encyclopaedia.

In September 1873, the U.S. economy entered a crisis. This followed a period of post-Civil War economic over-expansion that arose from the Northern railroad boom. It came at the end of series of economic setbacks: The Black Friday panic of 1859, the Chicago fire of 1871, the outbreak of equine influenza in 1872, and the demonetization of silver in 1873. The climax came in September 1873 when Jay Cooke & Company, a major player of the U.S. banking establishment, found itself unable to market several million dollars in Northern Pacific Railway bonds. Cooke's firm, like many others, had invested heavily in the railroads. At a time when investment banks were anxious for more capital for their enterprises, Cooke and other entrepreneurs had planned to build the second transcontinental railroad, called the Northern Pacific Railway. Cooke's firm provided the financing and ground was broken near Duluth, Minnesota, for the line on February 15, 1870. But just as Cooke was about to swing a US$300 million government loan in September 1873, reports circulated that the firm's credit had become nearly worthless. On September 18, the firm declared bankruptcy. The new railroad was not built. President Ulysses S. Grant's (1868-1877) monetary policy of contracting the money supply (again, also thereby raising interest rates) made matters worse for those in debt. While businesses were expanding, the money they needed to finance that growth was becoming scarcer.

In the 1874 congressional elections, the Democrats assumed control of the House. Public opinion made it difficult for the then Grant administration to develop a coherent policy regarding the Southern states. The North began to steer away from Reconstruction of the South. With the depression, ambitious railroad building programs crashed across the South, leaving most states deep in debt and burdened with heavy taxes. Retrenchment was a common response of southern states to state debts during the depression. It was a period of austerity. One by one, each Southern state fell to the Democrats, and the Republicans lost power everywhere except in the White House.

Meanwhile, the demise of those spectacular investment plans hit Wall Street like a 10-ton train engine. The New York Stock Exchange closed for ten days starting September 20, 1873. By November some 55 of the nation's railroads had failed, and another 50 went bankrupt by the first anniversary of the crisis. Construction of new rail lines, formerly one of the backbones of the economy, plummeted from 7,500 miles of track in 1872 to just 1,500 miles in 1875. An astonishing 18,000 businesses failed between 1873 and 1875. Unemployment peaked in 1878 at 8.25 percent. Building construction was halted, wages were cut, real estate values fell, and corporate profits vanished.

Steep wage cuts led railroad workers to launch the Great Railroad Strike in 1877. This stopped trains in their tracks across the country. Rutherford B. Hayes, another Republican, replaced Grant as President. President Rutherford B. Hayes (1877-1882) sent in federal troops to try to end the strike. In July 1877, the market for lumber crashed, sending several leading Michigan lumbering concerns into bankruptcy. Within a year, the effect of this second business slump reached all the way to sunny California. The depression did not lift until the spring of 1879. Even so, the tension between workers and the leaders of banking and manufacturing interests lingered on. The poor economic conditions continued.

The panic and depression hit all industrial nations. In Germany and Austria-Hungary, a like process of over-expansion had taken place. The period from German unification in 1870-71 to the crash in 1873 came to be called the Grunderjahre ("founders' years"). A liberalized incorporation law in Germany gave impetus to the foundation of new enterprises, such as the Deutsch Bank, and the incorporation of already established companies. Euphoria over the military victory against France in 1871 and the influx of capital from the payment by France of war reparations fuelled stock market speculation in railways, factories, docks, steamships—the same industrial branches that expanded unsustainably in the United States. In the immediate aftermath of Otto von Bismarck's victory against France he began the process of silver demonetization. The process began in November 23, 1871 and culminated in the introduction of the gold mark July 9, 1873 as the currency for the new united Reich, replacing the silver coins of all constituent lands. Germany was now on the gold standard. Demonetization of silver was thus a common element in the crises on both sides of the Atlantic Ocean.

On May 9, 1873, in lovely Vienna, the Stock Exchange crashed, unable to sustain the bubble of false expansion, insolvencies and dishonest manipulations. The crash of the Vienna Stock Exchange began on May 8, 1873 and continued until May 10, when the exchange was closed; when it reopened three days later, the panic seemed to have faded, and appeared confined to Austria-Hungary. A series of Viennese bank failures followed, causing a contraction of the money available for business lending. One of the famous private individuals who went bankrupt in 1873 was Stephan Keglevich of Vienna. He was a relative of Gabor Keglevich, who had been the master of the royal treasury (1842-48) and who in 1845 had founded, with some others, a financing association to fund the expansion of Hungarian industry and to protect the loan repayments, like the Kreditschutzverband of 1870. That made it possible for several new Austrian banks to be established in 1873 after the Vienna Stock Exchange crash. In contrast--in Berlin--the railway empire of Bethel Henry Strousberg crashed after a ruinous settlement with the Romanian government, bursting the speculation bubble in Germany. The contraction of the German economy was exacerbated by the conclusion of war reparations payments to Germany by France in September 1873. Coming two years after the foundation of the German Empire, the panic became known as the Grunderkrach or "founders' crash". Keglevich and Strousberg had come in the year 1854 in direct competition in a project in today's Slovakia, whereupon, in 1870, the Government of Hungary and finally in 1872 the Emperor-King Franz Joseph I of Austria resolved the question of these two competing projects.

Although the collapse of the foreign loan financing had been foreshadowed, the anticipatory events of that year were in themselves comparatively unimportant. The old capital of Hungary (Obuda and Buda) was officially united with Pest, thus creating the new metropolis of Budapest in 1873. The difference in stability between Vienna and Berlin had the effect that French indemnity payments to Germany were in excess of those to Austria and Russia, but these indemnity payments aggravated the crisis in Austria, which had benefited from the accumulation of capital not only in Germany, but also in England, the Netherlands, Belgium, France and Russia. Still, recovery from the crash happened much more quickly in Europe than in the United States. Moreover, German businesses managed to avoid the sort of deep wage cuts that embittered American labour relations at the time. There was an anti-Semitic component to the economic recovery in Germany and Austria as small investors blamed the Jews for their losses in the crash. Soon more luxury hotels and villas were built in Opatija and a new railway line was extended in 1873 from the Vienna-Trieste line to Rijeka, from where it was possible to go by train to Opatija. The strong increase of port traffic generated a permanent request for expansion. Also, 1875-90 became "the golden years" of Giovanni de Ciotta in Fiume (Rijeka).

The construction of the Suez Canal, which opened in 1869, was one of the causes of the Panic of 1873, because goods from the Far East had been carried in sailing vessels around the Cape of Good Hope and were stored in British warehouses. As sailing vessels were not adaptable for use through the Suez Canal because the prevailing winds of the Mediterranean Sea blew from west to east,

British entrepôt trade suffered. In Britain, the long depression resulted in bankruptcies, escalating unemployment, a halt in public works, and a major trade slump that lasted until 1897. In the wait for the end to the depression, for Britain it was a long goodbye.

The Long Depression

The long depression was a worldwide price and economic recession, beginning with the Panic of 1873 and running either through the spring of 1879 or 1890, depending on who's counting. It was the most severe in Europe and the United States, which had been experiencing strong economic growth fuelled by the Second Industrial Revolution in the decade following the American Civil War. The episode was labelled the "Great Depression" at the time, and it had that designation until the Great Depression of the 1930s. The United Kingdom is often considered to have been the hardest hit; during this period, it lost some of its large industrial lead over the economies of Continental Europe. While it was occurring, the view was prominent that the economy of the United Kingdom had been in continuous depression from 1873 to as late as 1895 and some refer to the period as the Great Depression of 1873-95.

In the United States, economists typically refer to the Long Depression or the Depression of 1873-95, kicked off by the Panic of 1873, and followed by the Panic of 1893, book-ending the entire period of the very wide Long Depression. The National Bureau of Economic Research dates the contraction following the panic as lasting from October 1873 to March 1879. At 65 months, it is the longest-lasting contraction identified by the NBER, eclipsing the Great Depression's 43 months of contraction. During the 65 months 18,000 businesses went bankrupt, including 889 railroads, which had fuelled the second industrial revolution. Unemployment peaked in 1878, long after the panic ended. Different sources peg the peak U.S. unemployment rate anywhere from 8.25 percent to 14 percent.

The Panic of 1873 was the first truly international crisis. By the same token the Long Depression was the first global depression. The optimism that have been driving booming stock prices in central Europe had reached a fever pitch, and fears of a bubble culminated in a panic in Vienna beginning in April 1873. Despite the collapse of the stock exchange in Austria, financial panic arrived in the America's only months later, Black Thursday, September 18, 1873 after the failure of the banking house of Jay Cooke and Company over the Northern

Pacific Railway. The Northern Pacific railway had been given 40 million acres of public land in the Western United States and Cooke sought $100,000,000 in capital for the company; the bank failed when the bond issue proved unsalable and was shortly followed by several other major banks. The New York Stock Exchange closed for ten days on September 20. The financial contagion then returned to Europe, provoking a second panic in Vienna and further failures in continental Europe before receding. France, which had been experiencing deflation in the years preceding the crash, was spared financial calamity for the moment, as was Britain.

Some have contended that the depression was rooted in the 1870 Franco-Prussian War that damaged the French economy and, under the Treaty of Frankfurt 1871, forced France to make large war reparations payments to Germany. Still, the primary cause of the price depression in the United States was the tight monetary policy that the U.S. followed to get back to the gold standard after the U.S. Civil War. The U.S. government was taking money out of circulation to achieve this goal; therefore, there was less available money to facilitate trade. Because of this monetary policy the price of silver started to fall causing considerable loses of asset values. By most accounts, after 1879 production was growing, thus further putting downward pressure on prices due to increased industrial productivity, trade and competition.

In the U.S. the speculative nature of financing due to both the greenback which was paper currency issued to pay for the Civil War and rampant fraud in building the Union Pacific Railway in 1869 culminated in the Credit Mobilizer panic. This was a panic within a panic. Railway overbuilding and weak markets collapsed the bubble in 1873. Both the Union Pacific and the Northern Pacific railroads were central to the collapse; another railway bubble was the railway mania in Great Britain and Ireland.

Because of the Panic of 1873, governments depegged their currencies to save money. That is, they freed their currencies from their ties to precious metals. The demonetization of silver by European and North American governments in the early 1870s was certainly a contributing factor. The U.S. Coinage Act of 1873 was met was great opposition by farmers and miners, as silver was more of a monetary benefit to rural areas than in banks in big cities. In addition, there were U.S. citizens who advocated the continuance of government-issued fiat money (United States Notes) to avoid deflation and promote exports. The western U.S. states were outraged—Nevada, Colorado, and Idaho were huge silver producers with productive mines, and for a few years mining abated. Resumption of silver dollar coinage was authorized by the Bland-Allison Act of 1878. The resumption of the U.S. government buying silver was finally enacted in 1890 with the Sherman Silver Purchase Act.

Monetarists believe that the 1873 depression was caused by shortages of gold that undermined the gold standard, and that the 1848 California Gold Rush, 1885 Witwatersrand Gold Rush in South Africa and the 1895-99 Klondike Gold Rush helped alleviate such crises. Other analysts have theorized that the Second Industrial Revolution was causing large shifts in the economies of many states, imposing transition costs, which may also have a role in causing the depression.

Like the later Great Depression, the Long Depression affected different countries at different times, at different rates, and some countries accomplished rapid growth over certain periods. Globally however, the 1870s, 1880s, and 1890s comprised an era of falling price levels and rates of economic growth significantly below the period preceding and following. Between 1870 and 1890, iron production in the five largest producing countries more than doubled, from 11 million tons to 23 million tons. Steel production increased twenty-fold (half a million tons to 11 million tons), and railroad development boomed. But at the same time, prices in several markets collapsed—the price of grain in 1894 was only a third of what it had been in 1857, and the price of cotton fell by nearly 50 percent in just the five years from 1872 to 1877, imposing great hardship on farmers and planters. This collapse provoked protectionism in many countries, such as France, Germany and the United States, while triggering mass emigration from other countries such as Italy, Spain, Austria-Hungary and Russia. Similarly, while the production of iron doubled between the 1870s and 1890s, the price of iron halved.

Many countries experienced significantly lower growth rates relative to what they had earlier in the 19th century and to what they experienced afterwards. This is illustrated in Table 6.1.

Table 6.1: Growth rates of industrial production (1850s-1913)

Countries	1850s-1873	1873-1890	1890-1913
Germany	4.3%	2.9%	4.1%
United Kingdom	3.0%	1.7%	2.0%
United States	6.2%	4.7%	5.3%
France	1.71%	2.5%	
Italy	0.9%	3.0%	
Sweden	3.1%	3.5%	

NOTES: The growth rates of industrial production are calculated at the mean for the various periods. The USA growth rate of 6.2% beginning in the 1850s can be attributed to the pre- and post-Civil War boom. GDP growth rates per capita for the USA (which would require population estimates) are provided for various years in Robert Gordon, *The Rise and Fall of American Growth* (Princeton, N.J.: Princeton University Press, 2016). See, for example, the table on p. 14;

The French experience was somewhat unusual. Having been defeated in the Franco-Prussian War, the country was required to pay 200 million pounds in reparations to the Germans and was already reeling when the 1873 crash came. The French adopted a policy of deliberate deflation while paying reparations. When the United states resumed growth for a time in the 1880s, the Paris Bourse crash of 1882 sent France careening into depression, one which lasted longer and probably cost France more than any other in the 19th century. The Union Generale, a French bank failed in 1882, prompting the French to withdraw three million pounds from the Bank of England and triggering a collapse in French stock prices.

Conclusions

The financial panic of 1873 triggered a widespread depression that ran from 1873 through 1879, even longer in some countries. It ignited a long Depression—hence, the long goodbye. It had more causes than the usual afflicted person with a dreadful disease. Let us enumerate them. From the top came the Post-Civil War inflation, rampant speculative investment (mostly in railroads), The demonetization of silver in the United States and Germany with a large U.S.

trade deficit, fallout from the economic dislocation in Europe from the Franco-Prussian War (1870-71), property losses from the Chicago and Boston fires in 1871 and 1872, and other factors that put a severe strain on bank reserves, especially in New York City in September and October 1873. The first symptoms showed up in lovely Vienna, the capital of the Austro-Hungarian Empire and spread to most of Europe and North America by 1873.

The cessation of minting Silver thaler coins in 1871 by Germany caused a decline in demand for silver. This was a knockout punch for silver mining in the United States, the main source of the metal. The Congress passed the Coinage Act of 1873, which put the U.S. on a gold standard. The effect was deflation in the price of silver which especially hurt mining interests in the West, which labelled the Act "The Crime of '73." The devaluation of silver greatly reduced the nation's money supply, raising interest rates and damaging farming. The climax came in September 1873 when Jay Cooke & Company was unable to market several million dollars in Northern Pacific Railway bonds. Cooke, like many others had invested mightily in railroads. Never built, the collapse of this massive investment hit Wall Street in the gut. Some 18,000 businesses failed between 1873 and 1875. Unemployment peaked at 8.25 percent, wages were cut, and corporate profits collapsed. The slashing of wages led to the Great Railroad Strike in 1877. The depression pall did not lift until spring 1879.Not soon enough to prevent the debacle from spreading globally.

Recovery from the crash happened much more quickly in Europe than in the U.S. For one thing, 1875-90 became "the golden years" of Giovanni de Clotta in Rijeka after the opening of the Suez Canal. It was not good for everyone. The opening of the Canal contributed to the Panic of 1873, for British entrepot trade was curbed resulting in bankruptcies and unemployment. It was part of the long goodbye in Britain. Not just in Britain, the long depression was worldwide and ran from the Panic until the spring of 1879 or 1880. It was most devastating in Europe and the United States. A panic within the panic, Railway over-expansion and weak markets pricked the bubble. It was not an equal opportunity panic.

Chapter 7
Rui Barbosa and Encilhamento

We begin with a brief biography of Rui Barbosa (1849-1923). He was a Brazilian polymath, diplomat, writer, jurist and politician whose name will always be associated with Encilhamento. Born in Salvador, Bahia, he was federal representative, senator, minister of Finance and diplomat. For his distinguished participation in the 2nd Hague Conference, defining the principle of equality among nations, he earned the nickname "Eagle of The Hague". He ran unsuccessfully for the Presidency of Brazil in 1910, 1914 and in 1919.

Barbosa gave his first public speech for the abolition of slavery when he was only 19. For the rest of his life he remained an uncompromising defender of civil liberties. Slavery in Brazil was finally abolished by the lci Aurea ("Golden Law") in 1888. Part of Barbosa's historical legacy is that he authorized, as minister of finance on December 14, 1890, the destruction of most government records related to slavery. The avowed reason for this destruction, which took several years to be enacted and was followed by his successor, was to erase the "stain" of slavery on Brazilian history. However, historians today agree that Barbosa aimed to prevent any possible indemnification of the former slave-owners for this liberation. Indeed, eleven days after the abolition of slavery, a law project was deposed at the Chamber, proposing some indemnification to the slave owners.

Barbosa's liberal ideas were influential in the drafting of the first republican constitution. He was a supporter of fiat money, as opposed to a gold standard, in Brazil. During his term as finance secretary, he implemented far-reaching reforms of Brazil's financial regime, instituting a vigorously expansionist monetary policy. The result was chaos and instability; the so-called fiat experiment resulted in the bubble of Encilhamento, a dismal political-economic failure. Due to his controversial role during it, in the following administration of

Floriano Peixoto, he was forced into exile until Floriano's term ended. Years later, after his return he was elected as a Senator. He headed the Brazilian delegation to the 2nd Hague Conference and was brilliant in its deliberations. As candidate of the Civilian Party in the presidential election of 1910, Barbosa waged one of the most memorable campaigns in Brazilian politics. He was not successful, losing to Marshal Hermes da Fonseca. He ran again in the elections of 1914 and 1919, both times losing to the government candidate. During World War I, he played a key role among the proponents of the Allied cause, arguing that Brazil should be more involved in the war. Barbosa died in Petropolis, near Rio de Janeiro, in 1923.

The Economic Bubble

The Encilhamento was an economic bubble that expanded in the late 1880s and early 1890s in Brazil, bursting during the provisional government of Deodoro da Fonseca (1889-1891) leading to the financial crisis. Two Finance Ministers, first, the Viscount of Ouro Preto and then Rui Barbosa, adopted a policy of unrestricted credit for industrial investments and for banks through an abundant issuance of money to encourage Brazil's industrialization. Instead, this policy of economic incentives created unbridled speculation, increased inflation, and encouraged fraudulent initial public offerings (IPOs) and takeovers.

The word "Encilhamento," literally "saddling-up," the act of girthing or mounting a horse, was a term borrowed from horseracing. It was used to refer to the speculative movement true to its analogy, the belief of trying to take advantage of get-rich-quickly opportunities... Further, it too is an analogy based on the popular Brazilian saying "An unmounted saddled horse doesn't appear twice".[38]

Throughout the 19th century the maturation of technological innovations, especially the development of rail transport, gas lighting and steamships, among others, all linked to the process of industrialization, created opportunities for large speculative movements, leading to an acceleration of the flow of capital in the world. A considerable volume of native capital was released with the prohibition of the slave trade in 1850; at the same time the Baron of Maua put in place the modern banking system in Brazil. Despite this feverish activity,

---

[38] Robert M. Levine, *Vale of Tears: Revisiting the Canudos' Massacre in North-eastern Brazil, 1893-1897* (Berkeley, CA: University of California Press, 1995), p. 330.

economic growth did not occur. This was because, at the beginning of the Republic, the Brazilian economy was tied to, among other things, restrictive economic legislation that was mainly due to the 1850 "Land Law" and the "barrier Act" of 1850. These laws inhibited the access to land ownership by former slaves and immigrants in a time when agriculture was economically predominant in the country and retarded for decades the development of Brazilian financial markets. Agriculture had become at the time, a kind of "notary oligopoly" under the control of few families. The rich families were represented by lawyers. Proposed changes in land legislation, for example, was one of the reasons why large landowners and former slaveholders supported the establishment of the republic. In this political environment, economic and social order was the pretext for the promotion of the process of industrialization of the country, industrialization at any cost.

The Major Players

Big Rentiers: They were holders of the native "big money" who went after the best rate of return for their capital. In Brazil in the late 19th century, they were predominantly big landowners, former slave dealers and owners, merchants, businessmen, and tradesmen (especially those involved with coffee and cotton exports), senior civil servants, politicians and lawyers with influence in formulation and implementation of public policies. They basically kept their financial resources within the country, with the most sophisticated investing being in foreign financial markets, mainly in the Parisian Bourse, City of London and Wall Street.

Financiers: They were institutional traders and investment bankers working for the big money, having contact with big business and having learned new forms of financial engineering. In Brazil of that time, the most illustrious figure was the Counselor Mayrink.

Economists-politicians: They were the makers of economic policies, usually also the middlemen of the renters and financiers' interests, eventually acting as junior partners of them. They also provided rhetoric to public opinion and the technical means to implement a regulatory model that served their interests. Of them, Rui Barbosa was the prominent figure at that time in Brazil.

Financial capital which from the mid-19th century was already organized to influence the life of nations provided the "ideal environment" for the business of the financiers. From that time on, the British banks were important and were led by the Rothschild's.

These were the major players of the encilliamento. The first step of Encilhamento took place during the end of the Monarchy under the command of Viscount of Ouro Preto, the last finance secretary of that period, when it was deregulated under a new Banking Act in November 1888. A rise in the Rio de Janeiro Stock Exchange that had already boomed in 1885 accelerated with the abolition of slavery two years later, having reheated again with the measures implemented by the new banking law (that reversed the 1850 "Barriers Act"), and in 1889 by the proposed changes in the Land and Real State laws. Along with the increase in market liquidity, modern financial mechanisms were introduced, enhancing the financial leverage possibilities. The reduction in the issuance of government bonds had also opened the opportunity for the expansion of stock issues. All this slowly led to an increase in speculation and inflation in general, embracing all economic sectors, from currencies to real estate, creating a big bubble from minor bubbles.

In this environment, the Viscount of Ouro Preto decided to create an institution to act as regulatory agency for the financial market--a private central bank in the European manner, a reserve bank or monetary authority to restore liquidity. The fact that Rui Barbosa had been a great opponent of such a system qualified him for an appointment by the military as finance secretary, when they set up the Republic. Ironically, when he took office, soon after the proclamation of the Republic, he put into practice all that he had criticized before. In January 1890, he enacted a new banking law, inspired by the ideas of the Counsellor Mayrink, his banker and friend, who he appointed as head of the new Central Bank, without even consulting the President. His signing the bill late at night caused a scandal that would be the first of a series until his departure for the secretary-ship. This however didn't stop the enactment of the new law, despite the protest and opposition from secretaries like Demetrio Ribeiro and Campos Sales, who, predicating the consequences of such measures got a central bank for Sao Paulo. This was not even a quid pro quo.[39]

The new law caused unregulated speculation to rise. It had reached all major sectors of the economy especially currency trading, where volume was high. Also, rogue trading in IPOs, despite its legality, led to the main political disaster of the whole process, due to the leniency of the new banking law that allowed

---

[39] Much of the above is based on Wikipedia, the Free Encyclopedia. See the site for "Encilhamento."

authorized issuers to act freely without any supervision or official punishment.

An example of such issues occurred not only when a company issued an IPO without any economic fundamentals to support it, but also whenever the company needed more money, more new subscriptions were issued. The "investor" who wouldn't accept the new offerings lost the rights to the old ones and all the money previously paid. The new law tied trading rights to the nominal value the stock. There were no official stock prices, and consequently, no way to negotiate them directly in the stock exchange to either minimize losses or maximize profits. This was the practice not only on restricted trading of securities on the over-the counter (OTC) market--congesting it by excess supplies--but also for new issues (IPO's) in the stock market. All this prevented legitimate business transactions, besides causing a net loss to many inexperienced investors.

Instead of helping to promote growth and structural change in the economy, the Encilhamento led to one of the worst inflation outbreaks of the country's history, and the Brazilian economy suffered a violent collapse. The Encilhamento's last straw came with the financial shock wave caused by the default of Argentine government bonds following the first collapse of the Baring Bank at the end of 1890.[40] Although the burst had been initiated then, it evolved slowly until 1892. On January 20, 1891, Rui Barbossa stepped down as finance secretary to head two companies that were created during the Encilhamento and in which he had a partnership with the counselor Mayrink. General Deodoro da Fonseca resigned on November 23 of that year, during the first naval revolt, under the imminent threat of deposition by the Republicans, represented by Vice President Marechal Floriano Peixoto who assumed "naturally" the Presidency.

Postlude

The success of the new stage of economic development, that in theory encouraged Encilhamento, depended on the creation of an enabling environment both regarding the relocation of domestic savings, as well as foreign investments. Because of the extraordinary powers given to the monetary authorities, the

---

[40] Wikipedia, under the heading "Baring Bank," states that the bank was founded in 1762 as the John and Frances Baring Company in London, which, at the time, was called Baring Banks. It was founded as a British merchant bank and had a long life until, notoriously, Nick Leeson, an English trader in Singapore, caused its collapse by 1997.

private interest in Encilhamento was overtaking the public interest. So, instead of a slow and steady promotion of development, economic growth, distribution of wealth, financial literacy and confidence, there was an increase in the concentration of wealth. These were due to profiteering at the expanse of productive activity and widespread bankruptcy. Moreover, there was an increase in ignorance and distrust about how politics and markets work. At the same time there was a geometric increase of debt and economic stagnation. So, there are three main reasons for the failure of this speculative movement or Encilhamento as a lever for development:

1. Lack of a true statesman to coordinate, correct and adjust the Encilhamento process as it progressed.
2. The choice of politicians and financiers who led the process, as their personal interests conflicted with the country's interests.
3. The fascination with "get-rich-quick schemes," both by the notary authorities of that time, who worked to benefit themselves as well as by the crowd of average amateurs who acted more like daydreaming gamblers rather than sober speculators. They hurt themselves by letting themselves being manipulated, helping to inflate a financial bubble. They participated in this process without having the least vocation, knowledge and experience required to attend to legal details and use personal trading strategies with proper risk and money managements, which would have prevented countless bankruptcies and their harmful consequences.

Following the effects of what was called "the burst," which ended the financial bubble, came the usual "witch hunt" to place blame that lasted until 1895. During the tenure of Floriano Peixoto some prominent Encilhamento figures had their assets frozen or seized, beyond having been prosecuted publicly and administratively. Among these was Rui Barbosa, who had to go into exile in Europe to escape persecution. Also, legislators convened to regulate the financial markets in Brazil, in a vain attempt to control their volatility. At the time the concept of financial fragility was unknown. This did not prevent a violent setback up until the time of the "Barriers Act," a lawyerly creature that limited holding periods for financial instruments. This Act lasted a long time: it was rescinded in 1965.

Although the bubble burst happened between 1890 and 1892, the economic and political effects were felt throughout the decade until the end of the Campos Sales administration, with the popular Francisco de Paula Rodrigues Alves, who had served as Treasury minister in the 1890's, in charge of the Brazilian economy until he died.[41] All this had a high social cost, due to the economic policy of austerity taken in accordance with the requests of big international capital. The economy was in shambles. Encilhamento had the opposite of its intended effects. Rui Barbossa was ruined and died in poverty in Paris.[42]

---

[41] The popular Rodrigues Alvis was elected President of Brazil and served until 1906. He died before he could be elected to a second term.

[42] See also James D. Henderson, Helen Delpar, Maurice P. Brungaardt & Richard N. Weldon, *A Reference Guide to Latin American History* (New York: M.E. Sharpe Inc., 2000), p. 172 and Jeffrey D. Needell, *A Tropical Belle Epoque: Elite Culture and Society in Turn-of-the-Century Brazil (*Cambridge, England: Cambridge University Press, 1987), P. 12.

Chapter 8
J.P. Morgan and the Panic Of 1907

The Panic of 1907 is also known as the 1907 Banker's Panic or Knickerbocker Crisis. It was a financial crisis that took place over a three-week period starting in mid-October, when the New York Stock Exchange fell almost 50 percent from its peak the previous year. Panic occurred, as this was during a time of economic recession, but it also was a time of numerous runs on banks and trust companies. The 1907 Panic eventually spread throughout the nation when many state and local banks and businesses entered bankruptcy. The primary cause of the bank runs included a retraction of market liquidity by several New York City banks and a loss of confidence among company directors, exacerbated by unregulated side bets at bucket shops. The bank runs were triggered by the failed attempt in October 1907 by Otis Heinze to corner the market on stock of the United Copper Company. Otis was the brother of F. Augustus Heinze who was a founder of United Copper Company. (More detail of this scheme will follow soon.) When this bid failed, banks that had lent money to the cornering scheme suffered runs that later spread to affiliated banks and trusts, leading a week later to the downfall of Knickerbocker Trust Company--New York City' s third largest trust. The collapse of the Knickerbocker spread fear thorough the city trusts as regional banks withdrew reserves from New York City banks.

Panic extended *across the nation* as vast numbers of people withdrew deposits from their regional banks.

The panic might have deepened then if not for the intervention of financier J.P. Morgan, who pledged large sums of his own money, and convinced other New York bankers to do the same, to shore up the banking system. At the time, the United States did not have a central bank to inject liquidity back into the market. In November, the financial contagion had largely ended, only to be replaced by a further crisis. This was due to the heavy borrowing of a large brokerage firm that used the stock of Tennessee Coal, Iron and Railroad Company (TC&I) as collateral. The collapse of TC&I's stock price was averted by an emergency takeover by (this time) Morgan's U.S. Steel Corporation—a move approved by anti-monopolist president Theodore Roosevelt. The following year, Senator Nelson W. Aldrich, father-in-law of John D. Rockefeller, Jr., established and chaired a commission to investigate the crisis and propose future solutions, leading to the creation of the Federal Reserve System.

The Dreadful State of the Economy

When U.S. President Andrew Jackson allowed the charter of the Second Bank of the United States to expire in 1836, the U.S. was without any sort of central bank, and the money supply in New York City fluctuated with the country's annual agricultural cycle. Each autumn money flowed out of the city as harvests were purchased and—to attract money, bank-interest rates were raised. Foreign investors then sent their money to New York to take advantage of the higher rates. From the January 1906 Dow Jones Industrial Average high of 103, the market began a modest correction that would continue through the year. The April 1906 earthquake that devastated San Francisco contributed to the market instability, prompting an even greater flood of money from New York to San Francisco to aid reconstruction. A further stress on the money supply happened in late 1906, when the Bank of England raised its interest rates, partly in response to UK insurance companies paying out so much to US policyholders, and more funds remained in London than expected, rather than flowing to New York. From their peak in January, stock prices had declined 18 percent by July 1905. By late September, stocks had recovered about half of their losses.

Figure 8.1 A scene on Wall Street during the Panic of 1907

The Hepburn Act, which gave the Interstate Commerce Commission (ICC) the powers to set maximum railroad rates, became law in July 1906. What followed was depreciation in the value of railroad securities. Between September 1905 and March 1907, the stock market slid, losing 7.7 percent of its capitalization. Between March 9 and 26, stocks fell a further 9.8 percent. This mid-March collapse is sometimes referred to as a "rich man's panic.".

The economy remained volatile through the summer. Several shocks hit the system: the stock of Union Pacific—among the most common stocks used as collateral—fell 50 points; that June an offering of New York City bonds failed; in July, the copper market collapsed; in august the Standard Oil Company was fined $29 million for antitrust violations. In the first nine months of 1907, stocks were lower by 24.4 percent.

On July 27, 1907 The Commercial & Financial Chronicle had noted that "The market keeps unstable—no sooner are these signs of new life in evidence than something like a suggestion of a new outflow of gold to Paris sends a tremble all through the list, and the gain in value and hope is gone."[43] Several bank runs occurred outside the U.S. in 1907: in Egypt in April and May; in Japan in May and June; in Hamburg and Chile in early October. The fall season was always a vulnerable time for the banking system: Combined with the roiled stock market, even a small shock could have grave repercussions.

The Real Panic Sets In

It all began not with gold, but with copper. There was a stock manipulation scheme to corner the market in F. Augustus Heinze's United Copper Company. Heinze had made a fortune as a copper magnate in Butte, Montana. In 1906 he moved to New York City, where he formed a close relationship with notorious Wall Street banker Charles W. Morse. Morse had once successfully cornered New York City's ice market, and together with Heinze gained control of many banks—the pair served on at least six national bank boards, ten state bank boards, five trust companies and four insurance firms.[44] More than ice was about to melt down.

Augustus's brother, Otto, devised the scheme to corner United Copper, believing that the Heinze family already controlled most of the company. He also believed that a significant number of Heinze's shares had been borrowed, and sold short, by speculators betting that the stock price would drop and that they could thus repurchase the borrowed shares cheaply, pocketing the difference. Otto proposed a short squeeze, whereby the Heinze's would aggressively purchase as many remaining shares as possible, and then force the short sellers to pay for their borrowed shares. The aggressive purchasing would drive up the share price, and, being unable to find shares elsewhere, the short sellers would have no option but to turn to the Heinze's, who could then name their price.

---

[43] Quoted by Robert F. Bruner & Sean D. Carr, *The Panic of 1907: Lessons Learned from the Market's Perfect Storm* (Hoboken, New Jersey: John Wiley & Sons, 2007), pp. 43-44.

[44] This took place before the attempt to prevent over-lapping membership on boards of trusts, before "trust-busting" became popular.

Figure 8.2
The Knickerbocker

To finance the scheme, Otto, Augustus and Charles Morris met with Charles T. Barney, president of the city's third largest bank, the Knickerbocker Trust Company. They were not like strangers on a train: Barney had provided financing for previous Morse schemes. Morse, however, cautioned Otto that he needed much more money than he had to attempt the squeeze and Barney declined to provide funding. Otto decided to attempt to corner the market anyway. On Monday, October 14, he began aggressively purchasing shares of United Copper, which rose the nest day from $39 to $52 per share. On Tuesday (Oct 15), he issued the call for short sellers to return the borrowed stock. The share price rose to nearly $60, but the short sellers could find plenty of' United Copper shares from sources other than the Heinze's. Otto had misread the market, and the share price of United Copper began its monumental collapse. The stock closed at $30 on Tuesday and fell to $10 by Wednesday (Oct. 16). Otto Heinze was ruined. The stock of United Copper was outside the hall of the New York Stock Exchange, literally an outdoor market "on the curb" (this curb market would later become the American Stock Exchange). After the crash, The Wall Street Journal reported, "Never have there been such wild scenes on the Curb, so say the oldest veterans of the outside market."[45]

The Contagion Spreads

The failure to corner the market on United Copper left Otto unable to meet his obligations and sent his brokerage house, Gross & Kleeberg, into bankruptcy. On Thursday, October 17, the New York Stock Exchange suspended Otto's trading privileges. Because of United Copper's collapse, the State Savings Bank of Butte Montana (owned by F. Augustus Heinze) announced its insolvency. The Montana bank had held United Copper stock as collateral against some of its lending and had been a correspondent bank for the Mercantile National Bank in New York City, of which F. Augustus Heinze was then president.

F. Augustus Heinze's association with the corner attempt and the insolvent State Savings Bank proved too much for the board of Mercantile to accept. Although they forced him to resign before lunchtime, by then it was too late. As news of the collapse spread, depositors rushed en masse to withdraw money from the Mercantile National Bank. The Mercantile had enough capital to withstand a few days of withdrawals, but depositors began to pull cash from the banks of the Heinze's associate Charles W. Morse. Runs occurred at Morse's National Bank of North America and the New Amsterdam National. Afraid of the impact the tainted reputations of Augustus Heinze and Morse could have on the banking system, the New York Clearing House (a consortium of the city's banks) forced Moore and Heinze to resign all banking interests. By the weekend after the failed corner, there was not yet systemic panic. Funds were withdrawn from Heinz-associated banks, only to be deposited with other banks in the city. A week later many regional stock exchanges throughout the nation were closing or limiting trading. For example, the Pittsburgh city's stock exchange closed for three months starting on October 23, 1907.

---

[45] Quoted by Robert F. Bruner and Sean D. Carr, *The Panic of 1907: Lessons Learned from the Market's Perfect Storm* (Hoboken, New Jersey: John Wiley & Sons, 2007)--a must read on this subject.

When Panic Hit the Trusts

In the early 1900s, trust companies were booming; in the decade before 1907, their assets had grown by 244 percent. During the same period, national bank assets grew by 97 percent, while state banks in New York increased by 82 percent. The trusts were clearly the new leaders. The lenders of the high-flying trusts were mainly prominent members of New York's financial and social circles. One of the most respected was Charles T. Barney, whose late father-in-law William Collins Whitney was a famous financier. Barney's Knickerbocker Trust Company was the largest trust in New York. Because of Barney's past association with Charles W. Morse and F. Augustus Heinze, on Monday, October 21, 1907 the board of the Knickerbocker asked that Barney resign (depositors may have first begun to pull deposits from the Knickerboker on October 18, prompting the concern). That day the National Bank of Commerce where J.P. Morgan was a dominant figure, announced it would no longer serve as a clearing house to the Knickerbocker. On October 22, the Knickerbocker faced a classic bank run. From the bank's opening, the crowd grew. As The New York Times reported, "as fast as a depositor went out of the place ten people and more came asking for their money and the police were asked to send some men be keep order."[46] Two vanloads of notes were quickly unloaded, yet even this failed to calm the panic-stricken depositors. Directors and other officials of the Trust forced their way through the crowd, assuring them that everyone would be paid. In less than three hours, $8 million was withdrawn from the Knickerbocker. Shortly, after noon it was forced to suspend operations.

---

[46] Quoted by Jon Moen & Ellis Tallman, "The Bank Panic of 1907: The Role of the Trust Companies," *The Journal of Economic History* 52 (3) 1992: 611-30. Some of my discussion of the trusts is based on this article.

Figure 8.3
A Bank Run, 1907

As news spread, other banks and trust companies were reluctant to lend any money. The interest rates on loans to brokers at the stock exchange soared to 70 percent and, with brokers unable to get money, stock prices fell to a low not seen since December 1900. The panic quickly spread to other large trusts—Hamilton Bank of New York, First National Bank of Brooklyn, International Trust Company of New York, Williamsburg Trust company of Brooklyn, Borough Bank of Brooklyn, Jenkins Trust Company of Brooklyn and the Union Trust Company of Providence. Few banks or trusts were spared.

Enter the Great Bulk of J.P. Morgan

When the chaos began to shake the confidence of New York's banks, the city's most famous banker was out of town. J.P. Morgan, the eponymous president of J.P. Morgan & Co., was attending a church convention in Richmond, Virginia. Morgan was not only the city's wealthiest and most well-connected banker, but he had experience with similar financial crisis—he famously had helped to rescue the US Treasury during the Panic of 1893. As the news of the crisis gathered, Morgan returned from his prayers to Wall Street late on the night of Saturday, October 19. The following morning, the library of Morgan's brownstone at Madison Avenue and 35th Street became a revolving door of New York City bank and trust company presidents to share information about (and seek help surviving) the impending crisis.

Morgan and his associates examined the books of the Knickerbocker Trust, and decided it was indeed insolvent so did not intervene to stop the run. Its failure, however, triggered runs on even healthy trusts, prompting Morgan to take charge of the rescue operation. Arriving on the afternoon of Tuesday, October 22, the president of the Trust Company of American asked Morgan for assistance. This, among other things such as the rapid deterioration of the trusts led Morgan to quickly take charge. That evening Morgan conferred with George F. Banker, the president of First National Bank, James Stillman of the National City Bank of New (the ancestor of Citibank) and the United States Secretary of The Treasury George B.Cortelyou'. Cortelyou' said that he was ready to deposit government money in the banks to help shore up their deposits. After an overnight audit of the Trust Company of America showed the institution to be sound, on Wednesday afternoon Morgan declared. "This is the place to stop the trouble then."[47]

Figure 8.4
J. P. Morgan

---

[47] See Bruner & Carr, *op. cit.* , pp. 87-88.

As a run began on Trust Company of America, Morgan worked with James Stillman and Banker to liquidate the company's assets to allow the bank to pay depositors. The bank survived to the close of business, but Morgan knew that additional money would be needed to keep it solvent through the following day. That night he assembled the presidents of the other trust companies and held them in a meeting until midnight when they agreed to provide loans of $8.75 million to allow the Trust Company of America to stay open the next day. On Thursday morning Cortelyou' deposited around $25 million into several new banks. John D. Rockefeller, the wealthiest man in America, deposited a further $10 million in Stillman's National City Bank. Rockefeller's massive deposits left the National City Bank with the deepest reserves of any bank in the city. To instil public confidence, Rockefeller phoned Melville Stone, the manager of the Associated Press, and told him that he would pledge half his wealth to maintain America's credit on a stock exchange on the edge of collapse. Despite the infusion of cash, the banks of New York were reluctant to make the short-term loans they typically provided to facilitate daily stock trades. Prices on the exchange began to crash, owing to the lack of funds to finance purchases. At 1:30 p.m. Thursday, October 24, Ransom Thomas, the president of the New York Stock Exchange, rushed to Morgan's offices to tell him that he, Thomas, would have to close the exchange early. Morgan was emphatic that an early close of the exchange would be catastrophic.

Morgan summoned the presidents of the city's banks to his office. When they started to arrive at 2 p.m., Morgan informed them that as many as 50 stock exchange houses would fail unless $25 million was raised in 10 minutes. By 2:15 pm., 14 bank presidents had pledged $23.5 million to keep the stock exchange afloat. The money reached the market at 2:30 pm. in time to finish the day's trading, and by the 3 o' clock market close, $19 million had been loaned out. Disaster was averted. Morgan usually shunned the press, but as he left his office that night he made a statement to reporters: "If people will keep their money in the banks, everything will be all right."[48] Friday, however, saw more panic on the exchange. Morgan again approached the bank presidents, but this time was only able to convince them to pledge $9.7 million. For this money to keep the exchange open, Morgan decided the money could not be used for margin sales. The volume of trading on Friday was two-thirds that of Thursday. The markets again narrowly made it to the closing bell.

---

[48] Quoted by Bruner & Carr, *op. cit.*,pp. 100-101.

The Crisis of Confidence

Morgan, Stillman, Banker and other city bankers were unable to pool money indefinitely. Even the U.S. Treasury was low on funds. Public confidence needed to be restored, and on Friday evening the bankers formed two committees--one to persuade the clergy to calm their usual Congregation on Sunday, and second to explain to the press the various aspects of the financial rescue package. Europe's most famous banker, Lord Rothschild, sent word of his "admiration and respect" for Morgan.[49] To gather confidence, the Treasury Secretary Cortelyou' agreed that if he returned to Washington it would send a signal to Wall Street that the worst had passed.

To ensure a free flow of funds on Monday, the New York Clearing House issued $100 million in loan certificates to be traded between banks to settle balances, allowing them to retain cash reserves for depositors. Reassured both by the clergy and the newspapers, and with bank balance sheets flush with cash, a sense of order returned to New York that Monday. Unbeknownst to Wall Street, a new crisis was being averted in the background. On Sunday, Morgan's associate, George Perkins, was informed that the City of New York required at least $20 million by November 1 or it would go bankrupt. The city tried to raise money through a standard bond issue but failed to gather enough financing. On Monday and again on Tuesday, New York Mayor George McClellan approached Morgan for assistance. To avoid the disastrous signal that a New York City bankruptcy would send, Morgan contracted to purchase some $30 million worth of city bonds. Morgan was paving the way for future interventions by a central bank.

The Drama Continues at Morgan's Library

Though calm was largely restored in New York by Saturday November 2, yet another crisis loomed. One of the exchange's largest brokerage firms, Moore & Schley was heavily in debt and in danger of collapse. The firm did what it could to stay afloat. It borrowed heavily, using shares of the Tennessee Coal, Iron and Railroad (TC&I) as collateral. This thinly traded stock was under pressure, and many banks called the loans of Moore and Schley on Monday, forcing an en masse liquidation of the firm's stock. This could trigger further panic in the market. To avert of the collapse of Moore & Schley, J. P. Morgan retired to his

---

[49] See Bruner & Carr, *Ibid.*, pp. 103-107.

library and called an emergency conference on Saturday morning. A proposal was made that the U.S. Steel Corporation, a company Morgan had helped form through the merger of the companies of Andrew Carnegie and Elbert Gary, would acquire TC&I. This would save Moore & Schley and avert the crisis. U.S. Steel studied the situation and offered to either loan Moore & Schley $5 million or buy TC & I for $90 a share. By 7 p.m. No agreement had been reached and the meeting adjourned.

Meanwhile, the omnipresent J. Pierpont Morgan was pulled into another situation. The Trust Company of America and the Lincoln Trust might fail to open on Monday due to the continuing runs by depositors. Some 40-50 bankers gathered on Saturday evening at the library to discuss the crisis with Morgan. The clearing-house bank presidents were in the East Room and the trust company executives in the West room. Morgan told his counsellors that he would agree to help shore up Moore & Schley only if the trust companies would work together to bail out their weakest brethren. Though the discussion among the bankers continued late into Saturday night, not much progress had been made. Around midnight, J. P. Morgan informed a leader of the trust company presidents that keeping Moore & Schley afloat would require a cool $25 million, but he would not commit these funds unless the problems with the trust companies could also be resolved. The trust company executives understood—they would have to finance any bailout of the two struggling trust companies.

Some 120 bank and trust officials assembled at 3 a.m. ostensibly to hear a full report on the status of the failing trust companies from Morgan. By now, the Trust Company of America was barely solvent, and the Lincoln Trust Company was about $1 million short of what it needed to cover depositor accounts. The bankers suddenly realized that Morgan had locked them in the library and pocketed the key to force a solution. It was the sort of strong-arm tactic that he had used in the past.

Morgan then entered the talks and advised the trust companies that they must provide a loan of $25 million to save the weaker institutions. Morgan told them that if they did not comply the entire banking system would collapse. At about 4:45 a.m. Morgan persuaded the unofficial leader of the trust companies to sign the agreement, and the rest of the bankers soon followed. Having these commitments in hand, Morgan unlocked the library door. On Sunday afternoon and into the evening, Morgan, Perkins, Baker and Stillman, along with U.S. Steel's Gary and Henry Clay Frick, worked at the library to complete the deal for U.S. Steel to buy TC&I and by Sunday night had a plan for acquisition. However, one obstacle was in their path: the anti-trust crusading President Theodore Roosevelt. He had made breaking up monopolies a focus of his presidency. Amazingly, Roosevelt eventually relented. "Teddy" later recalled the meeting: "It was necessary for me to decide on the instant before the Stuck Exchange opened, for the situation in New York was such that any hour might be vital. I do not believe that anyone could justly criticize me for saying that I would not feel like objecting to the purchase under these circumstances."[50] Wall Street was relieved as the final crisis of the panic had been averted.

Recession and a Central Bank in the Aftermath

A deep economic recession accompanied the financial crisis The National Bureau of Economic Research dates the recession between May 1907 and June 1908. The combination of contraction, bank panic and failing stock market created significant economic disruption. Industrial production dropped further than after any previous bank run, while 1907 saw the second-highest volume of bankruptcies to that date.

The final report of the National Monetary Commission was published on January 11, 1911. For nearly two years' legislators debated the proposal and it was not until December 23, 1913, that Congress passed the Federal Reserve Act. President Woodrow Wilson signed the legislation immediately and the legislation was enacted on the same day, December 23, 1913, creating the Federal Reserve System. Charles Hamlin became the Fed's first chairman and none other than Morgan's deputy Benjamin Strong became president of the Federal Reserve Bank of New York, the most important regional bank with a permanent seat on the Federal Open Market Committee. It was poetic justice that Strong had a major influence in shaping the policies of this new institution on. Absent J .P. Morgan, the American financial system would not have survived; absent Morgan, there would not have been a central bank to take over the role he had played.

The main lessons of this chapter are: (1): someone like J. P. Morgan can end a panic but not a recession and (2): the Panic of 1917 showed the need for a central bank and over time it was supplied. The panic of the depositors was from fear, afraid that they could not get their hands on their money in the banks and

---

[50] Quoted by Bruner & Carr, *op. cit.*, p 132.

trusts. Despite his great bulk, Morgan did not have be resources to end the recession. Later, that could be accomplished by timely fiscal policy by the Treasury and monetary policy by the central bank. The need for a central bank became obvious.

Chapter 9
The Great Crash of 1929

The Roaring twenties introduced most Americans not only to Zelda Fitzgerald and the Flapper but also to the automobile, starting a love affair that has yet to end. Scott Fitzgerald, the prophetic prophet of the Jazz Age, sent the final draft of *This Side of Paradise* (1920) to his publisher in August 1919, a month after John Maynard Keynes had fled Versailles in disgust with the terms of the peace treaty. In 1920, the now ubiquitous Model T was priced at $850 and some 25 percent of households owned cars; by 1930, despite economic hard times, the share had soared to 60 percent. Ford revolutionized the manufacturing process, and then cut prices. Lower price stimulates the number of cars demanded, increasing sales and facilitating long production runs, which allowed Ford to cut prices even further. In the 20 years ending in 1929, the sticker price of a typical Ford fell 80 percent. Better, Ford paid his workers enough to afford the car.

During the light-hearted decade of the 1920s the share of households with electricity almost doubled and the percentage with washing machines tripled. Households with inside flush toilets more than doubled. In 1929 it seemed as if everything was flush except bank accounts as consumer credit rose to about 15 percent of non-food purchases. Agriculture was the great exception. It was a decade-long depression in which agricultural prices fell by more than those of automobiles Farm income also fell. Agriculture worldwide had emerged from the Great War with excess capacity. The coming of the tractor (a by-product of automobiles) ploughed acreage once devoted to horses and mules but also increased the surpluses failing to create their own demands. The failure of Say's law was a failure for farmers.[51]

The values and institutions of capitalism had changed. The American Dream

---

[51] The simplified version of Say's law states that supply creates its own demand.

had shifted away from thrift, work effort and luck as ends and toward consumption and the making and use of financial instruments as the new means. Even Nick Caraway, Fitzgerald's narrator in The Great Gatsby (1925), was a bond salesman. We can learn something about the new values from the Bloomsbury circle, Jazz Age fiction, and the House of Morgan. Like F. Scott Fitzgerald's fictional Jay Gatsby, the noveau riche of the Jazz Age had huge fortunes but lacked the traditions associated with inherited wealth. Those with old money like Joseph Kennedy thought those with new money vulgar. Others, like Fitzgerald's Buchanan or the real world's Jack Morgan, son of Pierpont, had establishment wealth and thus possessed inherited traditions. They were more likely to corrupted by the purposelessness and ease their money provided.

Fashions of the Jazz Age—Flappers and More Or Less

Women's fashions expressly reflected the excesses of the Jazz Age. They were typified by less tailoring leading to an abandonment of the corset (goodbye corseted trophy wives). A tubular silhouette erased the typical feminine shape and a dropped waistline created a long, slim figure.

Not every woman was typical: Zelda Fitzgerald was an exception, who defined the Flapper as herself. Short shirts and flippant styles of the flappers were not copied by all women. In the early 1920s, irregular hemlines gave the appearance of shortening when uneven, scalloped, and handkerchief hems became fashionable. The short skirts of the Flapper and of Zelda were worn by younger women. The year Fitzgerald's The Great Gatsby was published (1925) was a tipping point for the Flapper, as skirts got shorter and shorter. Hems seemed to often move inversely with the stock-exchange as they went up during the Crash of 1929. The short skirt seemed to define Fitzgerald's concept of the modern women, which continued (more or less) during the 20th and 21st centuries.

Underwear became more visible as hemlines soared. Young women flattened their breasts with fabric bands to enhance a slim, boyish figure (this, the Age of the chemise, not the bra). Legs were suddenly and shockingly on display. Silk and rayon stockings and panties became the norm for the young. While dancing, flappers rolled their stockings to just below the knee to ease movement, especially for the Charleston.

Men's fashions were not as dramatic. The suits men wear today are still based, for the most part, on those worn in the late 1920s. Suspenders were extremely popular, often paired with knickers and a white or light blue dress shirt. Knickers, pants tucked in at the hem, were men's answer to the flapper. Gentleman's shoes went with the knickers. Bow ties also were more popular then than now. Newsboy caps were popular among men at the time and are seeing resurgence today. The watch fog was popular at the time.

A major innovation was the crease in the front of men's pants. You wouldn't be seen without a hat or without a neatly folded handkerchief in the breast pocket of your jacket. In addition to wool, tweed and flannel fabrics were popular. Sports stars such as tennis player Bill Tilden and golfer Bobby Jones were trendsetters and fans tried to emulate. Well-dressed young men might wear golfing knickers or loose, white flannel trousers and a sweater, sometimes V-necked sweater vests over a collared shirt. This was the case whether they played golf or tennis or neither. Zelda and Scott Fitzgerald often golfed and played tennis, helping to popularize these sporty clothes.

Figure 9.1
Other Colourful Fashions, Early 1920s

All That Jazz and Other Excesses

As would be expected, Jazz during the Jazz Age gained popularity in America and worldwide. New exuberant dances were devised to take advantage of the upbeat tempos' of jazz and Ragtime music. Jazz spread to dance halls and other venues, including speakeasies, all over America by the mid-1920s. The advent of radio and the ready availability of phonograph records which were selling in the tens of millions in the late nineteen-twenties introduced jazz to people living in even remote locations.

Strangely named dances inspired by African-style dance moves, like the shimmy, bunny hug, and the Charleston eventually spread to the general public. Today, few of these dances survive; the Charleston is a rarity. White audiences saw these dances first in vaudeville shows, then in clubs. Jazz was mostly to be listened to or observed. The popular Tin Pan Alley composers like Irving Berlin incorporated ragtime influence into their compositions, though they rarely used the musical techniques often used by jazz players. Paul Whiteman's band became popular in the late 1920s, with backup vocalist Bing Crosby. Crosby was considered the first "cool" white guy. Then, in Paris in 1921 there was Louis Armstrong and "all that jazz." Scott and Zelda Fitzgerald knew Berlin, Whiteman and "Satchmo." The fashions and the music was the light side of the Jazz Age, but as Fitzgerald's *The Great Gatsby* revealed, there was a dark side to the Age, part of which had to do with lopsided income and wealth distributions, to which we return.

J. Edward Stettinius, a J. P. Morgan partner during the 1920s, had six cars and several houses. It cost him $250,000 a year or $3,448,489 in 2019 dollars just to cover basic living expenses. Stock ownership was even more concentrated than the income distribution. This financial imbalance presented problems of its own, which would later emerge by the Thirties. Except for what is purchased as necessities, the large discretionary income of the rich is not dependably spent. It must go for mansions (like Jay Gatsby's), yachts, Rolls-Royces (such as the used one bought by the Fitzgeralds), and Caribbean travel or else be saved and thus be subject to the even less predictable behaviour of producers. It is one thing for producers to issue new equities and bonds to expand their facilities, it is quite another for rich people to buy and sell existing securities among themselves, changing only the pieces of engraved paper. The amount of unanchored cash chasing other pieces of paper probably had never been so high. Despite the obvious trouble that can be caused by cash on the loose, the average citizen threw caution to the restless winds, wanting nothing so much as getting rich quickly with a minimum of exertion.

These excesses began to bubble to the top well before 1929. By the mid-1920s, a classic speculative bubble inflated over balmy Florida. Miami, Miami Beach, Coral Gables—in fact the whole southeast coast as far north as Palm Beach—basked in the warmth of the great real estate boom. "Ocean view" lots often required telescopes, and Charles Ponzi's subdivision "near Jacksonville" was actually 65 miles west, closer to the Okefenokee swamp than to the Atlantic. Still nearly everybody acted as if prices of Florida real estate would go forever skyward, and it took not one but two hurricanes out of the autumn skies of 1926 to blow away the bubble. The bigger one showed "what a Smoothing Tropic Wind could do when it got a running start from the West Indies."[52] It killed four hundred people and launched yachts into the streets of Miami.

The collapse of the Florida land boom did not end speculation; it merely ended Florida's prosperity. The rise in stock prices had been rather steady beginning in the second half of 1924. Then the hurricanes blew away the Florida land bubble that October, the stock market dipped a bit, but a recovery soon began. The true stock market boom got underway in 1927, by the end of which the Times industrials, predecessor to the Dow, had gained 59 points to end at 245.

The Bubble

It is hard to say when the stock market boom of the nineteen-twenties began, though reasons for the beginning were sound. During these years, the prices of common stocks should rise because corporate earnings were good and growing. Moreover, in the early twenties stock prices were low and yields favourable. So, it is not surprising that in the final six months of 1924, the prices of securities began to rise, and the increase was continued and extended through 1925. At the end of May 1924, the New York Times average of prices of twenty-five industrial stocks was 108, by the end of the year it was 134. By December 31, 1925, it had gained nearly another 50 points and stood at 181. The advance though 1925 was steady; there were only a couple of months when values failed to show a net gain.

During 1926 there was a slight setback. Business was off a little in the early part of that year; it was thought by many that values the year before had risen unreasonably, a thought that did not persist as the twenties roared on. February brought a sharp fall in the market, and March a rather abrupt collapse. However, in April the market steadied and renewed its advance. Another mild setback occurred in October, just after a hurricane blew away the vestiges of the Florida land boom, but again recovery was prompt. At the end of the year values were about where they had been at the beginning.

In 1927 the increase began in earnest. Day after day and month after month the price of stocks went up. In the summer of 1927 Henry Ford rang down the curtain on the immortal Model T and closed his plant to prepare for Model A. The Federal Reserve Index of Industrial Production nodded its disapproval. The

---

[52] Frederick Lewis Allen, *Only Yesterday* (New York: Harper, 1932), p. 280.

effect on the market was imperceptible. At the end of the year by which time production had also turned up again, the Times industrials had reached 245, a net gain of 69 points for the year.

Still, until the start of 1928, even a man of conservative mind could believe that the prices of common stock were catching up with the advance in corporation earnings, the prospect for further increases, the peace and tranquillity of the times, and the certainty that the
Administration then firmly in power in Washington would take no more than necessary any earnings in taxes. Early in 1928, the nature of the boom changed. As John Kenneth Galbraith put it:

The mass escape into make-believe, so much a part of the true speculative orgy, started in earnest. It was still necessary to reassure those who required some tie, however tenuous, to reality. And, this process of reassurance—of inventing the industrial equivalents of the Florida climate—eventually achieved the status of a profession. However, the time had come as in all periods of speculation, when men sought not to be persuaded of the reality of things but to find excuses for escaping into the new world of fantasy.[53]

In March 1928, the industrial average rose nearly 25 points. News of the boiling market was frequently on the front pages of newspapers across the country. Individual issues sometimes made gains of 10, 15 and 20 points in a single days trading. On March 12, Radio, in many respects the speculative symbol of the time, gained 18 points. On the following day, it opened 22 points above the previous close. Then it lost 20 points on the announcement that because of the behaviour of the trading, the stock was being investigated by the Exchange. Then, Radio gained another 15 points and fell off 9. A few days later, on a strong market, it made another 18-point gain.

An important figure in all this was John J. Raskob. He had impressive associations. He was a director of General Motors, an ally of the Du Points and soon to be Chairman of the Democratic National Committee by choice of Al Smith. On March 23, 1928 on a trip to Europe, Raskob spoke favourably of prospects for automobile sales for the rest of the year and of the share in the business that General Motors would have. As the Times put it, such was "the magic of his name" that Mr Raskob's "temperate bit of optimism" sent the market into a frenzy. On March 24, a Saturday, General Motors gained nearly 5

---

[53] John Kenneth Galbraith, *The Great Crash, 1929* (Boston: Houghton Mifflin, 1955), Ch. 10.

points, and the Monday following it went to 199. The surge in General Motors set off a great burst of trading elsewhere. As luck would have it, among others who put their strength behind the market that spring was William Crapo Durant (1861-1947). Durant became manager of General Motors, after Raskob and the Du Ponts had been thrown out of the company in 1920. After a further adventure in the auto business, he had turned to full-time speculation in the stock market. His fame is such that he was a model for a character in a F. Scott Fitzgerald story. The seven Fisher brothers were also believed to be influential. They too were GM alumni and had come to Wall Street with the great fortune they had realized from the sale of the Fisher-body plants. The public was awestruck by their vision for the future and their boundless hope and optimism. It was not as though this market needed any more boasters!

Even this market did not go straight up. In June 1928, the stock market retreated 30 points or so. June12, a day of especially heavy losses, was a landmark. On that day, 5,052,790 shares changed hands. The ticker fell nearly two hours behind the market. Radio dropped 23 points. However, the announcement of the death of the bull market was as prescient as the announcement of the death of Mark Twain (1835-1910). In July, there was a small net gain and in August a strong upsurge On December 17, Roger W Babson told an audience that "if Smith would be elected with a Democratic Congress, we are almost certain to have a resulting business depression in 1929." He also said the "the election of Hoover and a Republican Congress should result in continued prosperity for 1929." Another reassurance came from the distinguished Andrew W. Mellon, who said, "There is not cause for worry. The high tide of prosperity will continue."

Herbert Hoover (1874-1964) was elected in a landslide in January 1929. The day after the election, three was a "victory boom," and the market leaders climbed 5 to 15 points. The Times industrial average made a net gain of 41.2 points on the day's trading—then considered an impressive advance. December was not so good. Early in the month came a bad break, and, on December 8, Radio fell a ghastly 72 points in one day. The market steadied and over the whole year of 1928 the Times industrial average gained 85 points, or from 245 to 331. Though it had never paid a dividend, Radio went from 85 to 420; Du Pont went from 310 to 525; Montgomery Ward from 117 to 440; Wright Aeronautic soared from 69 to 289. During the year 920,550,032 shares were traded on the New York Stock Exchange. At the same time there was a phenomenal increase in trading on margin. This meant that the public was borrowing money to buy stocks.

Buying on the margin is a magical thing. The buyer of securities on margin gets full title to this property in an unconditional sale. But he rids himself of the most critical burden of ownership—that of putting up the purchase price—by leaving his securities with his broker as collateral for the loan that paid for them. The buyer gets full benefit of any increase in value—the price of the securities goes up, but the loan that bought them does not. The buyer also gets any earnings of the securities he purchased. Banks supply funds to brokers and brokers to customers, and the collateral goes back to banks in a smooth and all but automatic flow. People were swarming to buy stocks on margin—to have the increase in price without the costs of ownership.

Even corporations found it profitable to trade on the margin. Instead of trying to produce goods with its manifold headaches and inconveniences, they confined themselves to financing speculation. They began to lend their surplus funds to Wall Street. New York banks profited from the situation. They could borrow money from the Federal Reserve Bank for 5 percent and re-lend it in the call market for 12. In practice, they pocketed the difference. There was a difference, or so it was claimed, between a gambler and a stock speculator. A gambler wins only because someone else loses. With a stock purchase, all gain. One buyer buys General Motors at $110, sells it to another for $150, who sells it to a third at $200. Everyone makes money; that is, everyone who bought at a low price and sold at a higher price. It simply looked as if everyone was getting rich from the stock market.

The Crash

The Wall Street Crash of 1929, also known as Black Tuesday (October 29), the Great Crash, or the Stock Market Crash of 1929 began on October 24, 1929 or "Black Thursday." It was the most devastating stock market crash in the history of the United States, when taking into consideration the full extent and duration of the after effects. The crash, which followed the London Stock Exchange's crash of September, signalled the beginning of the 10-year Great Depression that affected all Western industrialized countries. Were there harbingers of what was to come?

The Roaring Twenties, the decade that followed World War I led to the crash; it was a time of concentrated wealth and excess, a time of irrational exuberance.

Building on post-war optimism, rural Americans migrated to the cities in vast numbers throughout the decade with the hope of finding a more prosperous life in the ever-growing expansion of America's industrial sector.

While the American cities prospered, the overproduction of agricultural produce created widespread financial despair among American farmers throughout the decade. This would later be blamed as one of the key factors that led to the 1929 stock market crash. Despite the dangers of speculation, many believed that the stock market would continue to rise forever.

On March 25, 1929, after the Federal Reserve warned of excessive speculation, a mini crash occurred as investors started to sell stocks at a rapid pace, exposing the market's shaky foundation. It would not be the only time that the Federal Reserve would contribute to a crash. Two days later, banker Charles E. Mitchell announced that his company, the National City Bank, would provide $25 million in credit to stop the market's slide. Mitchell's move brought a temporary halt to the financial crisis and call money declined from 20 to 8 percent. Mitchell must have thought he was J. P. Morgan.

However, the American economy showed continuous signs of trouble. Steel production declined, construction was sluggish, automobile sales went down, and consumers were building up high debts because of easy credit. In the face of all these economic troubles, after market breaks in March and May 1929, stocks resumed their advance in June and the gains continued almost unabated until early September 1929 (the Dow Jones average gained more than 20 percent between June and September).

The market had been on a nine-year run that saw the Dow Jones Industrial Average increase in value tenfold, peaking at 381.17 on September 3, 1929. Shortly before the crash, economist Irving Fisher famously proclaimed, "Stock prices have reached what looks like a permanently high plateau." After this proclamation, professor Irving Fisher added on October 15, "I expect to see the stock market a good deal higher than it is today within a few months." Still, the optimism and financial gains of the great bull market were shaken after a well-publicized early September prediction from financial expert Roger Babson that "a crash was coming." The initial September decline was thus called the "Babson Break" in the press. This was the start of the Great Crash, although until the severe phase of the crash in October, many investors hailed the September "Babson Break" as a "healthy correction" and buying opportunity. The only disturbing thing, in these golden autumn days, was the steady downward drift in the market, like the falling leaves.

On September 20, the London Stock Exchange crashed when top British investor Clarence Hatry and many of his associates were jailed for fraud and forgery. The London crash greatly weakened the optimism of American investment in markets overseas. In the days leading up to the crash, the market was severely unstable. Periods of selling and high volumes were interspersed with brief periods of rising prices and recovery. Volatility was the order of the day.

Selling intensified in mid-October. On October 24 ("Black Thursday"), the market lost 11 percent of its value at the opening bell on very heavy trading. The huge volume meant that the report of prices on the ticker tape in brokerage offices around the nation was hours late, so investors had no idea what most stocks were trading for at that moment, increasing the panic. Several leading Wall Street bankers met to find a solution to the panic and chaos on the trading floor. The meeting included Thomas W. Lamont; acting head of Morgan Bank; Albert Wiggin, head of the Chase National Bank; and the redoubtable Charles E. Mitchell, president of the National City Bank of New York. They chose Richard Whitney, vice president of the Exchange, to act on their behalf.

With the bankers' financial resources behind Whitney, the wind was behind his sails, He placed a bid to purchase a large block of shares in U.S. Steel at a price well above the current market. As traders watched intently, Whitney then placed similar bids on other "blue chip" stocks. This tactic was like one that ended the panic of 1907. It succeeded in halting the slide. The Dow Jones Industrial Average recovered, closing down only 6.38 points for the day. The rally continued Friday, October 25, and the half-day session on Saturday the 25th but, unlike 1907, the respite was only temporary. Whitney too might have thought he was J. P. Morgan.

Over the weekend, the events were covered by the newspapers across the United States. On October 28, "Black Monday," more investors facing margin calls decided to get out of the market, and the slide continued with a record loss in the Dow for the day of 38.33 points, or 13 percent. The next day, "Black Tuesday", October 29, 1929, about 15 million shares traded as the panic selling reached its peak. Some stocks had no buyers at any price that day (called "air pockets" by the brokers) The Dow lost an additional 30 points or 12 percent. The volume of stocks traded on October 29, 1929, was a record that was not broken for nearly 40 years.

On October 29, William C. Durant, who headed General Motors, joined with members of the Rockefeller family and other financial giants to buy large quantities of stocks to demonstrate to the public their confidence in the market, but their great efforts failed to stop the large decline in prices. Due to the massive volume of stocks traded that day, the ticker did not stop running until about 7:45 p.m. that evening. The market had lost over $30 billion in the space of two days which included $14 billion on October 29 alone.

After a one-day reprieve on October 30, when the Dow regained an additional l28.40 points, or 12 percent, to close at 258.47, the market continued to fall, arriving at an interim bottom on November 13, 1929, with the Dow closing at a remarkable 198.60. The market then recovered for several months, starting on November 14, with the Dow gaining 18.59 points to close at 217.28, and reaching a secondary closing peak (i.e. bear market rally) of 294.07 on April 17, 1930. The following year the Dow embarked on another, much longer, steady slide from April 1931 to July 8, 1932, when it closed at an astonishing 41.22— its lowest level of the 20th century, concluding an 89 percent loss rate for all the market's stocks.

For most of the 1930s, the Dow began slowly to regain the ground it lost during the 1929 crash and the three years following its beginning on March 15, 1933 with the largest percentage increase of 15.34 percent, and the Dow Jones closing at 52.10, with an 8.25-point increase. The largest percentage increases of the Dow Jones did occur during the early and mid-1930s. In late 1937, there was a sharp dip in the stock market, but pries held well above the 1932 lows. The market would not return to the peak closing of September 3, 1929, until November 23, 1954. It had been a devastating long slide.

The Economic Fundamentals

What was happening to what economists call "the real variables" in the economy? The crash followed a speculative burst that had taken hold in the late 1920s and would not let go. During the latter half of the 1920s, steel production, building construction, retail turnover, automobiles registered, even railway receipts advanced from record to record. It was the Roaring Twenties! The combined net profits of 536 manufacturing and trading companies showed an increase for the first six months of 1929 of 35.5 percent over 1928, itself a record. Iron and steel, which had been driving the economy, led the way with doubled gains. Such figures set up a crescendo of stock-exchange speculation which had led hundreds of thousands of Americans to invest heavily in the stock market. A significant number of them were borrowing money to buy still more stocks. By August 1929, brokers were routinely lending small investors more than two-thirds of the face value of the stocks they were buying. Over $8.5 billion was out on loan—a record, more than the entire amount of currency circulating in the U.S. at the time.

The rising share prices encouraged more people to invest; people hoped the share prices would rise further. Speculation thus fuelled further rises and created an economic bubble. Because of margin buying, investors stood to lose large sums of money if the market turned down—or even failed to advance quickly enough. The average P/E (price to earnings) ratio of S&P Composite stocks was 32.5 in September 1929, clearly well above historical norms.

Fundamentals elsewhere were sound. Good harvests had built up a mass of 250 million bushels of wheat to be "carried over" when 1929 opened. By May there was also a winter-wheat crop of 560 million bushels ready for harvest in the Mississippi Valley. This oversupply caused a drop in wheat prices so heavy that the net incomes of the farming population from wheat were threatened with extinction.

Stock Markets are always sensitive to the future state of commodity markets, and the slump in Wall Street predicted for May by Sir George Paish arrived on time. In June 1929, the position taken, based on Paish's predictions, was saved by a severe drought in the Dakotas and the Canadian West, plus unfavourable seed times in Argentina and Eastern Australia. The oversupply would now be required to fill the big gaps in the 1929 world wheat production. From 97 cents per bushel in May, the price of wheat rose to $1.49 in July. When it was seen that at this figure the American farmers would get rather more for their smaller crop than for that of 1928, up went stocks again and from far and wide orders came to buy shares for the profits to come. In August 1929 wheat prices fell when France and Italy were bragging of a magnificent harvest, and the situation in Australia improved. This sent a shiver through Wall Street and stock prices quickly dropped, but a world of cheap stocks brought a fresh rush of "stags," amateur speculators and investors. Congress had also voted for a $11 million relief package for the farmers, hoping to stabilize wheat prices. By October though, the price had fallen to $1.31 per bushel.

As to other economic fundamentals, important economic barometers were also slowing or even falling by mid-1929, including car sales, house sales, and steel production. The falling commodity and industrial production may have dented even American self-confidence, and the stock market peaked on September 3 at 381.17 just after Labour Day, then started to falter aftermarket guru Roger Babson issued his prescient "market crash" forecast. By the end of September, the market was down 10 percent from the peak (the "Babson Break"). Selling intensified in early and mid-October, with sharp down days punctuated by a few up days. Panic selling on huge volume started the week of October 21 and intensified and culminated on October 24, the 28th and especially the 29th ("Black Tuesday"). Journalists were beginning to run out of "Black days" labels.

The president of the Chase National Bank said at the time, "We are reaping the natural fruit of the orgy of speculation in which millions of people have indulged. It was inevitable because of the tremendous increase in the number of stockholders in recent years, but the number of sellers would be greater than ever when the boom ended and selling took the place of buying."[54]

In 1932, the Pecora Commission was established by the U.S. Senate to study the causes of the crash. The following year the U.S. Congress passed the Glass-Steagall Act mandating a separation between commercial banks, which take deposits and extend loans, and investment banks, which underwrite, issue, and distribute stocks, bonds, and other securities. It was a much-needed tourniquet after most of the bleeding had taken place. The strictures of the Glass-Steagall Act have slowly eroded since.

After the 1929 crash, stock markets around the world instituted measures to suspend trading in the event of rapid declines, claiming that the measures would prevent such panic sales. However, the one-day crash of Black Monday, October 19, 1987, when the Dow Jones Industrial Average fell 22.6 percent, was worse in percentage terms than any single day of the 1929 crash (although the combined 25 percent decline of October 28-29, 1929 was larger than October 19, 1987, and remains the worst two-day decline ever).

Further Outcome's

This was not the end of the effects from the debacle. The Great Crash of 1929 propelled gold, a historically viable store of value and durable medium of exchange, to an unprecedented value. Economists have often referred to internationally-traded gold as a "relic," not so in and after 1929. In 2015

---

[54] Second Crash," *The Sydney Morning Herald*, Sydney, October 30, 1929, p. 17.

inflation-adjusted terms, the price of a single ounce of gold rose from $291 an ounce in 1929 to $539 in 1939, more than doubling in price. In 1930, 1,352 banks held more than $853 million in deposits; in 1931, one year later, 2,294 banks went down with nearly $17 billion in deposits. Many businesses failed (28,285 failures at a daily rate of 133 in 1931).

Together, the 1929 stock market crash and the Great Depression formed the largest financial crisis of the 20th century. The panic of October 1929 has come to serve as a symbol of the economic contraction that gripped the world during the next decade. The declines in share prices on October 24 and 29, 1929 were practically instantaneous in all financial markets, except Japan.

The 1929 crash brought the Roaring Twenties to a shuddering halt. There was a central bank, the Federal Reserve System, but it did not do its job. If anything, it made matters worse. There was no lender of last resort effectively present. The crash marked the beginning of widespread and long-lasting consequences for the United States. To this day historians still debate the question: did the 1929 Crash spark The Great Depression, or did it merely coincide with the bursting of a loose credit-inspired economic bubble? Only 16 percent of American households were invested in the stock market within the United States during the period leading up to the depression, suggesting that the crash carried somewhat less of a weight in causing the depression.

The psychological effects of the crash reverberated across the nation as businesses became aware of the difficulties in securing capital market investments for new projects and expansions. Business uncertainty naturally affects job security for employees, and as the American worker (as consumer) faced uncertainty with regards to income, the Keynesian propensity to consume declined. The decline in stock prices caused bankruptcies and severe macroeconomic difficulties including contraction of credit, business closures, firing of workers, bank failures, decline of the money supply, and other economically depressing events.

The rise of mass unemployment often is seen as a result of the crash, although the crash is by no means the sole event that contributed to the depression. The Wall Street Crash is usually seen as having the greatest impact on the events that followed and therefore is widely regarded as signalling the downward economic slide that initiated the Great Depression. True or not, the consequences were dire for almost everybody. Most academic experts agree on one aspect of the crash: It wiped out billions of dollars of wealth, and this immediately depressed consumer buying.

The stock market failure set off a worldwide run on U.S. gold deposits (i.e. the dollar) and forced the Federal Reserve to raise interest rates into the slump. Some 4,000 banks and other lenders ultimately failed. Also, the uptick rule, which allowed short selling only when the last tick in stock's price was positive, was implemented after the 1929 crash to prevent short sellers from driving the price of stock down in a bear raid.

The stock market crash of October 1929 led directly to the Great Depression in Europe. When stocks plummeted in New York, the world took immediate notice. Although financial leaders in England, as in the United States, vastly underestimated the extent of the crisis that would ensure, it soon became clear that the world's economies were more interconnected than ever. The effects of the disruption to the global system of financing trade, and production and the subsequent meltdown of the American economy were soon felt throughout Europe. During 1930 and 1931 unemployed workers went on strike, demonstrated in public, and otherwise took direct action to call public attention to their plight. Protests often focused on the so-called Means Test, which the Hoover government had instituted in 1931 to limit the amount of unemployment payments made to individuals and families. For working people, the Means Test seemed an intrusive and insensitive way to deal with the chronic and relentless deprivation caused by the economic crises. The strikes were met forcefully, with police breaking up protests, arresting demonstrators, and charging them with crimes related to the violation of public order.[55]

Concluding Comments

As to concluding comments, the briefer, the better. The 1920s roared not only because of the antics of the Fitzgerald's but because the fundamentals of the economy and the stock market were booming. One would expect the market to move up and down with fundamentals. But speculators would not leave well enough alone and drove prices into the stratosphere. Common people could not set at the side-lines of such profit opportunities and jumped on the bandwagon, just as they had done during Tulipmania. It was too much of a good thing.

---

[55] In this chapter when I was unsure of the facts or trends, I turned to John Kenneth Galbraith's classic *The Great Crash 1929* (New York: Houghton-Mifflin, 2009) for reassurance.

Women's fashions especially reflected the excesses of the Age. Hemlines went up and down with the stock exchanges. Men's fashions were less exuberant as indeed they remain. Moreover, the short skirt defined the Flapper and Fitzgerald's new woman. Not surprisingly Jazz, became popular during the Jazz Age, and along with F. Scott Fitzgerald, helped to define it. New dance crazes such as the Charleston were all the rage. It was an era of experimentation and innovation.

The excesses began to bubble to the top well before 1929. By the mid-1920s, a classic speculative bubble inflated over balmy Florida, only to be blown away by two hurricanes. This was a harbinger of what was to come in the stock market. As noted, the beginnings of the stock boom were sound. It just got out of hand. During 1926 there was a slight setback, but in 1927 the increase began in earnest. Day after day, week after week, month after month the market advanced. The mass escape into make-believe began in early 1928. Radio stock led the way with multiple gains. Then John J. Rascob, who had impressive associations, sent the market into a frenzy. The day after Hoover was elected in a landslide, there was a "victory boom." Buying on the margin was the final magic making the market froth. In retrospect, the crash was inevitable. It came on Black Thursday (October 24, 1929) and Black Tuesday (October 29, 1929) and was the most devastating stock market crash in the history of the United States, There were great private efforts to save the day, such as those of Richard Whitney of the New York Exchange, and William C. Durant, along with the Rockefeller family and others . But their great efforts failed to stop the large decline in prices. The Federal Reserve, the nation's central bank, set on its hands, even during the Great Depression that followed the 1929 debacle. Together, the stock market crash and the Great Depression formed the largest financial crisis of the 20th century. Worse, the 1929 crash led directly to the Great Depression in Europe and the aftermath.

Next, we come closer to modern times with The Stock Market Crash of 1987. After that, we will be ready for some comedy relief.

Chapter 10
The Stock Market Crash Of 1987

As we know by now, a stock market crash is a sudden dramatic decline of stock prices across a significant cross-section of a stock market, resulting in a significant loss of paper wealth. Such crashes are driven by panic as much as by underlying fundamentals, and often follow speculative stock market bubbles. All of this was true for the Crash of 1987.

We nonetheless can elaborate. Broadly, stock market crashes are social phenomena where external economic events combine with crowd behaviour and psychology in a positive feedback loop where selling by some market participants, especially the nouveau riche, drives more market participants to sell. Generally, crashes occur under the following conditions: a prolonged period of rising stock prices and excessive economic optimism, a market where P/E ratios exceed long-term averages, and extensive use of margin debt and leverage by market participants. Often a crash is followed by a bear market. This was not the case for the 1987 crash.

Can we put a number on it, such as the percentage decline in an index? The short answer is "no". It all depends. Some crashes are bigger than others. Suffice it to say that a major index such as the Dow-Jones Industrial Average, will fall sharply and significantly during a crash. Steep double-digit percentage losses in a stock market index over a span of several days will catch the attention of CNN, if not your local stockbroker, who is often in denial. A crash can be distinguished from a bear market wherein the decline in stock market prices is measured in months or years. While crashes are often associated with bear markets, they do not necessarily go hand in hand. The crash of 1987 did not lead to a bear market, mostly because fundamentals improved directly afterward. Likewise,, the Japanese bear market of the 1980s occurred over several years without a crash, only moans about the glacial movement of stock prices.

Does Mathematics Help?

One might think that a mathematician would have a field day with market crashes. And, they would be right, whether the math was or not. A conventional assumption has been that stock markets behave according to a random log-normal distribution, a random walk, as it were. This notion was popularized by Burton G. Malkiel.[56] Among other gurus, mathematician Benoit Mandelbrot suggested as early as 1963 that statistics prove this assumption incorrect. Mandelbrot observed that large movements in prices (crashes) are much more common than would be predicted from a log-normal distribution. Rather, market moves are generally much better explained using non-linear analysis and chaos theory. Put differently, a crack in the ice can cause an avalanche, which has been explained by chaos theory. Rather than numbers, chaos theory produces patterns of data that look like psychological Rorschach tests. The problem is lack of quantification. Still, chaos paints a pretty good picture.

Research at the Massachusetts Institute of Technology (MIT) suggests that the frequency of stock market crashes follows an inverse cubic power law.[57] This and other studies such as one by Professor Didier Sornette suggest that market crashes are a sign of self-organized criticality in financial markets. In 1963 Mandelbrot proposed that instead of a strict random walk, stock price variations executed a Levy flight. A Levy flight is a random walk that is occasionally disrupted by large movements. The definitive answer is not in sight as researchers continue to study the Levy flight, particularly using computer simulation of crowd behaviour, and the applicability of models to reproduce crash-like phenomena.

The Crash

The mid-1980s was a time of strong economic optimism. From August 1982 to its peak in August 1987, the Dow Jones Industrial Average (DJIA) grew from 776 to 2722. The euphoria was virtually worldwide; the rise in market indices

---

[56] See Burton G. Malkiel, *A Random Walk Down Wall Street*, 12th Edition (New York: W. W. Norton and Company, 2019).

[57] The inverse cubic power law comes from the physics notion of an inverse square law or any physical law stating that a physical quantity or intensity is inversely proportional to the square of the distance from the source. Simply put, intensity is approximated by 1//Distance Squared.

for the 19 largest markets in the world averaged 296 percent during this time. The average number of shares traded on the NYSE had risen from 65 million shares to 181 million shares.

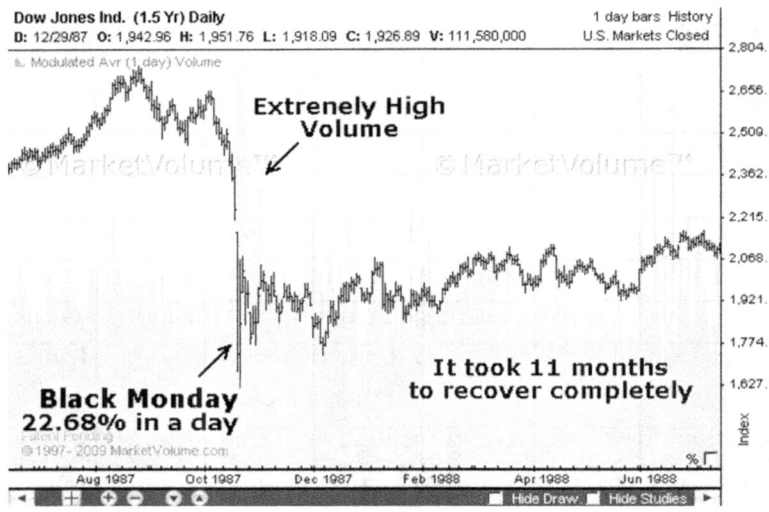

Figure 10.1
Dow Jones (1987-06-19 through 1988-01-19)

The U.S. Crash came on October 19, 1987, a date also known as "Black Monday," was the climactic culmination of a market decline that had begun five days before on October 14. The DJIA fell 3.81 percent on October 14, followed by another 4.60 percent drop on Friday, October 15. Then, suddenly, on "Black Monday", the Dow Jones Industrials plummeted 508 points, losing 22.6 percent of its value in a single day. The broader S&P 500 dropped 20.4 percent, falling from 282.7 to 225.06. The technology-oriented NASDAQ Composite lost only 11.3 percent, not because of restraint on the part of sellers, but because the NASDAQ market system failed. Deluged with sell orders, many stocks on the NYSE faced trading halts and delays. Of the 2,257 NYSE-listed stocks, there were 195 trading delays and halts during the day, with the NASDAQ market faring much worse. Because of its reliance on a "market making" system that allowed market makers to withdraw from training, liquidity in NASDAQ stocks dried up. Trading many stocks encountered a pathological condition where the bid price for a stock exceeded the ask price. These "locked" conditions severely curtailed trading. On October 19, trading in broadly-traded Microsoft shares on the NASDAQ lasted a total of only 54 minutes. The crash was the greatest single-day loss that Wall Street had ever suffered in continuous trading. Between October 14 and October 19, the DJIA lost 750 points, a decline of over 31 percent.

The United States exchanges are closely linked to foreign exchanges. As a result, the 1987 crash was worldwide. The[58] FTSE 100 Index, heavily weighted with international stocks traded in London, lost 10.8 percent on that gloomy Monday and a further 12.2 percent the next day.[59] During October all major world markets declined dramatically. On Thursday, October 15, 1987, Iran hit the American owned (and Liberian-flagged) super tanker, the Sjungari, with a silkworm missile off Kuwait's main Mina Al Ahmadi oil port. The next morning, Iran hit another ship, the U.S.-flagged MV Sea Isle City, with another silkworm missile. On Friday, October 16, the markets in London were unexpectedly closed due to the Great Storm of 1987, and the DJIA fell 108.35 points to close on record volume. Then-Treasury Secretary James Baker stated concerns about the falling prices. The crash began in Far Eastern markets the morning of October 19, accelerating in London time, largely because London had closed early on October 16 due to the Storm. By 9:30 a. m. the London FTSE 100 had fallen over 136 points. Later that morning, two U.S. Warships shelled an Iranian oil platform in the Persian Gulf in reaction to the earlier Silkworm attacks.

The least affected was Austria by the global stock slide (-11.4 percent) and the most afflicted was Hong Kong with a resounding drop of 45.8 percent. The stock exchange of Hong Kong, an international city, was influenced by both the East and the West. Of 23 major industrial countries 19 had a stock market decline greater than one-fifth.

Fashions of 1987

The big news in fashion in 1987 was the resurgence of the mini skirt. For some time, fashion designers had insisted that anything goes when it comes to the length of hemlines. Most women had accepted the idea but some abandoned

---

[58] FTSE 100 stands for the Financial Times Stock Exchange 100 traded in London. The 100 stocks are mostly international companies that are heavily capitalized. It is a gauge of prosperity for UK international companies listed on the exchange. The FTSE is closely watched by international traders.

[59] The FTSE 100 index is an average of the London stock exchange prices of the 100 largest British firms by capitalization. More informally, it is known as the "Footsie."

long skirts for short ones. Other women focused on the length they preferred. When fashion collections for fall 1987 were unveiled in the spring, however, it was clear that designers were surprisingly unanimous in their support of the short hemline. The new hemlines bared the knees and sometimes went to mid-thigh. The most popular skirt lengths measured to 21 inches from the waistband to the hem. The shorter lengths were the fashion choice for teenagers, but women of all ages began revealing their knees. Although the shorter skirts were designed for fall, women jumped the gun and began rolling up the waistbands or turning up their hemlines on their longer outfits to accommodate the new trend before the shorter fashion's hit the stores. Stores didn't go crazy. They still offered long skirts, but it was clear, short was in. Skirts seemed to go up and down with the stock market.

Causes of the Crash

So much for hemlines, though some uninformed persons linked hemlines to the stock exchange fluctuations. Many other explanations have been offered as causes of the crash.

Derivative securities and their effects: The initial blame for the 1987 crash centred on the interplay between stock markets and index options and futures markets. In the former people buy actual shares of stock; in the latter they are only purchasing rights to buy or sell stocks at particular prices. These options and futures are known as derivatives, because their values derive from stock prices and even though no actual shares are owned. The Brady Commission, which was appointed to investigate the causes of the crash, concluded that the failure of stock markets and derivatives markets to operate in sync was the major factor for the crash.

Computer Trading: Many analysts tie the yellow ribbon around the use of computer trading or program trading by large institutional investing companies. They say that computers were programmed to automatically order huge stock trades when certain market trends prevailed. However, this does not explain why other stock markets which did not use program trading also crashed, some with losses even more severe than from the 1987 U.S. Crash. Perhaps herd instinct and behaviour played a role in the latter case.

Illiquidity: Trading was terminated in many listed stocks. This insufficient liquidity may have had a significant effect on the size of the price drop. However, negative news to investors about the liquidity of stock, option and futures markets cannot explain why so many people decided to sell stock at the same time. Again, herd instinct and behaviour played a role.

U.S. Trade and Budget Deficits: Large trade and budget deficits during the third quarter of 1987 might have led investors into thinking that these deficits would cause a fall of U.S. Stocks relative to foreign securities (it was the largest trade deficit since 1960). This may have been a trigger for the collapse in the USA but cannot explain the decline in trade and budget surplus nations. Once again, it seems that a contagion was at work explained by herd instinct and behaviour.

Investing in Bonds as an Attractive Alternative: Long-term bond yields were rising, making them an attractive alternative to stocks, particularly at their very high P-E multiples. Yields had started at 7.6 percent in early 1987 and soared to about 10 percent the summer before the crash.

Overvaluation: Many stock analysts agreed that stock prices were overvalued in the fall of 1987. Historically, the P/E ratio is about 15 to 1. In October 1987 the P-E ratio for the S&P 500 had risen to 20 to 1.

While any one of these potential causes could have triggered the crash, it is likely that *all* caused the crash.

Consequences: The United States of America

Because the aftermath of the 1929 crash was the Great Depression of the 1930s, it was widely expected that recession would follow the 1987 crash. Rather, it was followed by general prosperity. One consequence was the introduction of the circuit breaker or trading curb on the New York Stock Exchange (NYSE). Based upon the idea that a cooling off period would help dissipate investor panic, these mandatory market shutdowns are triggered whenever a large pre-defined market decline occurs during the trading day.

Four concepts of power appear in discussions of circuit breakers: Economic power, psychological power, political power and statistical power. Breakers have economic power since they restrict what traders do and because they alter relationships among various classes of traders. They have psychological power because than can change how people think about trading and security values. Political power arises when we consider which circuit breakers markets will adopt. Finally, analysis of statistical power explains why empirical studies that attempt to examine the effect of circuit breakers cannot be convincing.

All circuit breakers limit trading activity in some way. Trading halts stop trading when prices have moved or will be expected to move by some specified amount. Trading resumes after some time interval. Price limits require all trade prices to be within a certain range. If traders are unwilling to negotiate prices within the limited range, trading will stop. Trading can resume anytime traders are willing to negotiate prices within the price limits. Transaction taxes restrict trading by taxing it. Margin requirements and position limits restrict the size of positions that traders can accumulate. Collars restrict access to computerized order submission systems. All forms of circuit breakers are aimed at limiting volatility in stock prices.

On March 8, 1995, a 217-point intra-day drop in the Dow almost triggered a halt. Partly in response to this close call, the exchanges changed their rules in July 1995 and February 1997. The revised rules now halt trading for one-half hour if the Dow drops 350 points and for an additional one hour if it drops 200 points more. These halts were triggered for the first time on October 27, 1997 when the Dow fell 350 points by 2:35 p.m. In the 25 minutes following the reopening at 3:05 p.m., the Dow fell an additional 200 points to trigger a second halt which closed the markets for the day. The October 13, 1989 "Mini Crash" triggered trading halts.[60]

Consequences: France

The French stock index is called the CAC 40. Price limits are used to decide halts in trading. Daily price limits are implemented in cash and derivatives markets. The securities traded are divided into three categories according to the number and volume of daily transactions. The price limits for each security varies by category. For example, for the more liquid category, when the price movement of such a security from the previous day's closing price exceeds 10 percent, the quotation is suspended for 15 minutes, and transactions are then resumed. If the price then goes up or down by more the 5 percent, transactions are again suspended for 15 minutes. The 5 percent threshold may apply once more before transactions are halted for the rest of the day. When such a suspension occurs, transactions on options based on the underlying security are also suspended. Furthermore, when more than 35 percent of the capitalization of the CAC 40 Index cannot be quoted, the calculation of the CAC 40 Index is

---

[60] For more details, see Bruce C. Greenwald and Jeremy C. Stein, "Transactional Risk, Market Crashes, and the Role of Circuit Breakers," Journal *of Business*, 1991, v64(4), 443-462.

suspended, and the index is replaced by a trend indicator. When less than 25 percent of the capitalization of the CAC 40 Index can be quoted, quotations on the derivative markets are suspended for half an hour or one hour, and additional margin deposits are requested.

The Global Reach of The Financial Crisis

Already, we have noted that the New York Stock Exchange is closely linked though exchange rates to the rest of the world. By the end of October, stock markets in New Zealand, Hong Kong, Australia, Spain, the United Kingdom, the United States and Canada had fallen from their peaks by 60 percent, 45.5 percent, 41.8 percent, 31 percent, 26.45 percent, 22.68 percent and 22.5 percent, respectively. New Zealand, Hong Kong, and Australia were hit especially hard. The Anglo-Saxon countries are tied together by both exchange rates and culture. New Zealand was a special case. It took several years to recover. The damage to the New Zealand economy was compounded by high exchange rates and the Reserve Bank of New Zealand's refusal to loosen monetary policy, in contrast to countries such as Germany, Japan and the United States whose central banks added to their portfolios. The increased bank liquidity that followed forestalled recession and they experienced economic growth in the next 2-3 years. This was soon to end in Japan.

The magnitude of the decline on "Black Monday"—the largest one-day percentage decline (23 percent or 707.99 points) in the DJIA's history—led to some panicked responses. Following "Black Monday", a gloomy day indeed, 33 eminent economists from various nations met in Washington, D.C. December 1987 to assess the damage. They collectively predicted that "the next few years could be the most troubled since the 1930s."[61] The United States economy was barely affected. It was a bubble with few victims, but those victims suffered greatly. And economic growth increased throughout 1987 and 1988, with the DJIA regaining its pre-crash closing high of 2,722 points in early 1989. This was not the Hollywood ending to the story. The quick rebound of the stock market greatly depended on the S&L business, which was already under scrutiny before its mid-1989 collapse. The new S&L collapse sent the economy into a hard landing late that summer. This, along with the abrupt demise of the leveraged

---

[61] "Group of 7, Meet the Group of 33," *The New York Times*, December 26, 1987. A day earlier and it could have been wrapped as a Christmas present.

buyout craze (which led to the Friday-the-13th mini-crash) brought a five-year recession late that year. In retrospect, the 1987 crash foreshadowed deeper problems in the United States economy.

The Mystery of the Kindleberger Omission

In his classic book, Kindleberger[62], later co-authored with Robert Aliber, the Crash of 1987 is notable for its absence. This is a curious omission. "They" listed the "Big Ten of Financial Bubbles" without including the Crash of "87", not even in the footnotes. Instead, at No. 6 he has "The bubble in real estate and stocks in Japan 1985-89," at No.7, "The 1985-89 bubble in real estate and stocks in Finland, Norway, and Sweden," at No. 8, "The bubble in real estate and stocks in Thailand, Malaysia, Indonesia, and several other Asian countries 1992-97 and the surge in foreign investment in Mexico in 1990-94," and No. 9, "The bubble in over the counter stocks in the United States 1995-2000".[52] These bubble swirl all about 1987 but never land there. This cannot be blamed on Kindleberger, whose last solo performance was well before the crash (1992); rather, this final listing must be the work of Aliber.

The curiousness is more perplexing because some of these episodes were related to what happened in 1987. The bubbles in real estate and stocks in Finland, Norway, and Sweden, as we have noted, were linked to the 1987 crash in the U.S. These real estate bubbles may have come first there and later in the U.S. The bubble in dot-com stocks may have characterized the 1995-2000 bubble in the United States (in a long stretch) but is usually tied to the 1998-2000 era. In 1987, it was the industrials index that collapsed. Still, the 1987 financial crash was a major financial bubble of the modern era: after all, it is the subject of this chapter. It ranks right up there with the 1929 debacle, except the aftermath was not as devastating.

Could the Crash Have Been Predicted?

The short answer to the above question is "yes" because it was. In an Atlantic Magazine article, John Kenneth Galbraith predicted the 1987 crash. Galbraith

---

[62] Charfles P. Kindleberger and Robert Z. Aliber, *Manias, Panics, and Crashes*, 7th edition (New York: Palgrave/Macmillan, 2015).

was not the only one. Nobelist Robert J. Shiller spends several pages on the crash, and writes.

The Wall Street Journal, on the morning of the 1987 crash, ran a plot showing the Dow in the 1980s and, just below it, a plot showing the Dow in the 1920s up to and for a month after the crash of 1929. The two plots were aligned so that the current date lined up with the date of the 1929 crash, and so the plot suggested that the crash of 1929 was about to repeat itself. Investors had the opportunity to see the plot at breakfast a matter of minutes before the start of the 1987 crash. The *Journal* was openly suggesting the possibility of a crash beginning that day.[63]

So, *The Wall Street Journal* was for once in agreement with Galbraith: It had also predicted the 1987 crash. Among Shiller's short discussions of the 1987 crash, he always links the two crashes of 1929 and 1987. He suggests: "In fact, in the crash of October 19, 1987 the Dow actually fell in one day almost the same amount as it did on October 28-29—22.6 % in 1987 versus 23.1% in 1929." It may have been a coincidence since it took two days for the market crash in 1929 compared with one day in 1987. As we have noted, investors were in the dark regarding how far the market had fallen in 1929. "However," according to Shiller, "many did have a rough impression of the extent of the 1929 plunge, and there was little other concrete information available to investors on October 19, 1987, to suggest when the market should stop falling."[64]

And, so, we reluctantly leave the story of the fascinating Crash of 1987. Next, we provide that comedy relief.

---

[63] Robert J. Shiller, *Irrational Exuberance*, Third Edition (Princeton & Oxford: Princeton University Press), 2015, pp. 118-119.

[64] *Ibid.,* p. 119.

Chapter 11
Rational Expectations and Bubbles: Comedy Relief

A Preliminary Summary

In his novel, *A Tenured Professor*, John Kenneth Galbraith's amiable maliciousness deftly uncovers society's hidden agendas in a morality parable that is both comic and timely. In broad outline the plot has Harvard's economics faculty looking for a professor with impeccable credentials, an impressive publication and the right political attitudes. They find Montgomery Marvin a scholar from all the right places (Harvard, Cambridge University and Berkeley--a road similar to the one travelled by Galbraith), a published treatise on the theory and mathematics of refrigerator pricing (symbolic of Galbraith's past as a price freezer during World War II), and the right political attitudes (liberal but responsible.) To their immense surprise and discomfort Harvard gets more than it bargained for. Professor Marvin has created a measure of excessive investor optimism and pessimism, the amazingly accurate Index of Irrational Expectations (IRAT) to counter any Index of Rational Expectations (IRE).

Goaded on by a very assertive wife (Marjie), Marvin and IRAT make millions in the stock market. Soon this respectable professor becomes a financial power player and--God, man and Harvard forbid--a successful corporate raider. If this quickly acquired wealth isn't galling enough for the Harvard bluebloods, the Marvin's decide to put their money where their progressive causes are. The faculty knives are unsheathed, and events spin out of control. As it turns out, spin control by the Marvin's involves a Harvard "bail out."

Rational Expectations

The summer between Marvin's undergraduate days at Harvard and a year at

Cambridge University is spent in nostalgic Vienna, a setting that enables Galbraith to give us "twin peaks" at Vienna and Budapest. Here is romance and sex as young Marvin falls in love near lovely Schoenbrunn, where many others have succumbed. With Galbraith as our guide, we glide down the Danube to Budapest and hear the tale of two great Hungarian economists—Nicholas Kaldor and Thomas Balogh, or "Buddha" and "Pest", as they were called. The transition from romance to money is smoothed by Marvin's musings regarding the perfect environment of Cambridge.

Figure 11.1
Inside the Schonbrunn Palace

To understand the incredible money-making machine soon to be invented by Marvin, the reader needs some introduction to the idea of rational expectations. All market participants have the same information and use it with equal efficiency. The market ends up being efficient in the sense that all profits have been exploited. No one can make any money because it has already been made (This is not satire. It is where rational expectations logically takes us. The naïve economist must wonder why speculators or investors would enter a market in which all profits already have been taken. Yet, unless people do enter the market, it doesn't exist.

At Cambridge, an old mentor (Let's call her "Joan" for Joan Robinson) advises Marvin to obtain tenure before revealing his liberalism or other broad interests. This caution does not prevent Marvin's contrary mind from drifting frequently to the delusions of the crowd--to South Sea Bubbles, the manic speculation of the late 1920s, and the financial genius of those men who communicated the errors of euphoria to others.

Marvin reads of the glowing reputations of the men who helped produce the stock market boom of the late 1920s. For example, "there was Richard Whitney, the quintessential Harvard clubman, deeply committed to his own economic acuity, a symbol of the highest standards of financial morality as expressed by the New York Stock Exchange, who passed quietly into Sing Sing." (We earlier ran into Richard Whitney in Chapter 10.) From this history emerges a principle of finance: "Find out who in any euphoric episode is the greatest hero, who is the most celebrated, and invest in his eventual fall." Donald Trump springs to mind, though Galbraith resists this forecast. As F. Scott Fitzgerald once wrote: "Show me a hero and I will write you a tragedy."

Charting Euphoria

At Berkeley where he is a graduate student doing research, Marvin realizes that he needs a measure of the euphoria in a company and its stock. Marvin takes measure of a banking legend, the Bank of America. With reality as 100, Marvin set the measure of euphoria in the bank as twice that figure. With the lights of Berkeley below, those of San Francisco aglow in the distance, he and his cooperative Canadian wife, Marjie, invent the Index of Irrational Expectations (IRAT). Galbraith, who predicted the 1987 stock market crash in an Atlantic article, is toying with the rational expectationists.

IRAT no doubt has some symbolic meaning. It reminds me of my first encounter with experimental economics. I was being interviewed by a university economics department which was generating experimental data on the "token economy." Rats were rewarded with tasty pellets (tokens) only if they behaved in a purely self-interested way. The behaviour of rats was exactly as predicted by orthodox economics, which puts capitalism on a pedestal. Through the methods of natural science, the economists claimed proof that capitalism worked because capitalists responded correctly to the proper market incentives. I, very young and irreverent, suggested that the experiments only proved that "capitalists are rats" I did not land the job.

Marvin had his own experiment to conduct with IRAT. Armed with the knowledge that eventual losses of the many clearly came from the eventual gains of the few, a short position in the Bank of America stock could lead to profits. Marjie understood: borrow stock, sell it at current prices and then when the price goes down replace it, keeping the difference.

Marvin is cautious, not so his aggressive wife. Marjie opens a Merrill Lynch account and makes all the right moves. The return was to give her "powerful leverage in influencing and indeed, governing Marvin in the years to come!" Marjie is the political flywheel that balances the faint-heated Marvin. By now the same Harvard that produced Marvin the undergraduate, has recruited Marvin, the Berkeley PhD.

Galbraith takes us along on a commentary-filled travelogue of the USA as Marvin and Marjie construct indices in Oklahoma and Dallas at a time prior to the oil, real estate and S&L debacle there. After a stop in Washington, D.C., they eventually settle in a comfortable apartment on Prescott Street behind the Faculty Club, only a block from Harvard Yard. Of course, Galbraith knows this terrain intimately. Marvin and spouse set up an elaborate computer network in their home in order to calibrate IRAT and apply it to stock market gains. Then, Marvin, attending his first economics department meeting is warmly congratulated on his cool work on refrigerator pricing.

Unlike most young Assistant Professors, Marvin is rich before he has tenure. Galbraith walks us through a very funny tenure meeting at Harvard, at which Marvin ultimately prevails. Of course, since no one knew of his exploits, no one was influenced by the newness of Marvin's wealth or the means of its acquisition.

Ken Galbraith, a life-long Democrat, manages to reach the Gipper and his economists with a few jabs. We are told of the "compelling doctrine that the rich were not working because they had too little money, the poor because they had too much." And......the Laffer curve?

The Laffer curve is appealing to the Marvin's as well as to Governor and President Ronald Reagan. Under the influence of Arthur Laffer, President Ronald Reagan managed to greatly reduce taxes on the top incomes. That left the Marvin's with a great deal more cash than would otherwise have been the case. According to accepted legend, the original Laffer curve had been drawn on a paper napkin, possibly toilet paper, and some critics of deficient imagination held that the paper could have been better put to its intended use.

By the mid-1980s, euphoria was becoming endemic and universal. Securities prices across the board were going up. The Marvin's discover index and program trading and begin to use heretofore undreamed-of-leveraging. At a time when Ivan Boesky is in descent for using inside information, the Marvin's carefully avoid any improprieties. They are honest speculators. The Marvin's, going short as usual, become very rich from the stock market crash of October 19, 1987.

The Green Light

The author of *The Great Crash 1929* makes much of the parallels between the roaring 20s and what I have called "the casino economy" of the 1980s. The stock market crash of October 1929 had extinguished the bright lights and levity of the 1920s. The memories of the gin, sex and dances of the 1920s took on an almost legendary aura in the grimness of the Great Depression. In *A Tenured Professor*, the yuppie--unisex, perhaps even giving the woman the edge--replace the Flappers of the 1920s. Soon, I suspect, we too will remember only the legends of the 1980s.

F. Scott Fitzgerald's' morality tale, *The Great Gatsby*, helped to define the earlier Jazz Age. The nouveau riches, such as Gatsby and those like him, made huge fortunes but lacked the traditions associated with inherited wealth and were therefore vulgar. Others, such as the Tom Buchanan's, who had establishment wealth and thus possessed inherited traditions, lacked the vulgarity, but were corrupted by the purposelessness and ease their money provided. Both kinds of wealth resulted in similar human failings, though they were manifested differently.

Gatsby's spirituality enables him to construct and preserve a vision. At the end of the first chapter, Gatsby appears in the attitude of a worshiper, alone and stretching his arms toward the single, faraway green light--the one that is at the end of a dock across the water—the visible symbol of his vision. Green is the colour of promise, of hope and renewal and ultimately, near the end of the final chapter, it infuses Gatsby's vision of the explorers who discovered the promise of a new continent.

In American culture as well as in Gatsby's personal dream, ideals are also always wrapped up with wealth, and so the means corrupt the ends. Gatsby's description of Daisy's voice as being "full of money" defines the charm she embodies for him. Youth and beauty are inextricably part of the package, imprisoned, and preserved by money. Daisy has an ethereal, insubstantial quality that radiates insincerity. The irony: Daisy is unworthy of the vision, and Gatsby's sole attraction is her "vulgar, meretricious beauty." The sacred green light becomes nothing more than a bulb burning at the end of Daisy Buchanan's dock.

As Galbraith suggested in *The Affluent Society*, the material aspect of the American dream is most prominently displayed in advertising. "Gatsby resembles an advertisement", remarks Daisy. Eternal youth, beauty, and wealth are on permanent display there. Daisy does not want Gatsby for what he is, but for the superficial illusion of what he represents. Gatsby's corruption is reflected historically to the destruction of America's early idealism by its involvement with a materialistic ethic. In Gatsby, Nick Carraway is the Scottish moralist (like Galbraith) who realizes that an ideal based on materialism alone is a corruption rather than a fulfilment of the American dream.

John Kenneth Galbraith is the moral presence in *A Tenured Professor*. Marvin embodies his economics and Marjie his penchant for political action. Galbraith the writer is one person expressing himself as many. The Marvin's had agreed that the wealth was just a means to a greater end. Galbraith lampoons the limousine liberal taking the high road paved with good intentions. The "positive power of wealth" imbues it with elevated purpose.

Limousine Liberalism

Liberalism resolves the moral dilemma confronted by Fitzgerald. The limousine liberal takes the vulgar out of wealth by using money to "do good" and to speed progress. The idealism of the American Dream is transformed into the new American prospect. Money nonetheless remains the lubricant.

Marjie teams with New Englander Henry Winthrop Wentworth in an effort to place a tag or sticker on products conveying the state of women in the executive ranks of the producer. Meanwhile, under increasing heat from Harvard as information of their activities become known, the Marvin's decide to "bail out" Harvard by offering to buy all of its securities subject to criticism because of corporate participation in the South African economy. Marvin's offer was at 10 percent over closing prices.

Harvard becomes anti-apartheid only after Marvin makes it profitable to do so. Old wealth again takes the easy street of Fitzgerald's Buchanan's, but new wealth (like that of Gatsby's), fails to fill the moral void. Galbraith's earlier story about the houses of Harvard takes on a new meaning. The original seven red-brick houses were to be named—like Dunster House—for Harvard presidents in their order of succession, a design that faltered with the presidency of Dr Leonard Hoar.

The novel also shows just how unpopular waging peace, one of Galbraith's lifelong missions can be. Marvin offers an endowment o $2.5 million to establish Professorships for peace in each of the three service academies. The academies are slow to respond. "What seemed to cause the greatest concern was whether this might make peace as a concept unduly prominent in the academies' routine." Critical congressional reaction was that "the professorships were a design for making the academies and their graduates soft on defence." The American Legion went further: the teaching was no less than an insertion of "subversive Communist propaganda into patriotic and otherwise sacred institutions." The error of training officers to prefer peace to war ultimately is overwhelmed only by the size of the endowments.

In *A Tenured Professor* there is no Daisy. Marjie has a well-defined progressive vision and knows how the make the conversion to reality. She can do what a Gatsby cannot, though Galbraith seems a bit put off by her apparent aggressiveness. Yet she is the necessary foil to Marvin's hesitant nature. Her sexual fidelity places her as such in the 1990s as Daisy's infidelity helped to define the Jazz Age.

Margie's special role enables Galbraith to continue his Ju jitsu. Marjie's new idea is to fight political action committees (PACs) with a countervailing PAC, the counter-Pac would provide dollars to the opposing candidate. "A liberal would get the money and then beat the moneyed interests with their own weapon." Margie's suggestion for the name of the New PAC, Political Rectitude and Integrity Committees or PRICs did not survive the indelicacy of its acronym because "it was considered sexist." Unwittingly, Marvin and Marjie "had crossed the great divide that separates benign and agreeable liberalism in which all politicians are known to be tolerant, from action, which often means serious and highly unwelcome trouble."

Stepping on the toes of congressmen inevitably leads to hearings and sometimes even action, actions taken by such regulatory agencies as the Securities and Exchange Commission (SEC). Galbraith provides a description of the hearing room and the hearing of the House Banking Committee that becomes more hilarious as it approaches accuracy. The hearings nonetheless do not prevent Marvin from a leveraged buyout of "special Electric" and a rumoured buyout of General Electric. A bill is introduced in the House and Senate forbidding any corporation with more than a one-half-billion-dollar commitment in the arms industry to own a TV station. The fictional president embraces the new law as "supporting the First Amendment. In an assurance of free, untrammelled speech, it removes our defence industry, the men and woman of our armed forces, all who so serve our county, from the effects of ill-motivated, ill-spirited, unpatriotic propaganda."

The Red Light

The turning point is provided by the SEC. The use of IRAT, it had been determined, constituted an illegal manipulation of the markets. It was a case of unfair competition with a certain winner. IRAT not only gave Marvin an unfair advantage, but those following his trades had inside information on his purchases and sales. Hence, the SEC had "a clear case of insider trading based on inside information on Marvin's insider trading on insider trading! Market failure is the product of the rational use of irrationality."

When the SEC denies Marvin the further use of IRAT, he buys stocks in a random walk, informs the SEC, and provides full information on his transactions to the press. Marvin's undiminished reputation is enough to bring others onto a bandwagon. Complete information shakes the markets. At the end Marvin still has tenure.

Galbraith once again is sending up the rational expectationists. But there is also subtle symbolism. Galbraith at Harvard always was an "outsider" because he sought a larger audience. His verbal dexterity, acerbic put-downs, and mordant understatements gained not only a wider audience but a Playboy interview and political clout in Democratic party circles. Galbraith became an insider in national politics by being an outsider at Harvard where the green might have represented envy rather than Gatsby-like hope. Galbraith nonetheless has brought hope to economists by reminding us of how much fun we could have if only we were more like him. Only perhaps devotees of rational expectations will find fault in the humour, as indeed they did.

Chapter 12
The Dot-Com Bubble and Crash

The dot-com bubble has almost as many names as Elizabeth Taylor had husbands. It is also known as the dot-com boom, the tech bubble, the Internet bubble, the dot-com collapse, and the information technology bubble. Some of these names are obviously euphemistic, but they all carry some information about what happened. It was a historic speculative bubble covering roughly 1995-2001 during which stock markets in industrialized nations saw their equity value rise rapidly from the growth in the Internet and related industries. The Internet boom refers to the steady commercial growth of the Internet with the advent of the World Wide Web (www). WWW was exemplified by the first release of the Mosaic web browser in 1993 and continuing. About the only thing that could end the Internet would be engulfment by Blockchain technology, to which we will return in Chapter 14. Let's just say that the Internet boom was punctuated by the dot-com collapse. And the information technology bubble was punctuated by that collapse. Dot-com and information technology were slowed, but they did not cave in.

The era was marked by the founding (and sometimes the spectacular failure) of several new Internet-based companies commonly called the Dot-coms. Small companies could cause their stock prices to soar by simply adding an "e-" prefix or a ".com" suffix to their names. A miraculous combination of rapidly rising stock prices, irrational exuberance regarding prospects, individual speculation in stocks and widely available venture capital created an environment in which many investors were willing to overlook traditional metrics, such as the P-E ratio, in favour of confidence in technological advancements. Most of these stocks, being tech stocks, were traded on the NASDAQ. By the end of the 1990s, the NASDAQ hit a P-E ratio of 200, a truly astonishing plateau that was to dwarf Japan's peak P-E ratio of 80 a decade earlier.

The Players

When the collapse came during 1999-2000, some companies, such as pets.com and Webvan, failed totally. Unlike Cinderella, these stocks did not have a prince in waiting. Others were revived as if someone had found the glass slipper and slipped it on in a perfect fit. Cisco, whose stock declined by 86 percent, lost a large portion of their market capitalization but remained stable and profitable. Others, such as eBay.com, later not only recovered but even surpassed their dot-com-bubble peaks. Equally prominent is Amazon.com. Its stock went on to exceed $700 a share, for example, after having gone from $107 to $7 in the crash. Some of the stocks were not Cinderella stories. Books-a-Million had seen its stock price soar by over 1,000 percent in one week simply by announcing an updated website The company's share price rose from off the floor at $3 a share to an all-time closing high of $38.04 on November 27, 1999, only to close again at $3 a share in 2000.

The Bubble Grows

Those were/are some of the players. Why did they behave like a herd of sheep? Something kept the bubble growing. Because of the rise of the Internet, venture capitalists expected record-setting growth. The dot-com companies had been around as penny stocks, but with the growth of the Internet and the availability of ready cash, they grew faster, experiencing meteoric rises in their stock prices. Venture capitalists were motivated to invest in fly-by-night companies, mitigating the risk by investing in many contenders and letting the marketplace decide which would succeed. They were bolstered by the low interest rates of 1998-99 and the cheer-leading by Alan Greenspan. The Federal Reserve allowed the money supply to grow and accommodate these highfliers.

A canonical Dot-Com company's business model relied on harnessing network effects by operating at a sustained net loss and building market share (sometimes a mental concept). Mental because these companies offered their services or product for free with the expectation that they could build enough brand awareness to charge profitable rates for their services latter. Their motto was "get big fast" and reflected this strategy. This strategy would not have "worked" in a different era. In the industrialized nations there was a campaign to reduce the "digital divide" in the late 1990s and early 2000s. Previously, individuals were not always able to access the Internet, sometimes because of lack of local access-connectivity to the infrastructure, some because of a lack of understanding that precluded the use of any such facilities. As connectivity grew, so did the potential for venture capitalists to take advantage of the growing industry. The impacts of this new technology eventually spurred on demand growth during this time.

The Crash

While virtually unbelievable, it's nonetheless true; with all the investment and excitement, stock values grew. NASDAQ went from around 1,000 points to more than 5,000 in 2000. Online retailing was one of the biggest drivers of this growth with sites like Pets.com getting big investors and gaining a place in American consumer culture. This happened in a relatively short time span. Companies were going to the marketplace with IPO s and fetching huge prices, with stocks sometimes doubling on the first day. This was an apparent wonderland, an Emerald City, where virtually anyone with an idea could start making money. This illusion could not last forever, no matter what was believed.

Everything started to change in March of 2000. On March 10, NASDAQ's combined values of stocks was $6.71 trillion. First, let us put a trillion dollars in perspective. A stack of a trillion dollar bills would go a quarter of the way to the moon and weigh about ten tons. Today, a trillion dollars would buy all the sports leagues in the nation. Would you rather buy a car? Recently a 1963 Ferrari 250 GTO was auctioned at $38 million and change. You could buy over 25,000 of these cars if you could find them. You, however, could put 8.33 million people though 4 years of a private college of your choice. If you are patriotic, you could pay down 5 to 6 percent of the national debt. Now, multiply the trillion by 6.71 and just imagine what that would buy.

We have already laid bare the dot-com bubble. What happened next? As the technology boom receded, consolidation and growth by market leaders caused the tech industry to come to more closely resemble other traditional USA sectors. As of 2014, ten information technology firms were among the 100 largest U.S. corporations by revenues: Apple, Hewlett-Packard, IBM, Microsoft, Amazon.com, Google, Intel, Cisco Systems, Ingram Micro and Oracle. Amazon.com and eBay.com are among the big three survivors. The fate of many others has been determined and are listed in Appendix 12, each with the usually sad story outlined. One of these is Pets.com that sold pet supplies to retail customers before going bankrupt. As Figure 12.1 illustrates, even the pets were perplexed by this bankruptcy. The owners of the stock were equally astonished.

Figure 12.1
A Boston Terrier is Perplexed by the Collapse of Pets.com

In 2000 everything was flying high, with new Internet-based companies popping up almost every week. On January 10, America Online, a dot-com favourite and pioneer of dial-up Internet access, announced plans to merge with Time Warner, the world's largest media company, in the second-largest merger & acquisition transaction in the global economy. The merger has been described as "the worst in history." In October 2003 Time Warner dropped "AOL" from its name.

Getting back to the crash, the dot-com bubble, which had been building up for almost three years, began to collapse. Companies folded and fortunes were lost, particularly by those who could "afford" to lose. On March 10, the combined values of stocks on the NASDAQ was $6.71 trillion, this before the crash beginning the next day. By March 30, the NASDAQ was valued at $6.02 trillion, on April 6, $5.78 trillion. In less than a month, some trillion dollars' worth of stock value had completely disappeared. A J.P. Morgan analyst told Time in April that many companies were losing between $10 and $30 million a quarter, which was unsustainable.

Pets.com was one that bit the dust while magazines, such as Time, began running stories advising "investors" to limit their exposure to the tech sector, believing that portfolios would take a beating if tied to e-retailers and the other companies dropping like flies. A sign of the times could be found in Super Bowl ad spots. In the 2000 Super Bowl, 17 dot.com companies paid $44 million for ad spots according to Bloomberg. The next year, only three dot-com companies ran ads during the game.

On March 10, 2000 the NASDAQ, home of the tech favourites, peaked at 5,132.52. Afterwards, the NASDAQ fell as much as 78 percent. One of the more important players, World.Com was found to be engaged in illegal accounting practices to exaggerate its profits on an annual basis. It was one of the last standing combined competitive local exchange and inter-exchange companies and was struggling to survive. It had been hit hard by the implementation of the Telecommunications Act of 1996. This Act favoured the Regional Bell Operating Companies and led to the demise of competition. Consolidation was the order of the day, leading to a current oligopoly ruled by lobbyist-saturated powerhouses AT&T and Verizon.

Many dot-coms ran out of capital and were either acquired or liquidated. World.Com stock plummeted. The domain names were picked up by old-economy competitors, speculators or cyber squatters. Those financing the dot-coms were not immune. The USA SEC fined top investment firms like Citigroup and Merrill Lynch millions of dollars for misleading "investors". Various supporting industries, such as advertising and shipping, reduced their operations as the derived demand for their services fell. Still, few dot-com companies became industry dominating mega-firms; they include "Amazon.com, eBay and Google."

While the September 11, 2001 attacks on the World Trade Centre accelerated the stock market drop, some 50 percent of the dot.com companies survived through 2004, even some small players endured the destruction of the financial market during the crash of 2002. It led to the loss of $5 trillion in the market value of companies from March 2000 to October 2002. As the technology boom receded, consolidation and growth by market leaders caused the tech industry to come to more closely resemble other traditional U.S. sectors. As of 2014, ten information technology firms are among the 100 largest U.S. corporations by revenues: Apple, Hewlett-Packard, IBM, Microsoft, Amazon.com, Google, Intel, Cisco Systems, Ingram Micro and Oracle.

This ends the Dot-com story for now, though there are some new attempts to enter the Dot-com territory. We leave that account to others. Next, we look at the financial crisis that began long after the Dot-com burst, the crisis of 2008-2009.

Appendix 12
List of Companies Significant to the
Dot-com Bubble

Boo.com – spent $188 million in just six months in an attempt to create a global online fashion store that went bankrupt in May 2000.

Books-a-Million – saw its stock price soar by over 1,000% in one week simply by announcing an updated website on November 25, 1998. The company's share price rose from around $3 previously to an all-time closing high of $38.94 on November 27 and an intra-day high of $47.00 on November 30, before quickly pulling back to around $10 two weeks later. By 2000, the share price had returned to $3.

Boadcast.com – Acquired by Yahoo! for $5.9 billion in stock, making Mark Cuban a multi-billionaire. The site is now defunct and redirects to Yahoo's home page.

e-Digital Corporation (EDIG) – long-term, unprofitable OTCBB-traded company founded in 1988 previously named Norris Communications. Changed its name to Digital in January 1999 when its stock was at $0.06 level. The stock rose rapidly in 1999 and went from closing price of $2.91 on December 31, 1999, to intraday high of $24.50 on January 24, 2000. It quickly retraced and has traded between $0.07 and $0.165 in 2010Y. As of 2013, the stock continues to trade low, ranging between $0.12 and $0.19 a share.

eToys.com – Online toy retailer founded in 1997, hit a high of $84.35 in October 1999. Only two years later in February 2001, it filed for bankruptcy with $247 million in debt. It was bought out by KB Toys, which also had to file for bankruptcy.

Freeintemet.com – Filed for bankruptcy in October 2000, soon after cancelling its initial public offering. At the time Freeintemet.com was the fifth-largest ISP in the United States, with 3.2 million users of Y Famous for its mascot Baby Bob, the company lost $19 million in 1999 on revenues of less than $1 million.

GeoCities – Purchased by Yahoo! for $3.57 billion in January 1999(. Yahoo! closed GeoCities on October 26, 2009--Globe.com – Social networking service, that went live in April 1995 and made headlines by going public on November 1998 and posting the largest first day gain of any IPO in history up to that date. The CEO became in 1999 a visible symbol of the excesses of dot-com millionaires.

GovWorks.com-Doomed dot-com featured in the documentary film Startup.com ink Tomi – Valuation of $25 billion in March 2000.

Info. Space – In March 2000 this stock reached a price $1,305 per share, but by April 2001 the price had crashed down to $22 a share.

Kozmo.com – offered one-hour local delivery of several retail items, from March 1998 to April 2001

Lastminute.com – IPO in the UK coincided with the bursting of the bubble.

The Seaming Company – bought by Mattel in 1999 for $3.5 billion, sold for $27.3 million in 2000 dot-com bubble.

Lycos – Purchased by Spanish telecommunications provider Telefonica for $12.5 billion in 2000 (to expand its Terra Networks online platform. It was sold in 2004 to Seoul, South Korea-based Daum Communications Corporation for $95.4 million in cash, less than 2 percent of Terra's initial multibillion-dollar investment. MicroStrategy – Shares lost more than half their value on March 20, 2000, following their announcement of re-stated financials for the previous two years. A Business Week editorial said at the time, "The company's misfortune is a wake-up call to all dot-com investors. The message: It's time, at last, to pay attention to the numbers."

Open.com – Was a big software security producer, reseller, and distributor; declared bankruptcy in 2001

Pets.com – Former dot-com enterprise that sold pet supplies to retail customers before entering bankruptcy in 2000

Pixelon – Internet streaming video company that hosted a $16 million launch party in 1999 hosting celebrities such as The Who and the Dixie Chicks. Failed less than a year later when it became apparent that its technologies were fraudulent or misrepresented.

Startups.com – "Ultimate dot-com start up that went out of business in 2002"
Think Tools AG – One of the most extreme symptoms of the bubble in Europe: market valuation of CHF 2.5 billion in March 2000, no prospects of having a substantial product (investor deception), followed by a collapse.

Tiscali – Important Italian telecommunications company whose share price grew from €46 (IPO in November 1999) to €1,197 in four months. The share prices fell to €40 afterwards in less than two months and have continued plummeted to well under 0.20 Euros.

VA Linux – A provider of built-to-order Intel systems based on Linux and other open source projects. They set the record for largest first-day IPO price gain; after the price was set at $30/share, it ended the first day of trading at $239.25/share, a 698% gain (9 December 1999). After that, its stock declined consistently. After several business transitions it became Geeknet. It provides the backdrop of the documentary Revolution OS.

Webvan--Online grocer that operated on a credit and delivery system; the original company went bankrupt in 2001. It was later resurrected by Amazon.com

World.Com – a long-distance telephone and internet-services provider that became notorious for using fraudulent accounting practices to increase their stock price. The company filed for bankruptcy in 2002 and former CEO Bernard Ebbers was convicted of fraud and conspiracy.

Xcelera.com (XLA) – Swedish investor in start-up technology firms that was one of the 421 greatest one-year rises of any exchange-listed stock in the history of Wall Street.

NOTE: The source is https://en.wikipedia.org/wiki/Dot-com_bubble 3/30/2018.

Chapter 13
The Great Financial Crisis of 2008-2009

The bankruptcy of Lehman Brothers Holdings, then the fourth largest US investment bank, in mid-September 2008 triggered the most severe financial panic and crash in a century. That is the assessment of Robert Z. Aliber, the co-author of a classic with Charles Kindleberger.[65] Others have come to the same conclusion, including this author. This makes sense, since Lehman's leverage in the capital market was huge. Lehman had been an aggressive buyer of mortgage-related securities. The firm used the money it obtained from selling its own short-term IOUs to buy long-term mortgages. True, every investment bank is heavily leveraged. But Lehman was exceptional. It was at the end of the spectrum in leveraging with assets more than thirty times its capital. Sometimes, Lehman's leverage may have been as much as forty times its capital. This was covered up by "window dressing". In other words, its reported leverage for the month appeared smaller than the leverage it had had in the previous months.

Leveraging is double-edged, for when an economy is prospering and real estate prices increasing, the greater the leverage, and the greater the profits. When property values increase, household net worth increases and leverage will appear to decline because the percentage increase in property prices is larger than the percentage increase in indebtedness. There is some irony in this: the borrowers appear wealthier, since the value of their assets has increased faster than the value of their liabilities. However, when the bubble is pricked, the high leverage means the percentage decline in net worth of the indebted households

---

[65] Robert Z. Aliber and Charles P. Kindleberger, *Manias, Panics, and Crashes* (New York: Palgrave Macmillan, 2015), p. 313, Chapter 14. Aliber was the author of this chapter in the 6th edition; Kindleberger is still listed as the co-author. He ended his solo run with the 4th edition.

and of the banks may be three or four times greater than the percentage decline in property values.

But there is much more to the story of the 2008-2009 crisis. There were early warning signs of what was to come, if only the monetary authorities had noticed them. On December 9, 1985, the cover of Business Week featured John Gutfreund, the CEO of Salomon Brothers and "The King of Wall Street". While Merrill Lynch was at the time the best-known Wall Street house and Goldman Sachs allegedly the best-managed, Salomon was the firm most feared by its competitors. It was the prototype of the thoroughly modern investment bank. It was built around a group of risk-taking bond trading dealers who were powered by "quants" recruited from academic institutions and filled with financial engineers, who designed new financial products. Four years later Michael Lewis's *Liar's Poker* (1989) would carve in stone the status of Salomon as the paradigmatic bank of the 1980s. The same decade produced Oliver Stone's Wall Street movie, with Gordon Gekko's famous "greed is good" speech. Wall Street was laughing all the way to its banks.

During the 1980s, Salomon was noted for its financial innovations in the bond market. It sold the first mortgage-backed security, a hitherto obscure species of financial instruments created by Ginnie Mae. There was no intention on Ginnie Mae's part to place this instrument in private banker's hands. Anyway, Salomon purchased home mortgages from thrifts throughout the US and packaged them into mortgage-backed securities, which it sold to local and international clients. Later, it moved away from traditional investment banking that helps companies raise funds in the capital market and negotiate mergers and acquisitions: Salomon began to engage exclusively in proprietary trading or the buying and selling of stocks, bonds, options, etc. for profit. Salomon had expertise in fixed income securities and trading based on daily swings in the bond market. The profits turned out to be too small for top management. So, the firm decided to imitate Drexel Burnham Lambert, using its investment bankers and its own money to urge companies to restructure or engage in leveraged buyouts. The firm went on to compete for the leveraged buyout of RJR Nabisco and the leveraged buyout of Revco Stores, ending in failure.[66] No less than Michael Lewis went through Salomon's training program and became a bond salesman at

---

[66] At the time of the September 11,2001 attacks, Salomon Smith Barney was by far the largest tenant in 7 World Trade Centre, occupying 64 percent of the building which included floors 28-45.

Salomon Brothers in London.

Salomon Brothers was weakened by a financial scandal which led to its acquisition by Travellers Group, and later Citigroup. The new parent company was culturally averse to the volatile profits (and losses) caused by proprietary trading. Instead, it preferred slower and steadier growth. Subsequently, most of its proprietary trading business was disbanded. The investment banking operations became known as "Salomon Smith Barney" and was renamed on April 7, 2003, "Citigroup Global Markets Inc". Two members of the Salomon Brother's bond arbitrage unit, were John Meriwether and Myron Scholes, who became a founder and a consultant for Long-term Capital Management, a hedge fund that collapsed in 1998. The final years of Salomon Brothers, culminating in its involvement in Long-Term Capital Management crisis, is told in the 2007 book A Demon of Our Own Design. There was enough wreckage for many books, but what survived were the financial innovations, to which we now turn.

The Role of Derivatives

By buying mortgages, guaranteeing their principal payments, and turning them into mortgage-backed securities, Fannie Mac and Freddie Mac provided funding for banks to make more mortgages and absorb some of the risk of the market. Besides that, secularization created many new ways for banks to make profits. Secularization created a new market for banks' loans, boosting volume. In turn investment banks, such as Salomon, had three new ways to make money. One: they exacted fees from each secularization they created. Two: they earned fees from selling the new mortgage-backed securities to investors. And, three: they made profits by trading these securities. The private growth of these securities was nothing short of spectacular. The volume of private mortgage-backed securities (excluding those issued by Ginnie Mac, Fannie Mae and Freddie Mac) grew from $11 billion in 1984 to over $200 billion in 1994 to close to $3 trillion in 2007. The Brave New World was 2007 rather than 1984.

Salomon Brother also pioneered arbitrage trading. Traders could make sure money by finding two securities that should, but did not have the same value; buying one, selling the other, and waiting for prices to converge. Or, the same goal could be achieved by buying the interest payments and the final principal payment on a 30-year bond separately while selling the whole 30-year bond (including interest and principal) for a higher price. While this may seem a bit complicated, nonetheless, arbitrage trading soon spread to other investment banks. And, there was more. The popularity of arbitrage fuelled the rapid growth of hedge funds which grew from less than $30 billion in assets in 1990 to over $1.2 trillion in 2005, and then on to $2 trillion in the troubled year of 2008.

Others got on the bandwagon of financial innovations. JP Morgan Bank popularized the credit default swaps in the late 1990s. This explosion of new products provided vast new profit-making possibilities for financial institutions. Moreover the credit default played an important role in the financial crisis. It is a form of insurance on debts; the buyer of the swap pays a fixed premium to the seller, who agrees to pay off the debt if the debtor fails to do so. Typically, the debt is a bond or a similar fixed income security, and the debtor is the issuer of the bond.

All these new sources of profits naturally made banks, especially investment banks, larger.

Not only bigger, they got broader. They not only had help from derivatives but also from commercial paper (short-term debt of private corporations). They began to look broadly matronly. This, despite the main traditional role of banks; being the provision of funds for corporations and other companies. There was once again a new innovator. In 1978, Bankers Trust began placing commercial paper issued by corporations with "investors". The Federal Reserve helped out by opening up another loophole in 1985. The Fed allowed commercial banks to set up affiliated companies (through a bank holding company) to deal in specific securities that were otherwise off-limits to these banks. It did not end there. Alan Greenspan, long the banker's friend, expanded the loophole, which began with commercial paper, government bonds and mortgage-backed securities, to include corporate bonds and equities.

The old traditional commercial banks were taking on the function of investment banks! This had been prohibited under the Glass-Steagall Act which in recent times is being ignored. Worse, at the same time, investment banks encroached on the business of commercial banks. For example, Merrill Lynch introduced the cash management account (CMA), a money market account with check-writing privileges. The major commercial banks used acquisitions not only to become larger, but also to move into investment banking. What was once a divide between commercial banks and investment banks and Merrill Lynch became a divide among mega-banks. These mega-banks became the new Wall Street.

Deregulation Aids the Mega-Banks

There was more to come. The mega-banks and their operations were aided and abetted by further deregulation. The final dismantling of the regulatory system built in the US during the 1930s was completed in the 1990s. The Riegle-Neal Act of 1994 mostly eliminated restrictions on interstate banking: it allowed bank holding companies to acquire banks in any state and allowed banks to open branches in new states. Further, the Gramm-Leach-Blilely Act of 1999 demolished the remaining barriers separating commercial and investment banking by allowing holding companies to own subsidiaries engaged in both businesses and insurance. At the same time the government refused to regulate derivatives. Why? It was thought that market forces would be sufficient to prevent fraud and excessive risk-taking. The view of Alan Greenspan was that the rapid growth of the derivatives market was proof that they were socially beneficial.

Greenspan was not flying solo. Others celebrated financial innovations. Timothy Geithner, then New York Fed president, in 2006 warned about potential risk management challenges for derivatives. But he had changed his mind by the pivotal year of 2008, when he said:

These developments provide substantial benefits to the financial system. Financial institutions are able to measure and manage risk much more effectively. Risks are spread more widely, across a more diverse group of financial intermediaries, within and across countries. These changes have contributed to a substantial improvement in the financial strength of the core financial intermediaries and in the overall flexibility and resilience of the financial system of the United States.[67]

Worse, in April 2009, during the financial crisis, Ben Bernanke, Greenspan's successor, said: "Financial innovation has improved access to credit, reduced costs and increased choice. You should not attempt to impose restrictions on credit providers so onerous that they prevent the development of new products and services in the future."[68] He was welcoming financial derivatives.

---

[67] Timothy F Geithner, "Risk Management Challenges in the US Financial System" (Lecture, Global Association of Risk Professionals, 7th Annual Risk Management Convention and Exhibition, New York, February 26, 2008).

[68] Ben S. Bernanke, "Financial Innovation and Consumer Protection" (Lecture, Federal Reserve System's Sixth Biennial Community Affairs Research Conference, Washington, D. C., April 17, 2009)

The U.S. Housing Bubble and Its Causes

A housing bubble became part of the banking crisis of 2008-2009. A multitude of forces accounted for the bubble in housing, which led the global housing bubble. The creation of financial innovations tells most of the story. The increased availability of mortgage loans combined with lower initial monthly payments increased homebuyers' ability to pay and pushed prices upward. Borrowers could always refinance when their mortgages become unaffordable: this made mortgage-backed securities and CDOs more attractive to "investors" and to the investment banks that created them. Thus, prices continued to climb. But there was more. The higher prices induced existing homeowners to take out home equity loans, which provided more raw materials for asset-backed securities and CDOs. Worse, the lower risk reduced the price of credit default swaps on mortgage-backed debt. This made CDOs and synthetic CDOs easier to create. The enhanced Wall Street demand for mortgages to feed the secularization pipeline funnelled cheap money to mortgage lenders. By the early 2000s subprime lending became a larger and larger share of the market, not only in the US but in much of the rest of the global economy.

In the boom years of 2005 and 2006 about 80 percent of the securities in CDOs were mortgage-backed, about 70 percent of these were below top-grade, and at least half were subprime or second-lien home equity lines. These were the same years the industry was pumping out some of the most egregiously irresponsible loans in history. Under the assumption of a permanent new era of very low defaults, it was possible to build families of bonds such that 80 percent of the issued bonds had triple-A and double-A ratings, even though 70 percent of the supporting assets were subprime. Analysts called the phenomenon "embedded Leverage". Two apparently identical offerings of triple-A-rated CDO bonds supported in partway subprime mortgages. A 3 percent default rate in portfolio one would require that 3 percent of the triple-A bonds be downgraded. The same default rate in the second portfolio would require that more than 50 percent of the bonds be downgraded. Moreover, the subprime mortgages have a variety of terms, some are fixed going to floating, second liens, negative interest, and so on. So, they are extremely hard to put together in the first place.[69]

US housing prices reached a peak before falling off a cliff, beginning around

---

[69] For much more detail, see Charles R. Morris, *The Trillion Dollar Meltdown* (New York: Public Affairs, 2008), pp. 74-79.

2006. In 2005 mortgages were already in trouble, as the housing boom approached its peak, a peak not reached, according to US census purchase prices, until the second quarter of 2007. The Shiller picture is made more dramatic by the inclusion of data from 1890 through the estimated value in 2010. With 1890 as the base year, US housing prices "doubled". The index is an accurate view of the real estate bubble in the US. The data are from major cities where the inflation was greatest. The bubble has a broad peak. This is only slightly different from the U.S. Census data. One thing is clear: speculators, as ever, were reluctant to leave the market, irrespective of their locale.

Nobelist Robert Shiller has a remarkable track record in identifying bubbles before they burst. He warned about the prospects for NASDAQ stocks just before the stock market crash of 2000. He again called the turn just before housing prices dropped in 2006. As a result, there are many housing indexes bearing Shiller's name. The bubble appears to peak in the second quarter of 2006 but there are little differences in the four quarters of the year. The bubble has a broad peak. This is only slightly different from the U.S. Census data.[70]

House sales began to pick up after 2009 in response to the US Treasury's home buyers tax credit, only to fall eight percent in September 2010. Shiller, for one, saw home prices more important than the foreclosure crisis. On November 2, 2010, he said, "If home prices drop further, homeowners will fall further underwater and lending institutions. Balance sheets will become more distressed. That could bring on another phase of the crisis." [71]

The Banks: Too Big to Fall

One might suppose that the banks—especially the giants—would get caught in the web of defaulting mortgages. After all, in 2006 borrowers unable to refinance their mortgages began defaulting in sharply rising number. In 2007 the mountain of assets based on housing values began to crumble as increasing defaults torpedoed the prices of mortgage-backed securities and CDOs. The avalanche almost brought down the global financial system by 2008. Nonetheless, it appeared that big, risk-taking banks had become crucial to the

---

[70] See Chapter 7 of E. Ray Canterbery, *The Global Great Recession* (Singapore, New Jersey, Hong Kong: World Scientific, 2011).

[71] Jennifer Schonberger, "Robert Shiller Sees More Housing Pain Ahead," Kiplinger at http://www.kiplinger.com/columns/dekaser-practical economics/archives/ Robert Shiller.

USA economy and to the American way of life.

How did the giants react? On October 13, 2008, with their stock prices in decline and the short-term viability of their firms in doubt, the heads of nine major banks—Bank of America, Bank of New York Mellon, Citigroup, Goldman Sachs, JP Morgan Chase, Merrill Lynch, Morgan Stanley, State Street, and Wells Fargo—arrived at the Treasury for a meeting with then Treasury Secretary Henry Paulson. Since Paulson had been CEO at Goldman Sachs until 2006, he would be favourable to the problems of the Big Nine. After the meeting with Paulson, the government stepped in to protect the massive USA financial system and, by extension, the global economy. The nine banks were judged too big to fail, as they were sitting on a mountain of crumbling assets.

The Treasury loaned the banks money, at an initial five percent yearly interest rate, that never had to be repaid. The purchases, which gave the banks free money, meant that the government now owned part of the banks. The government began guaranteeing debt issued by the banks, allowing them to raise money by selling bonds to private citizens who now knew that the government was guaranteeing their investments. While some of the big banks were saved, Lehman Brothers went bankrupt, Bear Stearns and Merrill Lynch were sold, and Goldman Sachs and Morgan Stanley slipped into the safety of bank holding company status. All were given enhanced access to emergency lending from the Federal Reserve. True, these investment banks were facing a liquidity crisis and desperately needed more capital. Still, the big five investment banks were not eligible for direct loans from the Federal Reserve.

To aid the investment banks, Paulson, Geithner, and Ben Bernanke, now Fed head, had to do some end runs. Bear Stearns, the weakest of the big five investment banks, was brought down by a modern-day bank run. What happened next would never be done for the little guy. It is a cautionary tale. Bear Stearns was more exposed to structured mortgage-backed securities than its rivals. The Fed first attempted to lend Bear Stearns money by using JP Morgan Chase as an intermediary. However, this did not bolster confidence and Paulson, Bernanke and Geithner attempted to broker the sale of Bear to JP Morgan for a miserly $2 a share. The CEO at JP Morgan was not willing to go along, even for a bargain price without government assistance. Enter the New York Fed which agreed to assume all the losses on $30 billion of Bear's illiquid securities. The deal was renegotiated to a purchase price of $10 a share. Thais was a coup for JP Morgan, which was paying for Bear Stearns about what its building was worth. To prevent the other investment banks from going the way of Bear Stearns, the Federal Reserve immediately created the Primary Dealer Credit Facility, which would allow investment banks for the first time to borrow money directly from the Fed. The safety net for the investment banks was dramatically expanded.

No one in the government or elsewhere knew how bad the situation was for the banks. However, the big banks were taking major write-downs on the value of their outstanding loans. As early as 2007, Citigroup took $29 billion in write-downs, Merrill Lynch $25 billion, Lehman $13 billion, Bank of America $1 billion, and Morgan Stanley $10 billion Then, in 2008, Citigroup took another $53 billion in write-downs, Merrill Lynch $29 billion, Bank of America $29 billion, Lehman $14 billion, JP Morgan Chase $10 billion, and Morgan Stanley $10 billion. If some of the banks had acknowledged the true decline in value of their assets, they might have been insolvent. For example, Merrill Lynch in mid-2008 sold its CDOs to Lone Star Funds for a mere twenty-two cents for each dollar of original face value.

Quasi-government institutions were not immune to the crises. In the spring of 2008, Fannie Mae and Freddie Mac came under pressure. Their balance sheets were also heavily exposed to the housing market, and declining housing prices were tearing a hole in their balance sheets, threatening their survival. Not to worry, in July 2008, Paulson obtained the right to back up Fannie and Freddie with taxpayer money. This proved insufficient. On September 7, a day to remember, Fannie and Freddie were taken over by the government, placed in a conservatorship. The conservatorship was tantamount to bankruptcy. In exchange for saving Fannie and Freddie, the government got a controlling ownership share and the right to manage them. Two other pillars of the financial system had been taken over because they too were "too big to fail".

Next was Lehman Brothers. It was short of cash. The Lehman collapse is considered by many as the climax to the 2008-2009 bubble. The demise of Lehman triggered a chain reaction that ripped the financial markets. Over the infamous weekend of September 12-14, 2008, Paulson and Geithner cast about for a buyer.[72]

---

[72] A book by a Wall Street TV reporter is devoted to this remarkable weekend. It provides a detailed account of the personalities, the many phone calls, the conflicts of the Wall Street CEOs with each other and with Fed and Government officials. See Maria Bartiromo (with Catherine Whitney) *The Weekend That Changed Wall Street* (New York:

This time no taxpayer money was used. When a plan for Barclays to reacquire Lehman fell through on Sunday, the backup plan was bankruptcy early on Monday morning. The American International Group (AIG), itself smuggling with derivatives, faced downgrades by all three major credit rating agencies (Ironically, the main business of AIG was supposed to be insurance.) These downgrades, in turn, would force it into bankruptcy. Not to worry, the Fed stepped in with an $85 billion credit line to keep AIG alive. If the insurer defaulted on its hundreds of billions of dollars in credit default swaps, its counter parties would suffer devastating losses or at the least, fear of such losses would end liquidity in world financial markets.

The Federal Reserve was not finished with Lehman Brothers. Because of its losses on Lehman, the Reserve Primary Fund, one of the largest money market funds, announced that it would "break the buck" on Tuesday. It no longer could return one dollar for each dollar put in by investors. This announcement reverberated through the money market funds. The flight of money market funds dried up demand for the commercial paper used by corporations to manage their cash, raising the spectre of major corporations unable to make payroll. Again, the Fed came to the rescue. The Fed established a program to buy commercial paper from leading corporations, lending money not just to banks, but directly to non-financial companies. This was changing the face of capitalism.

Despite all these efforts, the mighty continued to fall. Washington Mutual collapsed as depositors pulled out their money: it was at the time the largest bank failure in US history. Wachovia, on the brink of failure, was acquired by Wells Fargo. Because they were running out of cash, banks stopped lending. Rather, money moved toward the safety of US Treasury bills and stayed there. There was a liquidity trap: that is, overnight lending rates were near zero and could go no lower, no matter how fast the money supply was increased. As it turned out, the money supply was not increasing because banks were no longer lending and therefore were not creating any new demand deposits (the bulk of the money supply) as "inside" money.

Penguin, 2010). Roger Lowenstein contends that the financial crisis really got underway in 2008. We agree with his timetable but still see the climax coming with the fall of Lehman Brothers. See Roger Lowenstein, *The End of Wall Street* (New York: Penguin, 2010).

Consequences: Whither Fiscal Policy?

An inkling of what was to come happened in late 2007. Bank of America absorbed Countrywide and Merrill Lynch and saw its assets grow from $1.7 trillion at the end of 2007 to 2.3 trillion in September 2009. Likewise, JP Morgan Chase absorbed Bear Stearns and Washington Mutual and grew from $1.6 trillion to $2.0 trillion. Wells Fargo absorbed Wachovia and grew from $600 billion to $1.2 trillion.

By mid-2009, Bank of America, JP Morgan Chase, Wells Fargo and Citigroup controlled half the market for new mortgages and two-thirds of the market for new credit cards. They straddled commercial and investment bank activity. The US has had a rule since 1994 that prohibits any single bank from holding more than ten percent of total retail deposits. But in 2009 this rule had to be waived for JP Morgan Chase, Bank of America and Wells Fargo. Derivatives had become more concentrated. At the end of June 2009, five banks had over 95 percent of the market for derivatives contracts traded by US banks, led by JP Morgan Chase.[73] This explains why, for the most part, the rule had been violated.

By 2010 there were at least six Banks that were too big to fail. They included Bank of America, Citigroup, Goldman Sachs, JP Morgan Chase, Morgan Stanley and Wells Fargo. Today, the Bank of New York Mellon would be added to this group. Why is this a problem? "Too big to fail" creates three major problems for society. 1. These institutions have to be bailed out by the government when they do come to the brink of failure. 2. Giant financial institutions have a strong incentive to take excess risk, since the government will bail them out in an emergency. This is called a "moral hazard."[74] Giant financial institutions stifle competition, and this is a bad deal for society and the economy. Even during the midst of the financial crisis, the large banks could pay nearly 0.80 percentage points less for money than small banks.

The small banks cannot compete with the giants. Not surprisingly, small banks began to fail. In 2009, 140 US banks failed, the most since deposit insurance was introduced in the 1930s. By October 29, 2010, 139 banks (mostly small ones) had failed a pace well in advance of that of 2009. The failures

---

[73] These shares are baaed on data from the Office of the Comptroller of the Currency.

[74] A moral hazard occurs when a second (or third) individual or institution takes the risk for the first party. Whole life insurance companies engage in moral hazard activity as they take the risk that the insured will not die "too soon."

continued. The closings in 2010 included 29 in Georgia, 23 in Illinois, 20 in California and 18 in Florida. Week after week, Banks were failing—in Norcross, Georgia; Springfield, Illinois; San Clemente, California; and Fort Myers, Florida. While the failures in the bubble states of Arizona and Nevada were modest in 2010, but massive in 2008-2009. There were mounting losses on loans in the toughest economic climate since the 1930s. These failures have sapped billions of dollars out of the FDIC fund, which fell into the red during 2009. Its deficit was $20.7 billion as of March 31, 2010.The FDIC was originally established to protect ordinary depositors.

Why should we be concerned about the failures of small banks? After all, giant corporations such as IBM and Microsoft depend on the large banks, those already bailed out. It is a marriage made in Heaven. Some 64 percent of the loans of small banks are to USA small businesses, which in turn create about 65 percent of all new jobs and employ about half of the private sector workforce. Worse, the FDIC had 829 banks at risk of failure as of October 29, 2010, most of them small ones.[75] So, if we are interested in full employment and competitive markets, we should be defensive about small-town banks.

The remaining question: whither fiscal policy? Beginning with Alan Greenspan, normal fiscal policy whereby federal budgets were unbalanced to stabilize the economy was taken off the table. This prevailed in the US and globally. What about unconventional fiscal policy which is not focused on budget balances? Continuing our story, the Treasury and the Federal Reserve remained in crisis model. On September 18, 2008, Paulson and Bernanke (Greenspan's successor) asked Congress for $700 billion for the express purpose of buying toxic securities. Congress quickly responded by passing the Emergency Economic Stabilization Act on October 8. Now the Troubled Asset Relief Program (TARP had the $700 billion needed to buy "troubled assets" from financial institutions. Never had so much taxpayer money been designated to save an industry from the consequences of its own misdeeds.

Why did they use such unconventional actions? Simply put, there was a great deal at stake. With panic in the financial markets, a sudden evaporation of credit, coupled with rapid deleveraging by financial institutions and corporations

---

[75] The FDIC data and information is from the FDIC website. For a complete list of banks names of failures, go to http://www.fdic.gov/bank/individual/failed/banklist.html. For a detailed account of how the FDIC operates, see Massimo Calabrese, "Death of a Small-Town Bank," *Time*, September 1, 2010, pp. 57-60.

everywhere, we would have had a second Great Depression. The immediate threat was a panic—induced bank run, but the underlying issue was the toxic securities held by banks that were plummeting in value. Liquidation of these assets at then current market prices meant insolvency for many financial institutions, most of them being giants "too big to fail".

The policymakers had to be very inventive. They were transferring risk from banks to the federal government, and by extension, to taxpayers. If the Treasury paid enough to solve the banks' problems, that constituted a massive subsidy from the taxpayer. Instead, the government chose to recapitalize banks by giving them cash for preferred shares. For every $100 committed by the Treasury at that October 13th meeting, only $22 was a subsidy to the banking sector, though it clearly was still a subsidy.

The crisis continued. In November 2009 Citigroup was struggling to fend off concerns about its viability. The government announced a second bailout package. Besides another $20 billion payment the government agreed to guarantee a $305 billion pool of Citigroup assets against declines in value. In return the government received additional preferred stock. A similar asset guarantee was provided to Bank of America in January, in exchange for agreeing to complete the acquisition of Merrill Lynch in December. The government guaranteed a $118 billion pool of assets in exchange for a mere $4 billion in preferred stock of Bank of America. The government was taking ownership of the banks "too big to fail". Once again, this was changing the face of capitalism.

The banks had additional help from AIG. The banks had purchased credit default swaps from AIG to insure $62 billion in CDOs. The AIG bailout financed a new entity (Maiden Lane III) to buy CDOs so that AIG could then settle the credit default swaps. Maiden Lane III paid $30 billion at the market price to buy the CDOs from the banks, and AIG, under instructions from the New York Fed, then paid the banks $32 billion to retire the credit default swaps. As a consequence, the banks received.

100 Cents on the Dollar in This Backdoor Bailout

The mega-banks now faced even less competition, for Bear Stearns, Lehman Brothers, Merrill Lynch, Washington Mutual, and Wachovia had all vanished, and an entire class of non-bank mortgage lenders had evaporated with the bursting of the housing bubble. The banks had more options than ever before. They could raise money at low interest rates from depositors virtually for free;

they could borrow cheaply from each other at the near zero fed funds rate; they could borrow cheaply at the Fed's discount window; they could sell bonds at low interest rate; they could swap their asset-backed securities for cash with the Fed;; they could sell their mortgages to Fannie and Freddie, which could in turn sell debt to the Fed, and on and on. Despite all this aid to the banks, every type of bank loan became harder to get in every quarter of 2008, 2009, and through the first three quarters of 2010. Still, the overall strategy brought the financial system back from the brink of ruin: but, it did so without stimulating much lending to the real economy.

Could the banks have seen the bubble burst coming? Alan S. Blinder, a former Vice Chairman of the Fed, says they had reason to believe that the good times would continue to roll. He asks us to "imagine yourself as a banker in 2005".[76] House prices had been going up for at least eight years and there was little reason to think that this will go on forever. Mortgage delinquencies and defaults had plummeted to historic lows. From the banker's perch, mortgage lending, which had always been a safe form of lending, looked saver than ever. It was a veritable walk in the park, or so it was thought. The bond salesmen were saying the "mortgages never default".

The super-low delinquency rates continued for a while longer, then reversed with a vengeance beginning as early as 2006. By 2008, that dangerous year, mortgage lending did not seem so safe anymore. By 2009, the bankers' pleas would seem almost comical. Loss rates on home mortgages were at a Rocky Mountain High, though it was nothing to sing about. Alan Blinder here seems to miss the point. A herd mentality had taken over, and those financing new homes did believe that low interest rates and investment opportunities would go on forever. The delusion of the crowd had prevailed.

The Stock Market Crash

Despite the Federal Reserve's best efforts, commercial and industrial credit fell sharply after early 2008 and accelerated in 2009. By September 2010, despite having levelled off early in the year, commercial and industrial loans declined 10.2 percent from their level a year earlier. In contrast, the mortgage industry experienced slower downward changes. The mortgage market was cushioned by

---

[76] Alan S. Blinder, *After the Music Stopped* (New York City:: Penguin, 2011), p. 43. The title implies that the bankers and other mortgage dealers were simply playing musical chairs with the mortgages.

the presence of Fannie Mae and Freddie Mac, despite all their problems. This is not to deny the severe repercussions of the subprime debacle. These declines were highly correlated with stock market indices.

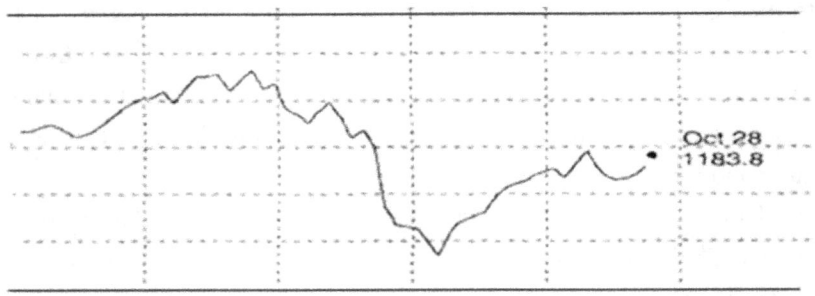

Figure 13.1
Stock Market Index: Standard and Poor's 500 Composite

As we know, there is more than one stock market index. One favoured by the general public and the media is the Dow Industrials, which is a blue-chip indicator. The broader index, and one favoured by the Federal Reserve, is Standard & Poor's 500 Composite Index. It peaked in late 2007 near 1600, then the S &I P 500 stair-steps its way downward and then falls off a cliff around mid-2008, reaching its near-term bottom early in 2009, only to begin a recovery punctuated by three dips. It had recovered to 1183.8 by October 28, 2010. It was being fuelled by low interest rates, especially short-term rates.

The 2008-2009 episode, was one of the worst financial collapses, except as I have suggested, it really began much earlier with the housing collapse. The Lehman Brothers debacle was the climax.

Chapter 14
Bitcoin Speculation and
the Blockchain Revolution

Introduction to the Bitcoin Blockchain

Once again, or so it appears, the technological genie has been unleashed from its bottle. As we learned from the 1960s TV show, *I Dream of Jennie*, once out of the bottle, she is very difficult to put back in. A brief survey will show how we came to this point, a tipping point, as it were. The first four decades of the Internet brought with it e-mail, the World Wide Web, dot-coms, social media, the mobile Web, big data, cloud computing, and the early days of the Internet of Things. It has reduced the costs of searching, collaborating and exchanging information. It also has lowered the barriers to entry for new media and entertainment, new forms of retailing, and various digital ventures. Through sensor technology, it has infused intelligence into our wallets or clothing, or automobiles, our buildings, our cities, and even our biology. Eventually, we will be so immersed in the technology that we will no longer "log on". We will already be online.

Some things the Internet cannot do. We still cannot identify someone or trust an entity to exchange money. An example is provided in The New Yorker. Peter Steiner's 1993 cartoon had one dog talking to another, "On the Internet, nobody knows you're a dog."

As early as 1981, innovators were attempting solve the Internet's problems of privacy, security, and inclusion with cryptography. Never mind, the Internet proved to be insecure because users had to divulge too much personal data. In 1993, the brilliant mathematician David Chaum invented eCash, a digital payment system that was "a technically perfect product which made it possible to safely and anonymously pay over the Internet". Then, however, users of the Internet were not concerned about security or privacy online and Chaum's Dutch company DigiCash went bankrupt in 1998. About that time, Nick Szabo, a Chaum associate, wrote a short paper called "The God Protocol," a slight twist on Nobel laureate Leon Lederman's phrase "the God Particle," in reference to the Higgs boson in modern physics. God, according to Szabo, could be designated as the third party in transactions.[77] Everyone would trust God. It's even engraved on USA coins. All inputs would be sent to God who would return the outputs. Faith, however, can only reach so far. One "God Particle" that was missing in the puzzle was an acceptable currency.

Later, in 2008, when the global financial industry was crashing, a pseudonymous person or persons named Satoshi Nakamoto outlined a new protocol for a peer-to-peer electronic cash system using a crypto-currency called bitcoin. Crypto-currencies (digital currencies) are different from traditional fiat currencies because they are not created or controlled by governments or central banks. A set of rules—in the form of distributed computations—ensured the integrity of the data exchanged among billions of devices without going through a trusted third party such as God. Bitcoins have excited or otherwise captured the imagination of the computing world and has spread like wildfire to businesses, governments, privacy advocates, social development activists, media theorists, and journalists, to name more than a few, everywhere. Despite exclamations, such as "My God, this is it!" God is held at a secular distance. No third party or middleman is required. Today, thoughtful people are trying to understand the implications of a protocol that enables mere mortals to manufacture trust through clever code. This has never happened before.

Of course, there is more to it than this. The protocol is the foundation of a growing number of global distribution ledgers called blockchains—of which the bitcoin blockchain is the largest. Blockchains enable us to send money directly and safely from me to you, without going through a bank or PayPal. It is the Internet of value or money. Big banks and some governments are implementing blockchains as distributed ledgers to revolutionize the way information is stored and transactions are made. The advantages are speed, lower cost, security, fewer errors and the elimination of central points of attacks and failure.

How does the bitcoin blockchain work? The digital currency isn't saved in a computer file somewhere like the Internet. Rather, it is represented by

---

[77] The word "protocol" has found its way into common expressions. Literally, it is a means for transmitting knowledge. The means is embodied in the protocol which can be written or said. There are different levels of complexity associated with the term.

transactions recorded in a blockchain—kind of like a global spreadsheet or ledger, which leverages the resources of a large peer-to-peer bitcoin network to verify and approve each bitcoin transaction. Each blockchain like the one that used bitcoin, is distributed; it runs on computers provided by volunteers around the world; there is no central database to hack. The blockchain is public; anyone can view it at any time because it resides on the network, not within a single institution charged with auditing transactions and keeping records. And the blockchain is encrypted.

Every ten minutes, like a slow heartbeat of the bitcoin network, all the transactions conducted are verified, cleared and stored in a block which is linked to the preceding block, thereby creating a chain. Each block must refer to the preceding block. This structure permanently time stamps and stores exchanges of value, preventing anyone from altering the ledger. If, say, you wanted to steal a bitcoin, you'd have to rewrite the coin's entire history on the blockchain in broad daylight, and that's practically impossible. Like the World Wide Web of information, it's the World Wide Ledger of value—a distributed ledger that everyone can download and run on their personal computer. This new platform enables conciliation of digital records regarding just about everything in real time.

The potential for blockchain goes beyond financial transactions. Blockchain mashes up cryptography and peer-to-peer networking to create what amounts to a shared database of transactions and other information—which can be open to all but controlled by no one in particular. It's not simply for securely recording payments in crypto-coinage; a blockchain can manipulate complex transactions, even entire contracts. Collaborators will be able to work together as free agents instead of under the hierarchy of bosses. The poetic vision of a blockchain society is a flock of starlings at dusk; decentralized yet perfectly coordinated. In the starling's vision, blockchain could replace lots of bankers, accountants, and lawyers, as well as escrow accounts, insurance, and everything else that society invented pre-21st century to verify payments and contracts.

The design of blockchain prevents the owner of a currency token from committing fraud by spending it twice.[78] The first time it is spent is recorded for all to see, so no one would ever accept it a second time. This "truth-telling" feature of blockchain makes it useful to banks, which have been among the first

---

[78] "Currency token" is often used to identify the currency unit such as bitcoin used as currency.

to start testing it. Last year Microsoft launched blockchain as a service. NASDAQ, an early adopter of blockchain, is using the technology to allow private companies to issue stock and stockholders of public companies to vote their shares. Everledger is using it to create a registry of diamonds to suppress trade in "blood diamonds" from zones of conflict.[79] This was the start of a revolution in payments. Some argue that it will never be possible to reduce the complex, fast-changing world of business to rules commanded by software. In practice, the system is elitist, controlled by those who build the new virtual machines and understand them. Machines are not God, but if we are to be the gods, we must take control of the technology before it takes control of us. It is a dilemma we face with robotic technology.

One of the most interesting applications of quantum mechanics is in computers—hence, in robotics. Quantum computers can take advantage of odd sub-atomic interactions to solve problems far faster than a conventional machine could. Such computers could speed advances in artificial intelligence. Investment in the arena from big business and the government, including intelligence agencies focused on breaking codes, is surging. The cryptographic tools commonly used to protect information online rely on very hard math problems, such as factoring large integers that normal computers can't solve in a reasonable time frame. Quantum computers, though, could probably make quick work of such equations. Hence, the possible application in robots.

How far have the blockchains gone? The financial services industry has already re-branded and privatized blockchain technology, referring to it as distributed ledger technology, to reconcile the best of bitcoin—security, speed, and cost--with an entirely closed system that requires a bank or financial institution's permission to use. Blockchains are considered more reliable databases than what they already have. Moreover, investing in blockchain start-ups is taking off, as did investing in Dot-com.

Breaking News—Bitcoin Rallies and Fads

Bitcoin was and is a hot investment. We can trace its past and recent ups and downs. Beginning in September of 2015 and continuing until summertime 2018, monthly bitcoin prices rose nonstop, with the rally accelerating in the final weeks. The virtual currency surged to $574.11 on a Sunday, more than double its

---

[79] References to these applications are found in Peter Coy and Olga Kharif, "This Is Your Company On Blockchain," *Business Week*, August 24-September 4, 2016, pp. 8-9.

low in September of $326.61, according to digital-currency news service CoinDesk. It is no longer the hot media topic it once was, but it doesn't matter. The volume of media articles and blogs mentioning bitcoin worldwide tanked in 2014, and has failed to recover even as the value of the virtual currency started rising again toward the end of 2018, according to Dow Jones & Co.

The media's diminished interest reflects the idea that most of the investment interest in bitcoin comes from far-away China. There, interest has grown as bitcoin has appreciated. Two Chinese bitcoin exchanges, Huobi and OKCoin, now account for 92 percent of all global trading in this currency, according to data from blockchain, info. Fears of a sudden devaluation of the yuan have led Chinese investors to bitcoin.

By contrast to the media's diminished attention to bitcoin itself, global interest in bitcoin's ledger technology, blockchain, continues to grow. Recently, J.P. Morgan Chase & Co. and Citigroup Inc successfully used blockchain to keep records on credit default-swap transactions. While bitcoin has lost its cool, blockchain has become the hot.com in the 1990s.[80] The rate of investment recent doubled annually. Another dramatic development: The Bank of England's top economist, Andrew Haldane, has proposed a national digital currency for the United Kingdom. Despite all this interest or perhaps because of it, bitcoin's price has fluctuated drastically, partly because the ownership of bitcoins is still concentrated. The bitcoin price hit a two-year high of $719 on June 14, 2016. In 2013 some 937 people owned half of all bitcoin, although that is changing daily. This relatively small number of owners helps to explain bitcoin's volatility. Still, huge institutions now control and own this new means of production and social interaction—its underlying infrastructure; massive and growing treasure troves of data; the algorithms that increasingly govern business and daily life; the world of apps; and extraordinary emerging capabilities, machine learning, and autonomous vehicles.

Economic power has gotten spikier, more concentrated and more entrenched. Rather than data being more widely and democratically distributed, it is being hoarded and exploited by fewer entities that often use it to control others and acquire more power. Worse, powerful digital conglomerates such as Amazon, Google, Apple, and Facebook—all Internet start-ups at one time—are capturing the treasure troves of data that citizens and institutions generate often in private

---

[80] See Jon Sindreu, "Bitcoin Rallies, but Lure Grows More Limited," *Wall Street Journal*, June 7, 2016, p. C4.

data silos rather than on the Web.

A New Look for the Global System

The current global system of finance is antiquated, built on decades-old technology that is at odds with our rapidly advancing digital world, making it oftentimes slow and unreliable. It is exclusive, leaving out billions of people with no access to basic financial tools. It is centralized, exposing it to data breaches, other attacks or outright failure. Moreover, it is monopolistic, reinforcing the status quo and stifling innovation. Blockchain promises to solve these problems and many more as innovations and entrepreneurs devise new ways to create value on this powerful platform. According to Don and Alex Tapscott, there are four characteristics of bitcoin Blockchain which will contribute to the transformation of the global financial system. These are as follows.[81]

Attestation: Two parties who neither know nor trust each other can transact and do business. The blockchain technology can establish trust when trust is needed by verifying the identity and capacity of any counter-party through a combination of past transaction history (on the blockchain), reputation scores based on aggregate reviews, and other social and economic indicators. The blockchain network clears and settles peer-to-peer value transfers, and it does so continually so that its ledger is always up to date. Anyone, anywhere, with a smart phone and an Internet connection could tap into the vast arteries of global finance.

Speed: Today remittances take three to seven days to settle. Stock trades take two or three days, whereas bank loan trades take an average of a staggering twenty-three days to settle. In contrast, the bitcoin network takes an average of ten minutes to clear and settle all transactions conducted during that period. Other blockchain networks are even faster, and new innovations, such as the Bitcoin Lightning Network, aim to dramatically scale the capacity of the bitcoin blockchain while dropping settlement and clearing times to a fraction of a second. The shift to instant and frictionless value transfers would free up capital

---

[81] Don Tapscott and Alex Tapscott, *Blockchain Revolution* (New York: Penguin Random House, 2018), pp. 31-35.

otherwise trapped in transit, bad news for anyone profiting from the float.[82]

Risk Management: Blockchain technology can mitigate several forms of financial risks. The first is settlement risk, the risk that your trade will bounce back because of some glitch in the settlement process. The second is counter-party risk, the risk that your counter-party will default before settling a trade. Finally, and most significantly is systemic risk, the total sum of all outstanding counter-party risk in the system. For example, during the financial crisis, one of the risks is that unscrupulous managers will exploit the cumbersome paper trail and significant time delay to conceal wrongdoing. "If I'm trading with somebody, how do I know they're going to settle on the other side"? Instant settlement on the blockchain eliminates that risk completely. Irreconcilability of a transaction and instant reconciliation of financial reporting would eliminate one aspect of risk.

Value Innovation: The bitcoin blockchain was designed for moving bitcoins not for handling other financial assets. Since, however, the technology is open source, it invites experimentation.

Some innovations are developing separate blockchains, known as altcoins, built for something other than bitcoin payments. Others are looking to leverage the bitcoin blockchain's size and liquidity to create "spin-off" coins on side-chains that can be "coloured" to represent any asset or liability, physical or digital—a corporate stock or bond, a barrel of oil, a bar of gold, a car, a car payment, a receivable or a payable, or of course a currency. Side-chains inter-operate with the blockchain though a two-way peg, a cryptographic means of transferring assets off the blockchain and back again without a third-party exchange, so much the worse for God. Blockchain technology is already being used to record, exchange, and trade assets and liabilities, and could eventually replace traditional exchanges and centralized markets.

Open Source: Being an open source technology means that blockchain can

---

[82] "The float" is a common term used in monetary economics and by central banks. It consists of the money in transit between banks, including Federal Reserve banks. It is possible for private and other banks to borrow from this float, usually at very low interest rates. Float can affect the money supply because it *is* money, but the effects are temporary. Float affects the amount of currency available to trade and countries can manipulate the worth their own currency by retaliating with coins replacing the amount of float available to them. For more details, see the section on Float (money supply) in Wikipedia, the Free Encyclopedia.

continue to innovate, repeat and improve, if there is a consensus in the network. In contrast, conventional financial services cannot be changed easily. It stands "twenty miles high and on the verge of teetering over".

Prospects

These benefits—attestation, dramatically lower costs at lightning speed, lower risks, great innovation of value, liquidity and adaptability through open source--argue Tapscott and Tapscott, have the potential to transform payments, the securities industry, investment banking, accounting and auditing, venture capital, insurance, enterprise risk management, retail banking, and other aspects of the financial industry. This is a very strong statement and not everyone will agree; still blockchain technology is getting a lot of attention. Moreover, as we have learned, there is much in conventional finance and its institutions to criticize.

Certainly, the financial services industry would change in many ways. There are eight core functions of finance that would be altered. **First**, there is authenticating identity and value. There would be verifiable and robust identities crypto-graphically secured. **Second**, it would be a way of moving value. The transfer of value can be in very large and very small increments. Since there is no middleman, these transfers can be made at dramatically lower costs and greater speeds. Retail banking, wholesale banking, payment car networks, money transfer services and telecommunications would be affected. **Third**, value could be stored, whether it be currencies, commodities or financial assets. The payment mechanism combined with a reliable and safe store of value reduces the need for typical financial services. Bank savings and checking accounts would become obsolete. Retail banking, brokerages, investment banking, asset management and telecommunications would be affected. **Fourth**, bitcoins have lending value—credit card debt, mortgages, corporate bonds, municipal bonds, government bonds, asset-backed securities and other forms of credit could be held on the blockchain ledger. Debt can be issued, traded and settled on the blockchain. This would increase efficiency, reduce friction and improve systemic risk. Wholesale, commercial and retail banking would be affected. **Fifth**, Value could be exchanged—speculating, hedging and arbitraging would take place. Blockchain takes settlement times on all transactions from days and weeks to minutes and seconds. Investment, wholesale banking, foreign exchange traders, hedge funds pension funds, retail brokerage, clearing houses, stock, futures, commodities exchanges, commodities brokerages, and central banks would be involved. **Sixth**, Funding and investing in an asset, company, start-up—capital appreciation, dividends, interest, rents, or some combination would take place. New models for peer-to-peer financing recording corporate actions such as dividends paid automatically through smart contracts would evolve. Investment banking, venture capital, legal audits, property management, stock exchanges and crowd funding would all be affected. **Seventh**, Value and management of risk could take place, protecting assets, homes, lives, health, business property and business practices, and derivative products. Using reputational systems, insurers will better estimate actuarial risk, creating decentralized markets for insurance. Derivatives would be made more transparent. Insurance, risk management, wholesale banking, brokerage and clearing houses would be affected. **Eighth**, the accounting for value would facilitate new corporate governance. Distributed ledger will make audit and financial reporting real time, responsive and transparent, and will dramatically improve the capacity of regulators to scrutinize financial actions within a corporation. As a mechanism for shared, decentralized and replicated transaction records, blockchain is a golden resource.

There are some obstacles in the way of blockchain. For now, most people have only a vague understanding of bitcoin and crypto-currency and very few have even heard of blockchain the technology. It would not be easy to locate a bitcoin exchange or a bitcoin ATM anywhere but in New York City or say, Athens. Smaller cities are not quite ready for bitcoins. In other words, blockchain may not be ready for prime time. Hashing, the process of running pending transactions though the secure hash algorithm 256 (SHA-256) to validate them and solve a block, burns a lot of electricity. Estimates liken the bitcoin network's energy consumption to the power used by nearly seven hundred average USA homes at the low end of the spectrum and to the energy consumed by the island of Cyprus at the high end. It would be greater than the aggregate output of the world's top five hundred supercomputers. This assumes that $3 billion worth of bitcoins is in circulation.

Also, would bitcoins be regulated by government? Our Greenbacks are currently regulated by the US Treasury and the Federal Reserve. President Trump said he would investigate, then said it was important to regulate bitcoin blockchain, then backed off again. After all, bitcoins have been used as currency. Still, to be able to persist, the blockchain network would have to hold its own against mighty central authorities. With the Internet, powerful corporations have captured much of the technology and are using it in their vast private empires to extract most of the value. Would they do the same with the blockchain technology?

Will the blockchain be a job killer? It's difficult to know. The 2015 World Economic Forum annual meeting in Davos Switzerland discussed the impact of technology on jobs. All agreed that although technological innovations may disrupt labour markets temporarily, overall, they generate new and incrementally more jobs. Would this time be different? The bitcoin community does not yet have formal oversight bodies such as the Internet Engineering Task Force, or the World Wide Web Consortium to anticipate development needs and guide their resolution. Moreover, the community prefers it this way; it eschews governance of any kind. Critics have also argued that, because the technology is decentralized, lightning quick, and peer-to-peer, criminals would exploit it. But there is nothing unique to bitcoin or blockchain technology that makes it more effective for criminals than other technologies. Anyway, all this is to say that the obstacles are formidable.

John Maynard Keynes once called for an international currency to replace the then dominant trading currency, the British pound, in international trade. Could the bitcoin be used as that international currency? It is doubtful since no international reserves are held in bitcoins; even the lowly Chinese yuan is held in modest reserves at the IMF. (Recently, the Chief Economist at the IMF said the in the future bitcoins might be held as reserves.) It would make more sense if the SDR were to become the international currency. It is already used as a unit of account and is currently held as international financial reserves. It would only need to be accepted as a trading currency.[83]

Cryptocurrency Bubbles

Bitcoin price prediction and chart analysts are among the most popular topics on Bitcoin-talk. There's nothing wrong with a little speculation, though a lot of speculation can be ruinous. But there is a lot more to making a profit than reading the charts and following the news. After all, 70-90 percent of traders are losing money; they could do better than that in Las Vegas at the gaming tables. In the trading game, you are betting against all other traders, and many are smarter than you. If there is a long-run tendency, it is for equity to flow from the many to the

---

[83] The author once proposed a Delayed Peg based on the SDR. It would be a way of preventing speculation in the dollar and other currencies, including the Bitcoin.

few.

In the Bitcoin World there are enough beginners to profit from, but eventually professionals will reach the Bitcoin trading market too. You are currently betting against bitcoin enthusiasts reading every thread on Bitcoin-talk. Soon you are betting against market professionals with 5 + years of experience in trading. The biggest problem is that results from the past offer no guarantee for the future. At times it's easy to predict the market, at other times markets are being irrational.

News can be very important for the price of bitcoins, but news does not age well. By the time you read the news it has already been factored in by the market. Bitcoin enthusiasts and investors are closer to the news sources than you are. Professional traders run news tickers that receive news minutes before it's on the websites and Google news. Bitcoin enthusiasts get it from the community forums. And firms like dataminr try to beat the news headlines by following trends on twitter. Sometimes you see a price surge, only to find out three hours later the news that caused it.

Bitcoins do have some value because they serve the functions of money. They have durability, portability, fungibility, scarcity, divisibility and are recognizable. Price is determined by supply and demand. However, there is only a limited number of bitcoins in circulation and new bitcoins are created at a predictable and decreasing rate by "miners" of bitcoins, which means that the price must follow the rate of inflation to be stable.[84] Because it is a relatively small market, it takes very small amounts of money to move the market price. Thus, the price of a bitcoin is remains very volatile. Bitcoin prices caught up with that old-time favourite Gold in late 2013. Since then, the price has soared as high as $2,500 on the way to $4,000+, well above the price of gold. Subsequently, bitcoin prices came back to earth.

Is Bitcoin a bubble? It takes more than a fast rise in prices to constitute a bubble. An artificial overvaluation that will lead to a sudden downward correction constitutes a bubble. Still, the rapid price rise in November and

---

[84] "Miners" of bitcoins and other cryptocurrencies are not deep in the earth digging for precious metals. Rather, these "miners" are housed in warehouses secretly located at strategic spots on the planet. Those who saw the 60 Minutes documentary on bitcoins have a visual understanding of what mining cryptocurrencies is like. It consists of a series of powerful computers wired to each other in sequence. They are stacked from floor to ceiling. These warehouses connected to each other, sometimes through tunnels, comprise the physical presence of blockchain.

December of 2014 and in August 2017 looks suspicious. However, what followed in 2014 would not qualify as a correction. The price proceeded to decline in a discernible trend. After reaching a high of nearly $1100, it steadily declined to about $300. No one can predict its future. We cannot rule out a bubble sometime in that future, especially since, in my judgement, it has constituted the greatest speculative bubble in history.

Conclusions

Is the Bitcoin subject to speculation? This is an easy one: the pattern of volatility makes it so. Is there more to bitcoins than this, in Bitcoin-talk? The blockchain revolution has been successful. We are now so immersed in this new technology that we are "already on-line" and have superseded the Internet.

Among the things that blockchain can do, and the Internet cannot, is to identify someone or trust an entity to exchange money and other contractual things. The "God Particle" that had been missing was an acceptable currency. Through the blockchain, bitcoin can be that acceptable currency. The new protocol is a peer-to-peer electronic cash system using bitcoins. Such a system is independent of government and private groups. This is because all transactions conducted are verified, cleared and stored in a block which is linked to the preceding block, thereby creating a chain. A transaction is permanently time stamped and stored as exchanges of value. It is a World Wide Ledger (WWL) of value. This potential has already gone beyond financial transactions to include all sorts of contracts.

Blockchain's design precludes fraud from the inside. Everledger, as only one example, has created a registry of diamonds to suppress trade in "blood diamonds" from zones of conflict. Because of bitcoins and other digital-currencies, economic power has gotten spikier, more concentrated and more entrenched. In short, blockchain promises to solve many global problems and the global financial system will be transformed. As suggested, it will be transformed by attestation, speed, risk management, value innovation, liquidity, and by its open source technology. What could end this promise? If bitcoins now constitute a bubble, a bubble that, if it is pricked, will burst. As we will see, this has already happened, though the price of bitcoins once near $10,000 recently landed at around $3,000, a Princely sum.

Bitcoin does not stand alone, though it has the largest capitalization at about $40.5 million. In second place is Ethereum, a blockchain of contracts (programs that will state contractual terms automatically). Ethereum at $26.7 million is far behind bitcoin's capitalization. Ethereum started the token craze. Out of a total of 900+ cryptocurrencies, only 25 have a capitalization of $270 million or more. Besides bitcoin, some 24 others could become bubbles. Why lobby venture capitalists or deal with regulators of public markets when you can attach a token coin to your idea and have speculators throw money at it. For example, Ethereum's value has skyrocketed more than 2,700 percent in the 12 months ending in July 2017 to $300 per token. On the way there is has flash crashed to only 10 cents and has hit a high of $415. As noted, bitcoin has been historically just as volatile.

There is $100 billion worth of cryptocurrency in play with little intrinsic value. While a long-lasting system may emerge out of this, a handful of visionaries and hucksters will take billions from the greater fools. Initial coin offerings (ICOs) now play a role once reserved for initial public offerings (IPOs) of common stocks. The leader in ICOs is Ethereum. The market capitalization of cryptocurrencies of these virtual issues has surged 870 percent in the twelve months ending in July 2017. Even though the number is a moving target that was more than six times the rise in stock market capitalization. Speculators are betting on something which is not real. Bitcoin does not even have the support of a central government or a precious metal mined from the earth.

We must not forget about blockchain. It can turn a virtual coin into an asset. As noted, the blockchain is essentially a secure, decentralized, constantly updated ledger system. The ledger system is inside of those connected warehouses and computers, sometimes only in the minds of the miners or their "consultants." While bitcoin allows you to do transactions only in bitcoin, the Ethereum network allows for software programs. Ethereum based currencies can act. As noted, however, Ethereum has crashed and burned more than once.

We end with a word of caution. The bitcoin dealers claim that the coin is free of government interference. This happens to be false. In China, Beijing had closed trading venues for virtual currencies. Bitcoin was down 10 percent, at $2,490, after the bitcoin-exchange operator shut down its Chinese trading business. Bitcoin had declined about 25 percent from its peak of $5,014 on September 2, 2017. In recent years China has become a big market for bitcoin, with traders there drawn to both the currency's speculative nature and its potential as a conduit to move money outside the country. Chinese authorities also issued a blanket ban on initial coin offerings, or offerings of digital tokens, which have been used as a new fundraising method for companies. The angst has been building in recent weeks around cryptocurrencies after their torrid rise in 2017. Bitcoin is still up about 270 percent in 2017. This looks like a bubble pricked by the Chinese authorities.

Next, we introduce the reader to real-world casinos and what I have called "The Casino Effect."

Chapter 15
Casinos and the Casino Effect

Casinos: The Real Things

Casinos have been around for a very long time. Beyond their history, we will ponder how real casinos help to explain "The Casino Effect". Casinos are an integral part of the gambling industry, though there is more to most of them than only gambling. Many casinos offer lodging, shows, dining and other nightlife and all of it goes into the bottom line. Still, without the gambling function, there would be virtually no casinos. More to our point, it is the gambling function that is most closely related to the casino effect.

The gambling operations of a casino run at a profit because of what is known as the "house edge," or "house advantage". However, the edge is mathematically operative only when games are played many times. Consider a simple example: a flipped coin will land in one of 3 ways—heads, tails or on its edge. What, therefore, is the probability of the coin landing on it edge? The answer reveals how "edgy" casinos are. Suppose there is a "nickel game" for a casino to play. For a price of only $1 the player is allowed to toss a nickel 50 times. If it lands on its edge,[85] the player is paid $100, not bad for a dollar bet. If not, the player loses $1. But what are the player's chances of winning? Mathematically, it will take 120 runs of 50 tosses each (6,000 tosses) before a nickel lands on its edge. True, the actual results will vary: a remarkably lucky player may get the edge on one toss. Or, the unlucky player may require 10,000 flips of the nickel. On average, the casino will need to pay out $100 for every $120 it takes in. The "law of large numbers" is at work. The profit after a month of flipping the nickel is only $400 for the flipper. If you are a doctor, the opportunity costs represented

---

[85] This probability was estimated by Canadian physicists Daniel B. Murray and Scott W. Teare, "Probability of a tossed coin landing on edge," *Physical Review E* (October 1993).

by your lost monthly income would be very high. The main point: the casino always has the edge.

At the most fundamental level, this is the calculus the casino uses to make money on gambling games. Some games are more mathematical than others. Craps and roulette are highly mathematical. On any given dice roll or wheel spin, the odds are well established. For slot machines pay-outs are programmed into the machine, determined mechanistically or electronically, and thus are completely random. It is a random walk.

The only game where the player still comes into play is 21 or Blackjack. And the house edge in all these games is much better for the player than the nickel game. Still, a casino may operate on an average edge of just 2 percent. This works out, because a great number of games are running at the same time and the law of large numbers applies. Still, predicted and actual results are closely (but never exactly) matched. That's why they call it "gambling". The gambling motive is related to the casino effect.

The profit-making of a casino is more complicated than the foregoing would suggest. Also, there are differences based on location—whether it be the United States, Europe or Asia. In the United States, casinos can make money because they serve alcohol—a tee-totalling US casino is a rarity. Under the influence the player is likely to have impaired judgment. If their judgment is not impaired, they may quit sooner and minimize their losses. Casinos are arranged in such a way that exits are hard to find. If you can't find your way out, you are more likely to stay and gamble some more. Even in small casinos it is difficult to leave without passing ways of losing money. Most players, unless professional gamblers do not know their games. Few people know the exact rules of any game of change. Fewer still will know how to play successfully. This condition of relative ignorance greatly benefits the casino. US casinos offer massive buffets in which overeating is likely. Overeating impairs judgment. If the buffets are no longer free, they are a profit source. Casinos, especially in the US, are open 24 hours a day. Gamblers may get up in the middle of the night, when they are not on top of their game. By accepting players at all hours of the night and day, the nickel, so to speak, gets tossed more times, increasing the casino's margin at the edge. In Las Vegas beautiful women are allowed to enter free and can be a distraction for the average male player.

The Romance of the Oldest Casinos

There are many casinos, many possibilities to take chances—at last count, over 3,000 with many in the USA. There is about 1 casino for every major city (100,000 population) in the world, though not every country or city has a casino. There are only 200 casinos in all of Asia, whereas only 3 countries in the Middle East allow casinos, with Israel having the most. In Africa, most of the casinos are concentrated in South Africa. There are 160 casinos in South America with 51 of these in Argentina; Brazil, the largest country has none. North America enjoys some 1,000 casinos, with 29 in Mexico and more than 100 in Canada, the larger balance being in the USA. There are 80 in Las Vegas alone, with the Bellagio leading; it is the capital city of casinos. The only game more universal than casino gambling is golf.

But we would be remiss not to consider the casino as a historical icon. An integral part in the revenues and evolution of the gambling industry resolve around the question: What is the oldest casino in the world? That is where the romance begins. The "casino di Venezia" can be traced back to 1638 and it is located along the canals of the scenic Italian city of Venice. Its entrance from the Grand Canal provides exquisite classical Venetian architecture and ensures visitors can feel the history linked with this venue. The building was initially built in 1509 as a residence for the elite Venetian nobility before it turned into a casino over a hundred years later. The echoes of the past are found in the design of the casino having not changed since the early 17th century, including the chandeliers and sculptures. Today the Casino offers classic casino games such as roulette, blackjack, Caribbean stud poker, Texas Hold 'em, Chamin de Fer, Trente et Quarante, and over 600 slot machines.

The Casino Weisbaden in Germany is also a contender for being the oldest gambling establishment in the world. It was originally built in 1810, but as a venue, it can be traced back to the time of the Roman Empire. Caesar might have visited it. It has a classy ambiance with statues from Greek mythology, mosaic art and chandeliers that set it apart from other casinos. It is famous for its 180 slot machines. Players can also indulge in some classic casino table games, including baccarat, blackjack, and roulette. Today, it looks as good as it did in the 19th century.

The members-only Crockford's Club in London opened in 1828 as a gentleman's club but gambling probably took place there a long time before that date. It has even been suggested that casino gambling as we know it began there.

It has an elite reputation for some of the richest and most illustrious individuals in British society. Some of the major political decisions in British history were probably made at Crockford's. The decor is sophisticated and regal to fit the clientele that frequent the casino. Players have a wide choice of casino games to sample.

The Casino de Monte Carlo is familiar to moviegoers who saw Ocean's Twelve, Goldeneye, and Casino Royale. Even today one might expect to see James Bond on the premises. It was first constructed in 1856 and is the preferred casino of some of Europe's wealthiest gamblers. Many classic casino games can be played at this picturesque casino such as Baccarat, Craps, Poker, Blackjack, American Roulette, French Roulette (of course), Chemin Fer, Punto Banco, and slot machines. As might be expected, this was one of the first venues to expand into the entertainment world with concert halls, cafes, restaurants, and a theatre all located on the premises.

We have not settled on which of these four casinos is the oldest, and it might be a moot point. The Casino de Venezia is perhaps the only one that has proof of when it was first built. The important things to know about these casinos is, the romance attached to them, they as historical icons, and their use of the edge to make profits, among other means. We move on to something slightly more abstract, "The Casino Effect," though it is related to the foregoing.

The Casino Effect

There are at least two ways of approaching what I have called "The Casino Effect". One way is to use balance sheets to find the values of what Kenneth Boulding and I called "the dynamics of T". This approach is a bit too difficult for our purposes here. The second way is to take the main variables associated with T and draw a circle. Most everyone has seen the equation for a circle; for those who have not, you will be introduced to a circle with values of real estate and values of mortgages. As we noted earlier, the subprime mortgage and real estate crisis led to the financial crisis of 2008-2009. In casino terms, the mortgage dealers had the edge or, literally, the house advantage. So, it is only fitting that we use symbols to represent the values of real estate and mortgages. With that brief introduction, we begin by drawing our circles.

Let RE be the value of real estate, K be the value of total mortgages held by the financial industry at any point in time (that change at the rate of time). Let W be the real value of wealth ("real" = deflated by goods and services prices) of the upper quintile of the distribution. This wealth is created by the dynamics of T. These values are connected in a circular way even though the circle can expand and contract in space. In the simplest model the circles do no intersect, so that:

$$[RE(t) - W(t)]^2 + [K(t) - W(t)]^2 = [W(t)]^2$$

In a system of curves or circles whose position depends on the value of real wealth (W) at any point in time (t). The centre of the circle is (W,W) and its radius is W. The following constraints define the curves: $0 <\_ RE <\_ W$, and RE $+ K <\_ W$. As W or wealth gets larger, the centre of the circle moves away from the origin along a line bisecting the angle between the axes (45-degree line), and the radius of the circle increases. Imagine gamblers tossing different-sized units of gold bullion (W) into a smooth-surfaced lake; the larger the volume of bullion, the greater the circle made from the ripples. I risk being accused of making a circular argument.

This simple model says that an increase in real wealth in the upper reaches of the wealth distribution will increase the potential values of RE and K. As in the casino, the rich hold the upper hand. Because the values of mortgages as financial assets are also co-linear with the value of real estate, RE and K most likely will follow the 45-degree line. If the real wealth of the top quintile declines, so too will the value of real estate and mortgages. If much of the real wealth is tied to real estate and the prices of real estate drop, the event can shrink the circle. This happens if real estate prices drop faster than goods prices in an economy. Contrary to the conventional wisdom in economics, it is the relative price of real estate and goods rather than the relative price of leisure that is critical in what I have called the "Casino Economy".

Now we arrive at the "Casino Effect" Although RE and K may move together with respect to real wealth, their time path need not be and has not been, linear. Rather, with respect to time the pattern would be exponential or where the a's are positive integers and the k's are positive fractions.

$$RE(t) = a \text{ sub } 1 \text{ e superscript k sub } 1 \text{ superscript W(t) } K(t) =$$
$$a \text{ sub } 2 \text{ e superscript } K2 \text{ subscript superscript W(t),}$$

As real estate values fall, the exponents will become negative. This sudden shift means that the initial state and conditions have changed indeed, the exponential pattern—up or down—did not characterize the years before the late 1960s. Events changed the initial state and conditions beginning at that time. First, income and wealth distributions became much more concentrated during the 1980s. This was the beginning of the Casino Economy. Second, the Carter and Reagan administrations turned dramatically toward the deregulation of the financial industry. Third, the deposit insurance systems and the lender of last resort stance of the Fed now seemed to take the risk out of over-expansion by the financial industry. This lack of supervision also characterizes the casino industry.

The Casino Effect suggests that historical speculative episodes must have been ignited by dramatic upward shifts in wealth (W). Why does this movement cause speculative bubbles? In other words, why does the Boulding-Canterbery T spin out of control and cause larger and larger circles?

One reason relates to ability to pay; the household needs wealth in excess of basic needs in order to "afford" to speculate. This does not preclude some speculating beyond their means, just as in the casino. However, such high-risk finance pays off during economic expansion, especially when there is a wealthier "greater fool" to bid assets still higher. Even generally cautious persons tend to jump onto the bandwagon. No less a cynic than Thorstein Veblen took an uncharacteristic dive into the stock market during the 1920s but mercifully died a few months before the Crash of 1929. Finally, in an environment of cutthroat competition in the financial industry, firms offer higher and higher interest rates to attract funds that in turn must be lent at still higher rates, requiring higher-risk loans. The compounding of the values of these assets and liabilities gives the exponential path.

We call such speculative episodes "speculative bubbles" for their tendency to burst. For example, by historical standards the decline in real estate values just prior to the 2008-2009 financial crisis was huge. Just as sharp rises in real estate values relative to goods prices led the parade of high-yielding mortgages, CDs and junk bonds, the decline in real estate values relative to modest inflation in goods prices produced nonperforming loans nearly to the point of extinction of the S&L industry and to the grave threat to the banking industry. Such innovations as junk bonds provided chips for new high-risk games Even the insurance industry was threatened with a possible run, as it had about twice the share of junk-bond assets than was originally reported. This contagion spread to households, which also were filling record numbers of bankruptcies. The values of assets and liabilities in T indeed were connected in a nearly unbroken circle.

The widening of the circle—once it had expanded—was reversed.

Before we leave the Boulding-Canterbery T, we should explain why it can go out of control. The definition of T goes a long way in this regard. The financial transfer's item or T is comprised of changes in the money supply held by business firms, changes in the net worth of the households, and dividends. All these changes can be volatile, depending on economic conditions. How does T then appear in the national income accounts? It depends upon which distributional model is deployed. In Model I, all variables are "given" so that changes are not involved. In this model, after doing the math, consumption is a positive function of the wage share, and investment is a positive function of the profits share. In turn, profits and wages also are determined by the levels of consumption and investment adjusted by transfers (T). At two extremes, all the product goes to wages, and at the other, all the product goes to wages. The real world, of course, is between these two extremes. Wages can vary and equal consumption minus T. Profits can vary and equal investment plus T. At any distribution, T equals profits minus investment. T also equals consumption minus wages. Variation is the financial transfer item (T) depends on both profits and wages, which is an unconventional conclusion. This does seem unconventional because it is: not to worry, the second model might help, though it is less intuitively obvious.

In Model II the wage and profit levels will be different at each level of output. In turn, those differences will result in different allocations of the output between household and businesses. This is the distributional aspect of the model. The level of investment is a positive function of profits, and consumption is a positive function of national income. Income, output and expenditures are simultaneously determined. This sounds like John Maynard Keynes and his determination of national income, except Keynes ignored distribution. He did not speak the language of profits and wages, which was his way of ignoring the wealth and income distributions. When he spoke of speculation, it was treated as a separate topic related mostly to foreign exchange.

Returning to Model II, transfers (T) can change so that the income distribution shifts in favour of profits relative to wages. Aggregate expenditures rise since consumption now is assumed independent of the wage share. Boulding separates the effect of the shift from profits to wages into a "transfer effect" plus an "income effect". The transfer effect simply is the amount of the transfer being added to total profits and subtracted from total wages. The income effect is the rise in national income due to the shift being divided between wages and profits, softening the fall in wages while hardening the rise in profits. The share of this division depends on the relative slopes of the consumption and investment functions. The steeper is the consumption function, the greater the increase in income that will accrue to wages. If consumption is reduced by the shift of wages to profits, as well it might be, this counters the output-increasing effect of a shift from wages to profits. If this effect is sufficiently large, there may be net output-decreasing effects, as in Model I.

Suppose, says Boulding, that consumption rises outside the model, say from a population increase. With no change in transfers or the relation of investment to profits, the wage curve will rise by the same amount as the consumption curve. At each output level profits will suffer relative to wages; this is because of the composition of output determines its distribution as in wages equal consumption—T. A rise in the wage bill in the consumption sector has no effect on absolute profits, but it will reduce the share of a larger national income going to profits. Only if the wage bill in the investment sector rises would profits and the profit share rise. This assumes that the bulk of the wages are paid in the consumer products sector.

Since Keynes, economists have chased equilibrium, especially income-output equilibrium, only to find it everywhere. Boulding was not exceptional in this respect. However, if transfers (T) vary with business investment and with dividends that, in turn, vary with profits, where would output and income settle? Boulding says as much when he concludes that "the dynamics of all these models is likely to be complicated by the dynamic instability of the transfer factor, and even of the consumption and investment functions themselves" [1050, 369]. The modelling of this instability goes beyond he mathematics used by Boulding. Since speculation in a "casino economy" suggests instability, any model of the dynamics of T is likely to lead away from stable equilibrium. This is because T contains elements subject to speculation.

Transfers and thus the financial system can alter the income distribution and the level of national income. Increases in consumer credit, decreases in the private bond sales to households, and an increase in dividends because of a more liquid business sector will reduce the absolute level of wages. The use of profits as the growth in net worth and the introduction of financial variables at the firm level are a fruitful means to model this interrelationship between households and business expenditures and the distribution of income between profits and wages. It has the merit of taking distribution theory out of the world of marginalism whereby factors, rather than people, receive income. At even the microeconomics level, the refinement of classical economics threw out the Ricardian baby with J.B. Say's bathwater. Still the notion of subsistence household expenditure should be resurrected as the complement of subsistence wages leaving a discretionary wage increment that determines discretionary spending. Discretionary spending is also the source of profits in the casino. A main theme emerges: profits decide business investment and consumption determines wages. There can be either profits inflation or wages inflation that leads to stock market expansion and the possibility of speculation. More chips mean more can play in the Casino Economy.

Next, we provide our summation.

Chapter 16
A Summation

Tulipmania defined the manias to come. They took on other names—bubbles, panics, crashes, crisis, casinos, or simply speculation. While there are many definitions of bubbles, the intuition remains the same. When the price of an asset is high today only because speculators believe that the price will be higher tomorrow, a bubble exists. That is, today's price is not explained by fundamentals or variables having a direct effect on future income streams from, say, bonds. Asset prices will move to the higher side if buyers believe they will: the asset in question yields a return (interest) equal to or greater than returns on alternative assets, including equities. Irrational exuberance seems to be present when fundamentals are violated. This is the case not only for bubbles, but for panics, cashes, crisis, casinos, or speculation.

As noted, this view is not the only one around. Contrary to irrationality is rationality. From rationality stems rational expectations. There are variations of such models, but they all boil down to the same thing. Rational expectationists have a strong faith in free markets, despite assurances that all markets are not perfectly free. All asset markets work smoothly and always reflect market fundamentals. Even "bubbles" are rational because buyers can hold two contrary beliefs simultaneously: an asset's price is above its fundamental value but is worth holding anyway. As shown in Appendix 1, despite the complex logic, the rational view can be expressed in simple mathematics.

It is comforting to know that most historians and economists favour the irrationality embedded in bubbles. The histories of bubbles presented in this book defy a rational explanation. These include tulipmania, the Mississippi Bubble, the South Seas Bubble, the Great Crash of 1929, and the Great Bull Market of the 1990s. One could argue that John Law, the British dandy behind the Mississippi and South Seas bubbles was himself rational, serving his own interests, but his followers nonetheless exhibited wild irrationality. Similar analogies apply to panics, which are based on fear rather than rational thinking. Attempting to cope with the panic of 1792, Alexander Hamilton was behaving rationally. We can argue analogously regarding the panic of 1819. President James Madison and Secretary of the Treasury Alexander Dallas were acting rationally when they attempted a revival of the Bank of the United States (BUS). The ultimate goal of the second BUS was to be a central bank, which was ahead of most thinking in the global community. In fact, the second Bank of the United States began operations in January 1817 as a fiscal agent of the US Treasury.

In an apparent contradiction, the trigger for the panic of 1819 was the second Bank (BUS).

It had initiated a sharp credit contraction beginning the summer of 1818. The timing turned out to be adverse. For example, Southwestern plantations were devastated when Britain began to increase its imports of East India cotton to avoid purchasing the high-priced U.S. Cotton. India had more land devoted to cotton production than the entire Louisiana Purchase. There was considerable rivalry. Tench Coxe was being rational when he warned about the adverse effects of foreign competition. The upshot: cotton prices threatened to burst a cotton bubble. The second Bank of the United States continued to make mistakes. The contraction of credit was approved by no less than U.S. President James Monroe and Nicholas Biddle as well as stockholders who wanted Bank leadership to be fiscally conservative and immune to political influence—that is, an independent bank. Tight money heightened the crisis.

The panic of 1873 was the mother of all panics, lasting from 1873 until 1879. While is began as a financial crisis, it triggered a depression in Europe and North America known as the "long depression". Hence comes the term "the long goodbye". Indeed, the Panic was known as the "great depression" until eclipsed by the events of the 1930s. It was the first truly international crisis. At the same time, the Long Depression was the first global depression.

The causes of the panic were unique. The crisis coincided with the end of the great railway boom. Then, the ending of minting Silver thaler coins by Germany caused a drop in demand for silver. This reverberated in the silver mining in the USA, the main source of the metal. In reaction, the Congress passed the Coinage Act of 1873, which placed the USA on a gold standard. The resultant deflation in the price of silver which hurt mining interests in the West was labelled "the crime of '73". In turn, the devaluation of silver greatly reduced the money supply.

This caused interest rates to soar and damaged farming interests. The climax came when Jay Cooke, who like many others had invested heavily in railroads, was unable to market several million dollars in Northern Pacific Railway bonds.

Rui Barbosa's (1849-1923) name is synonymous with Encilhamento. Known as the "Eagle of the Hague," he initially ran unsuccessfully for President of Brazil. He was a pioneer in advocating the freeing of slaves. His first public speech for abolition was given when he was only 19. During his term as finance secretary, he instituted a vigorously expansionist monetary policy, which resulted in chaos and instability. It resulted in the bubble of Encilhamento, which boomed in the late 1880s and early 1890s in Brazil. It burst during the provisional government of Deodoro da Fonseca, leading to a financial crisis. Barbosa's policy was unrestricted credit for industrial investments and for banks by an abundant issuance of money to encourage Brazil's industrialization. Instead, this policy led to unbridled speculation, increased inflation, and encouraged fraudulent initial public offerings (IPOs). The word "Encilhameno" literally is "saddling-up," the act of girthing or mounting a horse, a term borrowed from horseracing.

The major players were the big rentiers who were holders of the native "big money," the financiers who were institutional traders and investment bankers working for the big money, economist-politicians who were the makers of economic policies, providing rhetoric to public opinion, and haute finance, world financial capital which were already organized. Under a new law promoting and protecting these players, unregulated speculation rose. Instead of promoting growth and structural change in the economy, the process led to one of the worst inflation outbreaks of the country's history, and the Brazilian economy suffered a violent collapse. The Encilhamento's last straw came with the financial shock wave caused by the default of Argentine government bonds following the first collapse of the Baring Brothers bank at the end of 1890. Although the bubble burst happened between 1890 and 1892, the economic and political effects were felt throughout the decade until the end of the Campos Sales administration. Rui Barbossa was ruined and died in poverty in Paris.

What is the main lesson we can take away from Encihamento? Barbosa was apparently a rational actor serving the wrong people. The theory he used to spur economic growth was monetarism before it was invented by Milton Friedman. It failed to stimulate economic growth, much as it did in modern times. Once again, rational thought failed the general public.

The Panic of 1907 is also known as the 1907 Banker's Panic or Knickerbocker Crisis. It was a financial crisis that took place over a three-week period starting in Mid-October, when the New York Stock Exchange fell almost 50 percent from its peak the previous year. Panic ensued, as this was during a time of economic recession, but also there were numerous runs on banks and trust companies. The panic eventually spread throughout the nation when many state and local banks and businesses entered bankruptcy. The primary cause of the bank runs included a retraction of market liquidity by several New York City banks and a loss of confidence among directors, exacerbated by unregulated side bets at bucket shops. The bank run was triggered by the failed attempt in October 1907 by Otis Heinze to corner the market on stock of the United Copper Company. When this bid failed, banks that had lent money to the cornering scheme, suffered runs that later spread to affiliated banks and trusts leading a week later to the downfall of Knickerbocker Trust Company; New York City's finest. The collapse of the Knickerbocker spread fear through the city trusts as regional banks withdrew reserves from New York City banks. Panic gripped the nation as vast numbers of people withdrew deposits from their regional banks.

The panic might have deepened if not for the intervention of financier J.P. Morgan, who pledged large sums of his own money, and convinced other Now York bankers to do the same, to shore up the banking system. The United States did not have a central bank to act as lender of last resort, so Morgan filled that role. In November the financial contagion had largely ended, only to be replaced by further crisis. This was due to the heavy borrowing of a large brokerage firm that used the stock of Tennessee Coal, Iron and Railroad Company as collateral. Collapse of TC and I's stock price was averted by an emergency takeover by (again) Morgan's U.S. Steel Corporation, a move approved by anti-monopolist President Theodore Roosevelt. The following year, Senator Nelson W. Aldrich, father-in-law of John D. Rockefeller, Jr., established and chaired a commission to investigate the crisis and propose further solutions, leading to the creation of the Federal Reserve System.

There had been a bank which performed the functions of a central bank prior to the Fed. However, President Andrew Jackson allowed the charter of the Second Bank of the United States to expire in 1836, leaving the U.S. without a central bank. The money supply in New York City fluctuated with the country's annual agricultural cycle. Interest rates were subservient to the changes in the money supply. The Hepburn Act, which gave the Interstate Commerce

Commission (ICC) the power to set maximum railroad rates, became law in July 1906. What followed was depreciation in the value of railroad securities. The stock market slid, losing 7.17 percent, then fell further 9.8 percent. This March collapse is sometimes referred to as "rich man's panic".

The real panic began not with gold, but with copper. There was a stock manipulation scheme to corner the market in F. Augustus Heinze's United Copper Company. It was Augustus's brother, Otto, who devised the scheme to corner the market in United Copper, believing wrongly that the Heinze family already controlled most of the company. He also thought that Heinze's shares had been borrowed and sold short by speculators betting that the stock price would drop and thus they could repurchase the borrowed shares cheaply, pocketing the difference. Otto proposed a short squeeze, whereby the Heinze's would aggressively purchase as many remaining share as possible, and then force the short sellers to pay for their borrowed shares. The aggressive purchasing would drive up the share price, and, being unable to find shares elsewhere, the short sellers would have no option but to turn to the Heinzes, who could then name their price. The whole scheme was financed by Knickerbocker Trust. The plan did not work out as the share price of United Copper began a monumental collapse. The stock fell to $10 on October 15. Otto Heinze was ruined.

The failure to corner the market sent Otto's brokerage house, Gross U Kleeberg, into bankruptcy. As news of the collapse spread, depositors rushed en masse to withdraw money from the Mercantile National Bank, the correspondent bank for United Copper. Next, the panic hit the trusts. The National Bank of Commerce where J.P. Morgan was a dominant figure, announced it would no longer serve as a clearing house to the Knickerbocker. On October 22, the Knickerbocker faced a classic bank run. It was forced of suspend operations. As news spread, other banks and trusts were reluctant to lend any money. The interest rates on loans to brokers at the stock exchange soared to 70 percent, with brokers unable to get money, stock prices fell to a low not seen since December 1900. The panic quickly spread to other large trusts.

When the chaos began to shake the confidence of New York's banks, the city's most famous banker was attending a church convention in Richmond, Virginia. Morgan, not only the city's wealthiest and most well-connected banker, had experience with similar crisis—as noted, he famously had helped to rescue the U.S. Treasury during the Panic of 1893.

Morgan returned to Wall Street, and on October 20 the library of Morgan's brownstone on Madison Avenue became a revolving door of New York City bank and trust company presidents. When Morgan and his men examined the books of the Knickerbocker, they decided it was indeed insolvent and did not intervene to stop the run. Its failure nonetheless triggered runs on even healthy trusts, prompting Morgan to take charge of the rescue operation. Many rescues and loans later, the banks were stabilized.

Despite the infusion of cash into the banks, they were reluctant to make loans to facilitate daily stock trade. Prices on the exchange began to crash. When Morgan was told that the exchange would have to be closed, he said that an early close would be catastrophic. Then, Morgan called the presidents of the city's banks to his office. They were told that as many as 50 stock exchanges would fail unless $25 million was raised in 10 minutes. The bank presidents did raise $23.5 million to keep the stock exchange afloat. Disaster was averted. Morgan and the other bankers could not pool money indefinitely. They lacked the power to print money. To ensure the free flow of money, the New York Clearing House issued $100 million in loan certificates to be traded between banks to settle balances, allowing them to retain cash reserve for depositors. While a sense of order returned to New York banking, another crisis was occurring when Morgan's associate was informed that the City of New York required at least $20 million by November 1 or go bankrupt. Morgan, by contracting to purchase some $30 million worth of city bonds, was paving the way for future interventions by a central bank. Through several other interventions by Morgan and U.S. Steel, stability returned to New York banking.

A steep economic recession accompanied the financial crisis. Morgan could not end the recession, but his actions gave impetus for the establishment of a central bank. On December 23, 1913, Congress passed the Federal Reserve Act, establishing a central bank. None other than Morgan's deputy Benjamin Strong became president of the Federal Reserve Bank of New York. It was poetic justice that Strong had a major influence in shaping the policies of this new institution. Absent Morgan, there would not have been a central bank to take over the role he had played.

The Great Crash of 1929 demonstrated that the Federal Reserve could not be counted on to do the right thing. And, J.P. Morgan was not around to right the ship. The 1920s roared not only because of the antics of Scott and Zelda Fitzgerald but because the fundamentals of the economy and the stock market were booming. While we would expect the market to move up and down with fundamentals, speculators would not leave well enough alone and drove prices into the stratosphere. Common people could not set at the side-line of such profit opportunities and jumped on the bandwagon, just as the Dutch had done during Tulipmania. It was too much of a good thing. Women's fashions especially reflected the excesses of the Age: hemlines went up and down with the stock exchanges. Men's fashions were less exuberant as indeed they remain. Moreover, the short skirt defined the Flapper and Fitzgerald's new woman. Not surprisingly jazz became popular during the Jazz Age, and helped, along with Scott Fitzgerald, to define it. New dance crazes such as the Charleston were all the rage. It was an era of experimentation and innovation.

The excesses began to bubble to the top well before 1929. By the mid-1920s, a classic speculative bubble inflated over balmy Florida, only to be blown away by two hurricanes. This was a harbinger of what was to come in the stock market. While the start of the stock boom was based on fundamentals, speculators later took control. In 1927, the increase in prices began in earnest. Day after day, week after week, month after month the market advanced. The mass escape into make-believe began in early 1928. Radio stock led the way with multiple gains. Then John J. Rascob, who had impressive associations, sent the market into a frenzy. There was a "victory boom" the day after Hoover was elected in a landslide.

Buying on the margin was the final magic making the market froth. In retrospect, the crash was inevitable. It came on Black Tuesday (October 29, 1929) and Black Thursday and was the most devastating stock market crash in the history of the United States. There were great private efforts to save the day, such as those of Richard Whitney of the New York Exchange, and William C. Durant along with the Rockefeller family and others. But their great efforts failed to stop the large decline in prices. The Federal Reserve sat on its hands, even during the Great Depression that followed the 1929 debacle. Together, the stock market crash and the Great Depression formed the greatest financial crisis of the 20th century. Moreover, the 1929 crash led directly to the Great Depression in Europe.

After the angst and anguish of the preceding chapters, the reader deserves some comfort, which is provided by a chapter with comedy relief. The comedy is provided by John Kenneth Galbraith's novel, *A Tenured Professor,* which also critiques the idea of rational expectations. This is important because rational expectationists have their own view of speculative bubbles. The plot has Harvard's economics faculty looking for a professor with impeccable credentials, an impressive publication and the right political attitudes. They find these traits in Montgomery Marvin. As it turns out, they get more than they bargained for. Professor Marvin has created a measure of excessive investor optimism and pessimism, the amazingly accurate Index of Irrational Expectations (IRAT).

Goaded on by a very assertive wife, Marvin and IRAT make millions in the stock market. This quickly acquired wealth creates envy among the faculty and faculty knives are unsheathed and events spin out of control. Spin control by the Marvin's involves a Harvard "bail out".

To understand IRAT, the reader needs some introduction to the idea of rational expectations. All market participants have the same information and use it with equal efficiency. The market ends up being efficient in the sense that all profits have been exploited. No one can make any money because it has already been made. (This is not Galbraithan satire; it is where rational expectations logically deliver us.). The naive economist must wonder why speculators or investors would enter a market in which all profits already have been taken. Yet, unless people do enter the market, it doesn't exist.

Marvin's contrary mind drifts frequently to the delusions of the crowd—to South Sea Bubbles, the manic speculation of the late 1920s, and the financial genius of those men who communicated the errors of euphoria to others. He reads of the examples of such as Richard Whitney, a symbol of the highest standards of financial morality as expressed by the New York Stock Exchange, who passed quietly into Sing. From this history emerges a principle of finance: "Find out who in any euphoric episode is the greatest hero, who is the most celebrated, and invest in his eventual fall." Marvin realizes that he needs a measure of the euphoria in a company and its stock. He takes measure of a banking legend, the Bank of America. With reality as 100, Marvin set the measure of euphoria in the bank as twice that figure. He invents the Index of Irrational Expectations (IRAT).

He needed to experiment with IRAT. He concludes that a short position in the Bank of America stock could lead to profits. Borrow stock, sell it at current prices and then when the price goes down replace it, keeping the difference. Marvin and Marjie, his aggressive wife, open a Merrill Lynch account and make all the right moves. The Reagan administration reduces taxes on stock gains just in time to aid the Marvin's. By the mid-1980s, euphoria was becoming endemic and universal. Securities prices across the board were going up. The Marvin's discover index and program trading and begin to use heretofore undreamed-of-leveraging. The Marvin's, going short as usual, become very rich from the stock market crash of October 19, 1987.

As liberals, they face the dilemma of what to do with their wealth. Marjie teams with New Englander Henry Winthrop Wentworth in an effort to place a tag or sticker on products conveying the state of women in the executive ranks of the producer. Meanwhile, facing unceasing heat from Harvard for their activities, the Marvin's decide to "bail out." Harvard by offering to buy all of its securities subject to criticism because of corporate participation in the South African economy. Marvin's offer was at 10 percent above closing costs. Harvard becomes anti-apartheid only after Marvin makes it profitable to do so.

Going still further along the liberal path, Marvin offers an endowment of $2.5 million to establish Professorships for peace in each of the three service academies. "What seemed to cause the greatest concern was whether this might make peace as a concept unduly prominent in the academies' routine." There too was critical congressional reaction. The American Legion went further in attacking the idea. The error of training officers to prefer peace to war ultimately is overwhelmed only by the size of the endowments.

The turning point is provided by the SEC. IRAT, it has been determined, was an illegal manipulation of the markets. It was a clear case of insider trading based on inside information on Marvin's trading—insider trading based on insider trading? Market failure is the product of the rational use of irrationality. When the SEC denies Marvin the use of IRAT, he buys stocks in a random walk, informed the SEC and provides full information on his transactions to the press. Marvin's undiminished reputation is sufficient to bring others onto the bandwagon. Complete information shakes the markets. At the end Marvin still has tenure.

The dot-com bubble is also known as the dot-com boom, the tech bubble, the Internet bubble, the dot-com collapse and the information technology bubble. All these names carry some information about what happened. It was a historic speculative bubble covering roughly 1995-2001 during which stock markets in industrialized nations saw equity values soar from the growth in the Internet and related industries. The Internet boom was punctuated by the dot-com collapse. And the information technology bubble was punctuated in the same way. They were slowed, but did not cave in.

The era was marked by the founding (and sometimes the spectacular failure) of several new Internet-based companies commonly called the dot-coms. Small companies could cause their stock to soar by simply adding an "e-" prefix or a "com" suffix to their names. Irrational exuberance regarding prospects created an environment in which many investors were willing to overlook traditional metrics, such as the P/E ratio, in favour of confidence in technological advancements. Most of these stocks, being tech stocks were traded on the NASDAQ. By the end of the 1990s, the NASDAQ hit a P/E ratio of 200, a truly astonishing plateau.

When the collapse came during 1999-2000, some companies, such as pets.com and Webvan, failed totally. Others were revived—Cisco, whose stock declined by 85 percent, lost a large portion of their market capitalization but remained stable and profitable Others, such as eBay.com, later not only recovered but even surpassed their dot-com-bubble peaks. Equally prominent is Amazon .com. Alas, Books-a-Million had seen its stock price soar by over 1,000 percent only to fall to $3 a share in 2000.

What caused the relentless rise in stock prices? The unshakable faith in the Internet revolution led to irrational exuberance. No matter how high the NASDAQ went, it was thought to go higher. And it did, until the crash. As the technology boom receded, consolidation and growth by market leaders caused the tech industry to come more closely to resemble other traditional U.S. Sectors. On March 20, 2000 the NASDAQ peaked at over 50,000. Afterwards, it nosedived by as much as 78 percent. World.com, for one, was found be engaged in illegal accounting practices to exaggerate its profits. It was struggling to survive.

The Telecommunications Act of 1995 greatly favoured the monopolistic Regional Bell Operating Companies and this led to the demise of competition. Consolidation was the order of the day and World.com stock plummeted. As of 2014, ten information technology firms are among the 100 largest U.S. Corporations by revenues: Apple, Hewlett-Packard, IBM, Microsoft, Amazon.com, Google, Intel, Cisco Systems, Ingram Micro and Oracle. The fate of so many others has been determined. They went down with the dot-com-bubble.

The bankruptcy of Lehman Brothers Holdings, then the fourth largest US investment bank, in mid-September 2008 triggered the most severe financial panic and crash in a century. Lehman had been an aggressive buyer of mortgage-related securities. The firm used the money it obtained from selling its own short-term IOUs to buy long-term mortgages. Lehman was exceptionally leveraged: it was at the end of the spectrum in leveraging with assets more than thirty times its capital. This was covered up by "window dressing." Leveraging is a two-edged sword. When the economy is prospering and real estate prices are increasing, the greater is the leverage, and the greater the profits.

Deregulation greatly benefited the mega-investment-banks. The barriers once separating commercial and investment banking were torn down. At the same time the government and the Federal Reserve refused to regulate derivatives. Salomon Brothers, a major player, purchased home mortgages from thrifts throughout the US and packaged them into mortgage-backed securities, which it sold to local and international clients. Salomon began to engage in proprietary trading or the buying and selling of stocks, bonds, options, etc. for profit. Salomon Brothers was weakened by a financial scandal which led to its acquisition by Travellers Group, and later Citigroup. Their investment banking operations became known as "Salomon Smith Barney": and was renamed "Citigroup Global Markets". Salomon Brothers also pioneered arbitrage trading. Traders could make sure moves by finding two securities that should but did not have the same value; buying one, selling the other, and waiting for prices to converge. The popularity of arbitrage funded the rapid growth of hedge funds which grew from less than $30 billion in assets in 1990 to over $2 trillion in the troubled year of 2008. Others got on the bandwagon of financial innovations. JP Morgan popularized the credit default innovation.

A housing bubble became part of the banking crisis of 2008-2009. A multitude of forces accounts for the banking bubble, which led to a global housing bubble. The creation of financial innovations tells most of the story. In the boom years of 2005 and 2006 about 80 percent of the securities in CDOs were mortgage-backed, about 70 percent of these were below B grade. At least half were subprime or second-lien home-equity lines. These were the same years the industry was pumping out some of the most egregiously irresponsible loans in history. Under the assumption of a permanent new era of very low defaults, it was possible to build families of bonds such that 80 percent of the issued bonds had triple-A and double-A ratings, even though 70 percent of the supporting assets were subprime. Analysts called the phenomenon "embedded leverage". Two apparently identical offerings of triple-A-rated CDO bonds, supported in part by subprime mortgages. A 3 percent default rate in portfolio one would require that 3 percent of the triple-A bonds be downgraded. The same default rate in the second portfolio would require that more than 50 percent of the bonds be downgraded. Moreover, the subprime mortgages have a variety of terms some are fixed going to floating, second liens, negative interest, and so on. So, they are extremely hard to put together in the first place. It was a house of cards just ready to be toppled.

Real US housing prices reached a peak before falling off a cliff, beginning around 2005. In 2005 mortgages were already in trouble, as the housing boom approached its peak, a peak not reached until the second quarter of 2007. With 1890 as the base year, US housing prices had doubled. Speculators, as ever, were reluctant to leave the market.

One might suppose that the banks—especially the giants—would get caught in the web of defaulting mortgages. In 2007 borrowers unable to refinance their mortgages began defaulting in sharply rising numbers. In 2007 the mountain of assets based on housing values began to crumble as increasing defaults torpedoed the prices of mortgage-backed securities and CDOs. The avalanche almost brought down the global financial system by 2008. Nonetheless it appeared that big, risk-taking banks had become crucial to the US economy and to the American way of life. They were too big to be allowed to fail. The government stepped in to protect the massive USA financial system and, by extension, the global economy. The Treasury loaned the banks money, at an initial five percent yearly interest rate, that never had to be repaid. The loans, giving the banks free money, mean that the government now owned part of the banks. While some of the big banks were saved, Lehman Brothers went bankrupt, Bear Stearns and Merrill Lynch were sold, and Goldman Sachs and Morgan Stanley slipped into the safety of bank holding company status. Still, there were losses: Merrill Lynch in mid-2008 sold its CDOs to Lone Star Funds for a mere twenty-two cents for each dollar of original face value.

Despite all efforts, the mighty continued to fall. Washington Mutual collapses as depositors pulled out their money. At the time it was the largest bank failure in US history. Wachovia, on the brink of failure, was acquired by Wells Fargo. Because they were running out of cash, banks stopped lending. The money supply was stagnant.

In 2008, when the global financial system was crashing, a pseudonymous person or persons named Satoshi Nakamoto outlined a new protocol for a peer-to-peer electronic cash system using a cryptocurrency called Bitcoin. Cryptocurrencies (digital currencies) are different from traditional fiat currencies because they are not created or controlled by government or central banks. A set of rules—in the form of distributed computations—ensures the integrity of the data exchanged among billions of devices without going through a trusted third party such as God. Bitcoins have excited or otherwise captured the imagination of the computing world and has spread like wildfire to businesses, governments, privacy advocates, social development activists, media theorists, and journalists, to name more than a few, everywhere. Despite exclamations such as "My god, this is it!"[86] God is held at a secular distance. No third party or middlemen is required. Today thoughtful people are trying to understand the implications of a protocol that enables mere mortals to manufacture thrust through clever code. This has never happened before.

The protocol is the foundation of a growing number of global distribution ledgers called blockchains—of which the Bitcoin blockchain is the largest. The digital currency is represented by transactions recorded in blockchain—a kind of global spreadsheet or ledger, which leverages the resources of a large peer-to-peer Bitcoin network to verify and approve each Bitcoin transaction. Each blockchain like the one used for Bitcoin, is distributed: it runs on computers provided by volunteers around the world. There is no central database to hack. The blockchain is public; anyone can view it at any time because it resides on the network, not within a single institution charged with auditing transactions and keeping records. And the blockchain is encrypted.

All the transactions conducted are verified, cleared and stored in a block which is linked to the preceding block, thereby creating a chain. This structure permanently time stamps and stores exchanges of value, preventing anyone from altering the ledger. If say, you wanted to steal a Bitcoin, you would have to rewrite the coin's entire history on the blockchain in broad daylight, and that's practically impossible. It's the world-wide Ledger of value, a distributed ledger that everyone can download and run on their personal computer. This new platform enables conciliation of digital records regarding just about everything in real time. NASDAQ, an early adopter of blockchain, is using the technology to show private companies to issue stock and stockholders of public companies to vote their shares. In fact, the financial services industry has already re-branded n privatized blockchain technology, reconciling the best of Bitcoin—security, speed, and cost with an entirely closed system that requires a bank or financial

---

[86] Much of the discussion on the blockchain revolution is based on E. Ray Canterbery, *Supra-surplus Capitalism and Inequality* (Singapore, London, Hong Kong: World Scientific, 2017), the first part of Chapter 10.

institution's permission to use. It could transform global financial systems.

Bitcoin price prediction and analysts are the most popular topics on Bitcoin. In the Bitcoin world, there are enough beginners to profit from, but eventually professionals will reach the Bitcoin trading market too. You are currently betting against Bitcoin enthusiasts trending every thread of Bitcoin talk. Soon you are betting against market professionals with 5+ years of experience in trading. News can be very important for the price of Bitcoin, but news does not age well. By the time you read the news, it has already been factored into the market. Bitcoin enthusiasts and investors are closer to the news sources than you are. And firms like Datminr try to be before the news by following trends on twitter. Sometimes you see a price surge, only to find out three hours later the news that caused it. This does not stop speculators from trying to make profits.

Is Bitcoin a bubble? It takes more than a fast rise in prices to constitute a bubble. An artificial overvaluation that will lead to a sudden downward correction constitutes a bubble. Still, the rapid price rise in spring 2017 looks suspicious.

Casinos have been around for a long time. They are an integral part of the gambling industry, though there is more to some of them than only gambling. The gambling operations of a casino run at a profit because of what is known as the "house edge" or "house advantage". The edge is mathematically operative when games are played many times. Some games are more mathematical than others. The odds are well-established for craps and roulette. For slot machines, pay-outs are programmed into the machines. The results are completely random, as in a random walk. The only game where the player still comes into play is 21 or Blackjack.

Gambling is popular: there is one casino for every major city in the world, though not every country or city has a casino.

The only game more universal than casino gambling is golf, on which bets can be made. The romance begins with the oldest casinos. The "casino di Venezia" can be traced back to 1618 and is located along the canals of the scenic Italian city of Venice. Its entrance is from the Grand Canal. Today, its casino offers classic casino games such as roulette, blackjack, Caribbean stud poker, Texas Hold 'em, Chamin de'Fer, Trente et Quarante and over 600 slot machines. The Casino de Monte Carlo is familiar to moviegoers who saw Ocean's Twelve, Goldeneye and Casino Royale.

All of which brings us to the "Casino Effect". There are at least two ways of approaching it. One way is to use balance sheets to find the value of what Kenneth Boulding and I called "the dynamics of T": The second way, which is easier, is to take the main variables associated with T and draw a circle. Most everyone has seen the equation for a circle. As we noted earlier, the subprime mortgage and real estate crisis led to the financial crisis of 2008-2009. In casino terms, the mortgage dealers had the edge or, literally, the house advantage. So, it is only fitting that we use symbols to represent the values of real estate and mortgages. This simple circular model says that an increase in real wealth in the upper reaches of the wealth distribution will increase the potential value of real estate. As in the casino, the rich hold the upper hand. If the real wealth of the top quintile declines so too will the value of real estate and mortgages. This happens if real estate prices drop faster than goods prices in an economy.

With the "Casino Effect," the value of real estate and mortgages move together with respect to real wealth, their time path need not be and has not been, linear. Rather, with respect to time the pattern would be exponential. The Casino Effect suggests that historical speculative episodes have been ignited by dramatic upward shifts in wealth; this movement causes speculative bubbles as the circles become larger and larger. The Boulding-Canterbery T spins out of control.

This concludes the summary.

www.ingramcontent.com/pod-product-compliance
Lightning Source LLC
Chambersburg PA
CBHW070234190526
45169CB00001B/177